Practicing Islam in Egypt

Following the ideological disappointment of the 1967 Arab–Israeli war, an Islamic revival arose in Egypt. Yet, far from being a mechanical reaction to the decline of secular nationalism, this religious shift was the product of impassioned competition among Muslim Brothers, Salafis, and state institutions and their varied efforts to mobilize Egyptians to distinct projects. By pulling together the linked stories of these diverse claimants to religious authority and tracing the social and intellectual history of everyday practices of piety, Aaron Rock-Singer shows how Islamic activists and institutions across the political spectrum reshaped daily routines in an effort to persuade followers to adopt novel models of religiosity. In so doing, he reveals how Egypt's Islamic Revival emerged, who it involved, and why it continues to shape Egypt today.

Aaron Rock-Singer is Visiting Assistant Professor in the Department of Near Eastern Studies at Cornell University. He holds a Ph.D. in Near Eastern Studies from Princeton University.

Practicing Islam in Egypt

Print Media and Islamic Revival

AARON ROCK-SINGER
Cornell University, New York

CAMBRIDGE
UNIVERSITY PRESS

CAMBRIDGE
UNIVERSITY PRESS

University Printing House, Cambridge CB2 8BS, United Kingdom

One Liberty Plaza, 20th Floor, New York, NY 10006, USA

477 Williamstown Road, Port Melbourne, VIC 3207, Australia

314–321, 3rd Floor, Plot 3, Splendor Forum, Jasola District Centre, New Delhi – 110025, India

79 Anson Road, #06–04/06, Singapore 079906

Cambridge University Press is part of the University of Cambridge.

It furthers the University's mission by disseminating knowledge in the pursuit of education, learning, and research at the highest international levels of excellence.

www.cambridge.org
Information on this title: www.cambridge.org/9781108492058
DOI: 10.1017/9781108590877

First published 2019

Printed and bound in Great Britain by Clays Ltd, Elcograf S.p.A.

A catalogue record for this publication is available from the British Library.

Library of Congress Cataloging-in-Publication Data
Names: Rock-Singer, Aaron, author.
Title: Practicing Islam in Egypt : print media and Islamic revival / Aaron Rock-Singer.
Description: New York : Cambridge University Press, 2018.
Identifiers: LCCN 2018042448 | ISBN 9781108492058 (hardback)
Subjects: LCSH: Islam – Egypt. | Islam and politics – Egypt. | BISAC: POLITICAL SCIENCE / Government / International.
Classification: LCC BP64.E3 R63 2018 | DDC 297.0962–dc23
LC record available at https://lccn.loc.gov/2018042448

ISBN 978-1-108-49205-8 Hardback

For Cara

Contents

Figures

Acknowledgments

This book was born as a dissertation in Princeton's Department of Near Eastern Studies. Its origin, however, can be traced to the Fall of 2004, when I first studied with Heather Sharkey as an undergraduate at the University of Pennsylvania. Heather's combination of modesty, knowledge, and perspective gave me the compass to navigate research, and a model of what it means to be both a scholar and a teacher. In a case of fortune begetting fortune, I then had the opportunity to study at Oxford with Walter Armbrust, who introduced me to the critical study of media and to the discipline of Anthropology.

It was then at Princeton that this project officially took root. Muhammad Qasim Zaman and Cyrus Schayegh carefully and perceptively read each chapter over the course of several years, Michael Cook gave me an exhilarating crash course in the nuts and bolts of the Islamic scholarly tradition, and Jonathan Gribetz and Satyel Larson challenged and deepened this study through their nuanced and thoughtful comments. It is my hope that these pages bear the mark of the erudition, sensitivity, and commitment to critical inquiry that all modeled for me.

I am also deeply grateful to Cambridge University Press. I would like to thank Maria Marsh for seeing potential in this project and shepherding it to completion; Abigail Walkington for her editorial support; Cassi Roberts for efficiently yet thoroughly bringing this manuscript into book form; Mary Starkey for precise and perceptive copy-edits; and Sri Hari Kumar Sugumaran for the production. Portions of Chapter 2 formed an article entitled "A Pious Public: Islamic Magazines and Revival in Egypt, 1976–1981," which was published in the *British Journal of Middle Eastern Studies*. A version of Chapter 5 entitled "Prayer and the Islamic Revival: A Timely Challenge" was published in the *International Journal of Middle East Studies*.

Numerous colleagues have taken the time to read and engage with different parts of this manuscript. In particular, I wish to thank Megan Brankley Abbas, Joel Blecher, Vaughn Booker, Jeff Culang, Simon Wolfgang Fuchs, Angela Giordani, Samuel and Tally Helfont, Hilary Kalmbach, Leo Katz, Daniel Lav, Nadirah Mansour, Elizabeth Nugent, Jacob Olidort, Christian Sahner, Emilio Spadola, Daniel Stolz, Lev Weitz, Arthur Zarate, Oded Zinger, and members of Princeton Islamic Studies Colloquium and the Center for the Study of Religion and Culture, also at Princeton. I'm particularly grateful to Steven Brooke and Susanna Ferguson, who read and commented on the entirety of the manuscript with a keen eye for both argument and minute detail. This study has benefited immensely from all these individuals and the intellectual communities that they played such a vital role in building and maintaining, often through the unsung work of organizing workshops and commenting on others' work. Just as important are the friends who have been with me going back to childhood, particularly Teddy Fassberg and Pete Silberman.

I must also thank individuals in both Israel and Egypt who helped to make this project possible. In Israel, Meir Hatina hosted me at the Levtzion Center for Islamic Studies at the Hebrew University of Jerusalem during the 2014–15 academic year when I wrote most of the original dissertation; I must also thank Meir and Sasha Schneidermann for their help in accessing a rare printed collection of the sermons of ʿAbd al-Hamid Kishk. Just as importantly, Uzi Rabi at Tel Aviv University provided generous access to the Dayan Center's Arabic Press Archives, which proved crucial to this project. On the other side of the Egyptian–Israeli border, I wish to thank members of the Muslim Brotherhood and the Jamʿiyya Sharʿiyya who assisted me in this project. In light of the current political circumstances, many of them must go nameless, but I hope that, if this book is ever translated into Arabic, they will recognize their contributions to it.

The transformation of my dissertation into a book occurred thanks to the support of Bill Burke-White and Mike Horowitz at the University of Pennsylvania's Perry World House. It was during my year at Penn – a period in which Bill and Mike worked diligently to discourage me from even considering teaching a course – that I revised the dissertation while adding two new chapters. As I went through the process of revising and finalizing this manuscript, David Powers continuously provided me with both sound advice and necessary perspective; in this, as in all matters of research and teaching, David encapsulates what it means to be a professional.

Ultimately, though, this study is the product of a lifetime of love and support of family. Since I was young, my parents have encouraged and made it possible for me to explore my passions; I hope that they will see themselves – and the intellectual and personal journey to which have they been so central – in these pages. My siblings, Patrick and Miriam, have also provided encouragement and gentle mockery, helping me keep my sanity when dozens of pages stared back at me. I would also like to thank all the wonderful family whom I inherited through marriage – Craig and Judy Singer, Ellen Singer Coleman and Michael Coleman, Sarah and Nathan Gregoire, Matt and Rachel Busman Rosen, Chad Singer and Cari Mondragon Mesa, and Rachel Bishop, for their love and support.

This book, though, is for Cara who, for going on eight years, has supported me, personally and intellectually. While I might have finished a book without her, it would have been a lesser product, and I certainly would have been a lesser person. And our daughter, Liora Daphne, has also played her own powerful role, grounding me with her deep sweetness, endless curiosity, and sharp wit. And as I write these words, Cara, Liora, and I await a new addition to our family. In this moment, as in so many others, it is my family that gives these professional milestones meaning.

Aaron Rock-Singer

A Note on Transliteration and Spelling

Transliteration of Arabic terms follows a modified version of the style of the *International Journal of Middle East Studies*. I employ full diacritical marks for technical terms, and, for non-technical terms, indicate the *ʿayn* and the initial and medial *hamza*. For the sake of clarity I exclude the final *hamza* (thus *ʿulama* rather than *ʿulamaʾ*). I render personal names based on this system, with the exception of the names of Egypt's first two president, Jamal ʿAbd al-Nasir and Anwar al-Sadat, which I render according to *IJMES* conventions.

Introduction

For many, the signal event in the history of Islamic activism in Anwar al-Sadat's Egypt is his stunning assassination in October 1981 by the Jihad group, members of which would go on to form al-Qaeda. Other accounts of this period have examined the ways that the Muslim Brotherhood steadily rebuilt their shattered organization around a "Parallel Islamic Sector" operating on the margins of state control. These events, however, were only one manifestation of a much deeper and broader trend of Islamic revival that would redefine social norms. Under al-Sadat, Egyptian society saw a decisive turn in public debate and practice: from calls for the application of Islamic law to the crowded mosques across Egyptian cities to the self-consciously modest dress and pious comportment, Egyptian Muslims increasingly applied Islam to their daily lives. These projects, however, did not spring ready-made from an Islamic tradition of revival and reform, nor from a distinct Islamist tradition of religio-political challenge; instead, they emerged out of a battle between Egypt's Islamist opposition and key state religious bodies for control of Islam's position at the heart of state institutions.

In turning to Islam, Egyptian state institutions, Islamic movements, and the society from which they emerged and on which they acted were far from an outlier. Whether in Saudi Arabia, which saw an Islamic Awakening (*ṣaḥwa*) movement,[1] state-sponsored Islamization under Zia al-Haqq in Pakistan (r. 1977–88),[2] the emergence of an Islamist movement in Turkey under the leadership of Necmettin Erbakan,[3] or

[1] Stéphane Lacroix, *Awakening Islam: The Politics of Religious Dissent in Contemporary Saudi Arabia*, trans. George Holoch (London: Harvard University Press, 2011), esp. 129–32.

[2] Seyyed Vali Reza Nasr, *Islamic Leviathan: Islam and the Making of State Power* (Oxford: Oxford University Press, 2001), 130–57.

[3] Iren Ozgur, *Islamic Schools in Modern Turkey: Faith, Politics, and Education* (New York: Cambridge University Press, 2012), 41–51.

the Iranian Revolution of 1979,[4] the 1970s saw a broad transformation in the relationship between religion and politics across Muslim-majority countries of the Middle East and South Asia. Nor were such revivals limited to Muslims: in Israel, Messianic Zionism rose to new prominence under the leadership of Rabbi Tzvi Yehuda Kook in Israel,[5] and in the United States, an Evangelical named James ("Jimmy") Carter was elected President in 1976.

The rise of an Islamic Revival in Egypt, the most populous Arab state and a longtime regional religious and cultural center, offers a chance to revise current state–society dichotomies in the study of religious change across the Middle East. This book, in turn, is a social and intellectual history of a period in which Statist religious elites and Islamist movements competed to shape society by asserting control over the daily rhythms of life within state institutions and, in the process, produced novel models of religiosity. As they sought to redefine longstanding practices of education, prayer, and gender relations, members of the Muslim Brotherhood and select Islamist–Salafi thinkers and activists within Jamʿiyya Sharʿiyya clashed with the scholars of the Islamic Research Academy and the bureaucrats of the Supreme Council for Islamic Affairs. Far from a story of religious elites or their institutional centers alone, the genesis of the Islamic Revival in Egypt reveals how broad-based religious change emerged across, rather than outside, state institutions.

This book is the first study to draw on Statist, Islamist, and Salafi publications in telling a history of religious change in Egypt. During this period Islamic print media served as a key means of social mobilization; these projects, premised not only on ideological outreach but also on the crafting of practical programs, depended on readers to report the successes and the failures of their programs locally. Accordingly, this study melds analysis of articles published by leading figures within Egypt's key religious institutions and movements and fatwa requests and letters to the editor by their audiences to reconstruct how, why, and where religious change arose under al-Sadat.

The first magazine on which this study draws is also the best known: *al-Daʿwa* (The Call), was the official publication of the Muslim Brotherhood under the editorship of ʿUmar al-Tilmisani (d. 1986).

4 Said Amir Arjomand, *The Turban for the Crown: The Islamic Revolution in Iran* (New York: Oxford University Press, 1988), esp. 91–94.

5 Gideon Aran, *Kukizm: Shorshe Gush Emunim, Tarbut Hamitnahalim, Te'logya Tsiyonit, Meshihiyut bi-Zemanenu* (Jerusalem: Karmel, 2013).

At this time the Brotherhood's grassroots infrastructure was in tatters following the repression of the 'Abd al-Nasir period (1952–70)[6] and the surveillance of the early years of the al-Sadat period (1970–76),[7] and it lacked access to television, radio, or daily newspapers. Consequently, *al-Da'wa* represented the sole site where the Muslim Brothers could safely address a national audience and lay claim to a vision of Islamizing state and society through contemporary organizational forms.[8]

This Islamist opposition, however, was not limited to the Brotherhood. Among the most prominent organizations of this time was the Jam'iyya Shar'iyya, which melded a commitment to fighting un-Islamic innovation (*bid'a*) characteristic of Purist Salafism with a Brotherhood-inspired ambition to reform state and society beyond the mosque. While the organization itself steered clear of affiliation with a given magazine, its leading scholars, most prominently Ahmad 'Isa 'Ashur (d. 1990) and the organization's Imam, 'Abd al-Latif Mushtahiri (d. 1995), wrote and edited *al-I'tisam* (Adherence).[9]

[6] Technically, 'Abd al-Nasir only ascended above his fellow leader, Muhammad Najib, in 1954.

[7] While the period of 'Abd al-Nasir's rule (1954–70) saw wide-scale arrests and executions of the Muslim Brotherhood, the first half of al-Sadat's rule (1970–76) involved a comparatively modest effort to restrict public expression.

[8] This is not to suggest that *al-Da'wa* reached a still-substantial illiterate portion of Egypt's population. Rather, it is to claim that the circulation of this magazine, which surpassed 60,000 copies per issue, far exceeded the audience available to the Brotherhood by any other means. For a more detailed discussion of magazine circulation, see Chapter 2.

[9] This periodical's title refers to Surat al-'Umran 3:103, which reads: "And hold tight to the rope of God (*wa-a'taṣimū bi-ḥabl Allāh*) all together and do not become divided." I translate the title as "Adherence" to convey the joint emphasis of this verse on religious fidelity and unity. The question of whether the Jam'iyya Shar'iyya is Salafi requires elaboration. On the one hand, its Imam, 'Abd al-Latif Mushtahiri, emphasizes the organization's commitment to the "straight path of the Salaf (*ṣirāṭ al-Salaf al-mustaqīm*) ... We work day and night to adhere to the principles of monotheism (*al-tawḥīd*)." See "al-Jam'iyya Shar'iyya wa Sum'atuha fi al-Bilad al-'Arabiyya wa-l-Islamiyya," *al-I'tisam*, June 1978/Rajab 1398, 41. Indeed, in a 1960 lecture given at the Ansar al-Sunna headquarters in Cairo, Mushtahiri had explained that "the theology of the members of the Jam'iyya Shar'iyya (*'aqīdat a'adā' al-jam'iyya al-shar'iyya*) is the same as that of Ansar al-Sunna al-Muhamadiyya ... and it is the theology of the Salaf ... of the Quran and Sunna." This claim was reproduced in Ansar al-Sunna's *al-Hadi al-Nabawi* without critical comment, and an AS-sanctioned organizational history affirms that Mushtahiri as well as a second leading writer within *al-I'tisam*, Mahmud 'Abd al-Wahhab Fayyad, were "inclined to the

In the case of *al-I'tisam*, the term Islamist–Salafis refers not to an all-encompassing ideological description of the journal (though there were participants whose ideas fit both adjectives) but rather to the combination of Salafi and Islamist views among participants.

Less prominent yet no less significant were the Jam'iyya Shar'iyya's allies in fighting illicit innovation, the Quietist Salafis of Ansar al-Sunna al-Muhammadiyya, who published *al-Tawhid* (Monolatry)[10] in close conversation with Salafi scholars in Syria and Saudi Arabia.[11] Together, these periodicals reveal the contrasting ways in which these two organizations' leaders, many of whom were prominent Salafis, sought to shape religious practice in a time of Revival. For the sake of clarity, I will use the term Islamists to denote both the Brotherhood and those Islamist–Salafis of the Jam'iyya Shar'iyya, and the term Salafis to indicate both Islamist and Quietist subdivisions of this movement.

State institutions were not merely a site of negotiation, but were also a source of distinct religious projects. The Ministry of Endowments' Supreme Council for Islamic Affairs (al-Majlis al-A'la l-il-Shu'un al-

Salafi Call (*yumīlūn ilā al-da'wa al-salafiyya*)." This statement does not imply affiliation with the Alexandria-based Salafi organization the Salafi Call. For the former, see "Akhbar al-Jama'a," *al-Hadi al-Nabawi*, February 1961/Ramadan 1380, 50, and for the latter, see Ahmad Muhammad al-Tahir, *Jama'at Ansar al-Sunna al-Muhamadiyya: Nasha'tuha–Ahdafuha–Manhajuha–Juhuduha* (Mansura: Dar al-Fadila li-l-Nashr wa-l-Tawzi'/Dar al-Hadi al-Nabawi, 2004), 149. Here I differ with Richard Gauvain, who argues that the Jam'iyya Shar'iyya should not be considered Salafi because "despite … similarities, the main representatives of al-Gam'iyya al-Shar'iyya have never claimed the movement to be Salafism in ideology or practice" (Richard Gauvain, *Salafi Ritual Purity: In the Presence of God* [London: Routledge, 2013]), 37–38. Yet Gauvain also rightly points out the existence of Ash'arite theology within significant sectors of the organization. Accordingly, I specifically use the term "Salafi" with reference to particular leading figures within the JS rather than to describe all writers in *al-I'tisam* or members of the JS.

10 I consciously translate the magazine's title – and the theological concept within Salafi thought on which it is based – as Monolatry, rather than Monotheism, in acknowledgment of the centrality of practices of worshiping God, rather than monotheistic belief, to Salafism. See Daniel Lav, "Radical Muslim Theonomy: A Study in the Evolution of Salafi Thought" (unpublished dissertation, Hebrew University of Jerusalem, 2016), 24–26.

11 I categorize Ansar al-Sunna as Salafi first and foremost, based on its use of distinctly Salafi concepts. In the case of Ansar al-Sunna, the back cover of *al-Tawhid* noted the organization's commitment to "pure monotheism (*al-tawḥīd al-khāliṣ*), cleansed of all impurities (*al-muṭaharra min al-shawā'ib*)." To do so, they rely on the Quran and the authentic Sunna (*al-sunna al-saḥīḥa*). For example, see *al-Tawhid*, March 1979/Jumada al-Ula 1399, back cover.

Islamiyya) published *Minbar al-Islam* (The Pulpit of Islam). The magazine served to complement the Ministry's provision of Friday prayer leaders (sing. *imām*, pl. *a'īma*) and preachers (sing. *khaṭīb*, pl. *khuṭabā*) to mosques throughout Egypt, and sought to seize the mantle of religious legitimacy from the Islamist opposition by providing religious legitimization for state policies. Finally, the Islamic Research Academy (Majma' al-Buhuth al-Islamiyya), a body within al-Azhar University, the premier Sunni seminary located in Cairo, published *al-Azhar* as it attempted to uphold the primacy of a Statist project of religious regulation in the face of both bureaucrats within the Supreme Council for Islamic Affairs and Islamic movements which sought to remake state institutions and, by extension, society.

The religious shifts that these movements and institutions spearheaded cast light on the genesis of the key religious networks and societal practices that have undergirded the emergence of piety as a norm rather than an exception in Egypt over the past four decades. Moving beyond a focus on calls for the application of Islamic law (the shari'a) or the relative success or failure of Islamist parties at the ballot box, this book makes three linked interventions regarding the key actors, sites, and practices of religio-political change in Egypt.

First, it argues that key practices that have defined religious change in Egypt over the past four decades emerge primarily from Modernist notions of order and social change and secondarily from a longer Islamic tradition of piety. Second, it shows that, contrary to previous scholarship that has offered parallel stories of state and Islamist claims to Islam, Islamist projects of mobilization emerged within and were deeply shaped by state institutions. Finally, it demonstrates that state institutions, far from being ideologically uniform – let alone coherent – sites of transmission, hosted subtle negotiations over the role of Islam in daily life during this crucial period of religious change.

These linked arguments are significant for understanding the key axes of competition and cooperation to define the relationship between religion and politics in Egypt over the past forty years. By emphasizing the contribution of both state institutions and Islamic movements to the emergence of daily religious practice as a key axis of Egypt's Islamic Revival, this book shows the ways in which state-sponsored claims to shape daily practice both drive and are driven by independent religious movements, even as these movements themselves are deeply shaped by logics of order transmitted by state institutions. Though these two camps may be political competitors, and even enemies, they are ideological cousins. This observation extends to studies of Islamism and piety beyond Egypt, casting light on the mechanics of Islamists' engagement with state institutions, and on the ways in which ostensibly traditional projects of piety reflect distinctly modern assumptions of order.

My argument is that religious change in Egypt emerged out of intellectual cross-pollination between Statist and Islamist visions and a competition to reform society by reshaping state institutions. I unfold this argument across six chapters, which trace the roots, genesis, and consolidation of an Islamic Revival in Egypt between 1970 and 2015. In the first chapter I show how religious elites came to understand themselves as living in an age of Islamic Revival, while in the second chapter I profile the participants in these competing projects of piety. The next three chapters of the book explore the ways in which the Islamic Revival transformed the daily lives of middle-class Egyptians by reformulating and redefining key practices of religious education, public prayer, and gender relations at the intersection of local communities, on the one hand, and ideological and political platforms, on the other. The concluding empirical chapter (Chapter 6) then examines a peculiar legacy of the Islamic Revival under the rule of Hosni Mubarak (r. 1981–2011): the transformation of women's public participation from being a matter of educational or economic necessity that threatened public order to representing a necessary condition of public morality.

The Roots and Sites of Religious Change

In 1969 Richard P. Mitchell published *The Society of the Muslim Brothers*, which would soon become a classic and frequently cited study of Egypt's leading Islamist organization. In the preface to this work Mitchell argued that the Brotherhood's recent clashes with the Egyptian government represented

> the predictable eruption ... caused by an ever-dwindling activist fringe of individuals dedicated to an increasing level relevant "Muslim" position about society. ... Our feeling, for some time now shared by others, is that the essentially secular reform nationalism now in vogue in the Arab world will continue to operate to end the earlier appeal of this organization.[12]

[12] Richard P. Mitchell, *The Society of the Muslim Brothers* (New York: Oxford University Press, 1993 [1969]), xxiii–xxiv.

Writing in the shadow of modernization theory's claims about the ongoing and inevitable secularization of society,[13] Mitchell's position seemed uncontroversial. By the 1980s, however, it had become clear that this prediction was woefully inaccurate, and a series of English-language histories of Egypt's Islamic Revival were soon published, telling a story of a "turn" to Islam that emerged, seemingly full-formed, out of the disappointment of the 1967 Arab–Israeli war and the early euphoria of the 1973 war. These studies narrated this shift by focusing on prominent leaders, most notably Sayyid Qutb and ʿAbd al-Salam Faraj, on their landmark ideological contributions, and on the ways in which medieval scholarly debates came to acquire new relevance from the 1970s on.[14]

Political scientists and historians alike responded to this emphasis on religious elites by utilizing Social Movement Theory (SMT) to study the emergence of Islamist organizations within and beyond Egypt through a focus on local practices of outreach. These scholars have drawn on SMT to explore the broader political, economic, and social processes through which the grassroots educational and political apparatus of the Muslim Brotherhood developed during the Islamic Revival, while also accounting for the social contexts in which individual Egyptians came to participate not merely in acts of religious piety but also in Islamist political activism.[15] Yet the strength of these narratives – a deductive focus on how established social movements mobilize followers – obscures the ways in which change can pivot less on distinct ideological visions offered by particular movements than on social practices that emerge organically through competition among movements.

[13] For a landmark text of this school, see Daniel Lerner, *The Passing of Traditional Society: Modernizing the Middle East* (London: The Free Press of Glencoe, 1958).

[14] See Emanuel Sivan, *Radical Islam: Medieval Theology and Modern Politics* (New Haven: Yale University Press, 1990) and Gilles Kepel, The Roots of Radical Islam, trans. Jon Rothschild (London: Saqi, 2005). For works that analyze this trend beyond Egypt, see Fouad Ajami, *The Arab Predicament: Arab Political Thought and Practice since 1967* (Cambridge: Cambridge University Press, 1992), 60–88 and Seyyed Reza Vali Nasr, *Mawdudi and the Making of Islamic Revivalism* (New York: Oxford University Press, 1996).

[15] Carrie Rosefsky Wickham, *Mobilizing Islam: Religion, Activism, and Political Change in Egypt* (New York: Columbia University Press, 2002); Abdullah al-Arian, *Answering the Call: Popular Islamic Activism in Sadat's Egypt* (Oxford and New York: Oxford University Press, 2014).

In parallel, anthropologists have explored practices of ethical cultivation within Egypt's contemporary Islamic Revival. These studies have cast light on the importance of audiocassette sermons,[16] mosque study groups and ritual prayer,[17] and the use of religious dreams to transcend the barrier between the physical and spiritual worlds (known as the *barzakh*).[18] These authors and others emphasize the formation and performance of pious subjectivities across the social landscape, whether in taxicabs, mosques, or homes, and the ways in which a state of moral purity is both the result of pious practice and the precondition for its further performance.[19] Most prominently, Mahmood and Hirschkind situate these projects of subject formation primarily within a diachronic Islamic tradition of ethics and only secondarily in relation to state projects of religious regulation that they and others term "secularism."[20] The story told by this scholarship, however, significantly overstates the continuity between contemporary practices of piety and a longer Islamic tradition of ethical cultivation.

These narratives of grassroots mobilization and piety exist alongside a third body of scholarship on Islam and state power. In the specific case of Egypt, previous studies have highlighted primary and secondary religious education in public schools,[21] the increasing politicization of al-Azhar,[22] the activities of Dar al-

[16] See Charles Hirschkind, The Ethical Soundscape: *Cassette Sermons and Islamic Counterpublic* (New York: Columbia University Press, 2004).

[17] See Saba Mahmood, *The Politics of Piety: The Islamic Revival and the Feminist Subject* (Princeton: Princeton University Press, 2005).

[18] See Amira Mittermaier, *Dreams That Matter: Egyptian Landscapes of the Imagination* (Berkeley: University of California Press, 2011).

[19] See Hirschkind, The Ethical Soundscape, 30; Emilio Spadola, *The Calls of Islam: Sufis, Islamists, and Mass Mediation in Urban Morocco* (Bloomington: Indiana University Press, 2014), 126.

[20] Mahmood states: "Piety activists seek to imbue each of the various spheres of contemporary life with a regulative sensibility that takes its cue from the Islamic theological corpus rather than from modern secular ethics "(Mahmood, *The Politics of Piety*, 35). Similarly, Hirschkind notes that "we might say that Egypt's Islamic counterpublic is inscribed within the government rationalities and institutions of national public life but also oblique to them, incorporating orientations and modes of practical reason that exceed or cut across modern normativity" (Hirschkind, *The Ethical Soundscape*, 138–39).

[21] Gregory Starrett, *Putting Islam to Work: Education, Politics and Religious Transformation in Egypt* (Berkeley: University of California Press, 1998).

[22] See Malika Zeghal, "Religion and Politics in Egypt: The Ulema of al-Azhar, Radical Islam and the State (1952–94)," *International Journal of Middle East Studies*, 31:3 (1999), 371–99.

Ifta,[23] and how the Islamic Research Academy has used censorship to claim religious orthodoxy in the battle over "Cultural Islamism."[24] Beyond Egypt, numerous studies examine how governments from the Indian Ocean to the Mediterranean Sea use Islam as a means of extending the control of state institutions further into society,[25] while other research highlights the ways in which state policies decisively shape the particular form that Islamic movements take.[26] Although such research on the role of states in shaping a changing relationship between Islam and politics represents a valuable counterbalance to an exclusive focus on Islamic movements, it ultimately reproduces an intellectual and social binary between these movements and state institutions, and tells us little about how religious change is negotiated by ideologically diverse claimants within these institutions.

A focus on the intellectual roots and contextual performance of particular religious practices enables us to move beyond an exclusive concern with either Islamic movements or state institutions. Yet previous studies of Egypt's Islamic Revival provide little concrete detail as to the particular practices that define this shift. Saba Mahmood defines the Islamic Revival as referring

[23] Jakob Skovgaard-Petersen, *Defining Islam for the Egyptian State: Muftis and Fatwas and Dār al-Iftā'* (New York: Brill, 1997); Hussein Ali Agrama, *Questioning Secularism: Islam, Sovereignty and the Rule of Law in Modern Egypt* (Chicago: University of Chicago Press, 2012).

[24] Ismail examines the Islamic Research Academy's censorship role in the late 1990s through analysis of several decisions to either permit or ban specific books. See Salwa Ismail, *Rethinking Islamist Politics: Culture, the State and Islamism* (London: I. B. Tauris, 2006), 58–81, esp. 63–68 and 71–77.

[25] Mona Hassan, "Women Preaching for the Secular State: Official Female Preachers (Bayan Vaizler) in Contemporary Turkey," *International Journal of Middle East Studies*, 43:3 (2011), 451–73; Samuel Helfont, *Compulsion in Religion: Saddam Hussein, Islam, and the Roots of Insurgencies in Iraq* (Oxford: Oxford University Press, 2018); Nabil Mouline, *The Clerics of Islam: Religious Authority and Political Power in Saudi Arabia*, trans. Ethan S. Rundell (New Haven: Yale University Press, 2014); Nasr, *Islamic Leviathan*; and Donald Porter, *Managing Politics and Islam in Indonesia* (London: Routledge Curzon, 2002).

[26] For example, see Jocelyne Cesari, *The Awakening of Muslim Democracy: Religion, Modernity and the State* (Cambridge: Cambridge University Press, 2014); Mansoor Moaddel, *Jordanian Exceptionalism: A Comparative Analysis of State–Religion Relationships in Egypt, Iran, Jordan, and Syria* (New York: Palgrave Macmillan, 2002); and Colin J. Beck, "State Building as a Source of Islamic Political Organization," *Sociological Forum*, 24:2 (2009), 337–56.

not only to the activities of state-oriented political groups but more broadly to a religious ethos or sensibility that has developed within contemporary Muslim societies . . . [which has] a palpable presence in Egypt, manifest in the vast proliferation of neighborhood mosques and other institutions of Islamic learning and social welfare, in a dramatic increase in attendance of mosque by both men and women, and in marked displays of religious sociability.[27]

Along similar lines, Wickham notes that "a much broader segment of Egyptian society have been touched by the revival of private faith and observance than are committed to an Islamic project of transformative social and political change."[28] Finally, Hirschkind notes: "Its broadest section has always remained grounded in grassroots efforts to revitalize Islamic forms of knowledge, pedagogy, comportment, and sociability."[29] While these definitions certainly note key practices and central sites of performance around which Egypt's Islamic Revival pivoted, they do not ground these practices historically within particular institutions, nor do they analyze them as the product of negotiation among competing factions, Statist and Islamist.

As a result, SMT studies of Islamism and ethnographies of piety have both focused almost exclusively on those spaces outside the state in which piety is lived. Scholars utilizing SMT tell a story of Islamist preachers speaking to a growing segment of the population through audiocassettes, pamphlets, and magazines, while Islamist organizers function either on the urban periphery[30] or within "open" space provided by Egyptian universities.[31] Similarly, projects of ethical cultivation proceed entirely at a distance from the state within a broad array of charitable and educational organizations supported by the "Parallel Islamic Sector."[32] While this approach valuably captures the emergence of alternative networks of religious practice and activism, it does not conceptualize the state as both an actor and a site of religious contestation whose institutions intersect with these alternative networks.

27 Mahmood, *The Politics of Piety*, 3. 28 Wickham, *Mobilizing Islam*, 136.
29 Hirschkind, *The Ethical Soundscape*, 6.
30 See Wickham, *Mobilizing Islam*, 121–25.
31 See al-Arian, *Answering the Call*, esp. 105–45.
32 See Wickham, *Mobilizing Islam*, 93–118. Though Saba Mahmood does not discuss the funding of the Women's Mosque Movement, it is fair to assume that the same sources of funding identified by Wickham go to support these activities. See Mahmood, *The Politics of Piety*, 41–48.

By tracing the intellectual and social formation of Egypt's Islamic Revival, I cast light on the roots of piety in contemporary Egypt, the sociological boundaries of Islamist activism, and the relationship between Islamist organizations and state institutions. Historical studies of the Islamic Revival foreground the revitalization of longstanding models of Islamic thought, while the ethnographic literature on piety in post-1970s Egypt argues that these projects emerged directly out of a diachronic Islamic tradition of ethical cultivation.[33] This study, by contrast, places a longer Islamic tradition, political and ethical, on the margins of the Islamic Revival; instead, it is the fusion of Modernist notions of social change and order with Islamist visions of mobilization that undergird the key projects of the Islamic Revival.

A second central question relates to the study of Islamism. Scholars of Islamist movements in Egypt, Turkey, Pakistan, and Jordan have focused exclusively on "Islamist" sites of cultivation, rightfully highlighting the importance of local networks formed around mosques and college campuses.[34] By contrast, examining the rise of the Islamic Revival as a story of state institutions, Islamist organizations, and the mobilization of those who frequented state institutions on a daily basis reveals the intellectual and social ties that bind these projects with state-allied religious elites and the institutions under their control. Far from

33 For Egypt, see Hirschkind, *The Ethical Soundscape*; Mahmood, *The Politics of Piety*, and Mittermaier, *Dreams That Matter*. For Lebanon, see Lara Deeb, *An Enchanted Modern: Gender and Public Piety in Shi'i Lebanon* (Princeton: Princeton University Press, 2006). For Pakistan, see Robert Rozehnal, *Islamic Sufism Unbound: Politics and Piety in Twenty-First Century Pakistan* (New York: Palgrave Macmillan, 2007). For Indonesia, see Rachel Rinaldo, *Mobilizing Piety: Islam and Feminism in Indonesia* (New York: Oxford University Press, 2013). For France and Germany, see Jeanette S. Jouili, *Pious Practice and Secular Constraints* (Stanford: Stanford University Press, 2015).

34 This is distinct from highlighting the ways in which Islamists have "captured" official positions (such as that of leadership of student unions) within state institutions. See al-Arian, *Answering the Call*; Hazem Kandil, *Inside the Brotherhood* (Walden, MA: Polity, 2015); Wickham, *Mobilizing Islam*; and Carrie Rosefsky Wickham, *The Muslim Brotherhood: Evolution of an Islamist Movement* (Princeton: Princeton University Press, 2013), esp. 46–75. Examples of such studies outside Egypt include Jenny White, Islamist Mobilization in Turkey: A Study in Vernacular Politics (Seattle: University of Washington Press, 2002), and Janine A. Clark, Islam, Charity and Activism: Middle-Class Networks and Social Welfare in Egypt, Jordan and Yemen (Bloomington: Indiana University Press, 2004). Also see Quintan Wiktorowicz, *The Management of Islamic Activism: Salafis, the Muslim Brotherhood, and State Power in Jordan* (Albany: State University of New York Press, 2001).

being marginal sites of religious practice, state institutions – along with their particular ideological missions – continue to shape the performance of piety in Egypt as elsewhere.

Finally, this study shows that the relationship between state institutions and Islamist movements cannot be understood through a one-sided model in which one faction shapes the possibilities of the other. While it is certainly the case that state institutions exercise influence in shaping the local possibilities available to Islamist organizations, and that Islamist organizations have sought to capture state institutions, particular projects of piety in Egypt's Islamic Revival emerged through subtle and continued competition among religious elites, and between these elites and Egyptian men and women. How can critical use of print media help to cast light on the subtle negotiation of social change within state institutions?

Media, Social Change, and an Islamic Revival

In his 1996 study of textual culture and social change in early twentieth-century Berlin, Peter Fritzche documents how newspapers served as indispensable "guides" to their readers as they traversed an increasingly complex city. This process was expansive yet also incoherent:

> [As] an encompassing symbolic order [which] informed the city and left behind countless versions and editions ... popular newspapers did more than introduce the metropolis ... they fashioned ways of looking in addition to fashioning looks, and they trained readers how to move through the streets and crowds in addition to guiding them among sensational sites.[35]

Without the aid of newspapers, readers were lost in the city even as the newspapers continually sought to reshape the city through their own narratives. Conversely, the centrality of newspapers to the lives of their readers stemmed not only from industrialization or the spread of literacy, but also from the repositioning of the paper as an "encyclopedia of daily life."[36] Through a dynamic interaction between the city as a physical site and newspaper narrativization, editors and writers sought to guide their readers, and their readers applied this guidance with varying degrees of success.

35 Peter Fritzche, *Reading Berlin 1900* (Cambridge, MA: Harvard University Press, 1996), 16.
36 Fritzche, *Reading Berlin 1900*, 61.

Like Berlin's newspapers, Egypt's Islamic magazines provided alternative guides to a diffuse project of individual and collective religiosity anchored in urban environments; questions of religious education, public prayer, and gender relations raised new challenges when performed on public buses and subways or within state offices and educational institutions. If newspapers provided "keys to moving about the city and thus corresponded to the ability to master the city" in Berlin,[37] Islamic magazines guided daily acts of piety in the turbulent political, social, and economic environment of Egyptian cities.

In contrast to Fritzche's model, however, the syllabus by which readers navigated the city and the keys necessary to master it were not the creation of textual elites alone. Three of these five magazines – *al-Da'wa, al-I'tisam*, and *Minbar al-Islam* – featured numerous letters to the editor and fatwa requests in each issue. This space provided a forum for readers to both affirm and contest the religious claims of Islamic magazine editors and writers, while informing these elites of the challenges faced by their visions on the ground.[38] *Al-Azhar* and *al-Tawhid*, by contrast, feature relatively little correspondence from these periodicals' readers, a structural feature that both reflected and determined organizational priorities.

The use of letters to the editor and fatwa requests to represent reader participation also necessitates consideration of whether these sources were actually composed by readers. Previous scholarship on fatwas has highlighted the practice of muftis creating questions for themselves to answer.[39] It appears unlikely, however, that editors of the Fatwa and Letters to the Editor sections in these three magazines would have done so again and again – over 2,000 times among the three publications – in correspondence that often included numbered street addresses throughout Cairo, Alexandria, and the Nile Delta. If anything, editors had insufficient time to *read* all the letters, let alone to fabricate them.[40]

[37] Fritzche, *Reading Berlin 1900*, 90.

[38] *Al-Azhar* and *al-Tawhid*, by contrast, featured comparatively scarce popular correspondence between 1976 and 1981, though by the end of the period each had incorporated greater reader input.

[39] See Muhammad Khalid Masud, Brinkley Messick, and David Powers, "Muftis, Fatwas, and Islamic Legal Interpretation," in Muhammad Khalid Masud, Brinkley Messick, and David Powers (eds.), *Islamic Legal Interpretation: Muftis and their Fatwas* (Cambridge, MA: Harvard University Press, 1996), 22.

[40] For example, *Minbar al-Islam* editor Fu'ad Hayba apologized to readers in March 1979 that he had not read, let alone had time to select among, all their

Responding to reader input was not only a question of logistics, but also of practical goals: the Letters to the Editor and Fatwa sections of *al-Daʿwa, al-Iʿtisam*, and *Minbar al-Islam* served as a crucial means for religious elites to gauge the grassroots reception of their projects; in the case of the Brotherhood, their magazine was the only means of doing so. These projects, premised not only on ideological outreach but also on the crafting of practical programs, depended on readers to report the successes and the failures of their programs locally.

The editors, writers, and muftis of these periodicals could loosely be grouped as a "religious elite," and were divided among advocates of Statist, Islamist, Islamist–Salafi, and Quietist Salafi positions. In Bourdieuian terms, they were distinguished by their possession of a high level of "embodied cultural capital" (which assumes a process of cultivation requiring financial capital) and similarly high levels of "social capital" (i.e. access to social networks which in turn provide access to various forms of monetary capital).[41]

The audiences of these elites, by contrast, lacked this cultural and social capital; yet their position was not merely that of an undifferentiated mass. Instead, as Chapter 2 will show, they represented a slice of literate Egyptian middle-class readers who aspired to both socioeconomic mobility and religiosity. Put differently, these readers sought a "religious respectability"[42] in which they were both defined as pious subjects by religious elites and played an active role in defining their own subjectivities. This project of "educated piety," available to a literate yet economically heterogeneous middle class, was not available to working-class Egyptians, who remained captive to a narrower set of religious prescriptions and at continual risk of "incorrect" behavior. Just as significantly, these projects advantaged men's voices over

letters. See "Maʿa al-Qurra," *Minbar al-Islam*, March 1979/Rabiʿ al-Awwal 1399, 174.

41 See Pierre Bourdieu, "The Forms of Capital," in A. H. Halsey, Philip Brown, Hugh Lauder, and Amy S. Wells (eds.), *Education, Culture, Economy and Society* (New York: Oxford University Press, 1997), 48–51.

42 I adapt this term from Beverly Skeggs' 1987 ethnography of working-class white women in northwest England. As Skeggs notes, "Respectability contains judgments of class, race, gender and sexuality and different groups have differential access to the mechanisms for generating, resisting and displaying respectability" (Beverly Skeggs, *Formations of Class and Gender: Becoming Respectable* [London: Sage, 1997], 2). This approach, which draws inspiration from the work of Pierre Bourdieu, analyzes processes of subject formation that reflect, but are not defined, by capital.

women's; the editors and writers of these periodicals were overwhelmingly male, as were the readers whose letters appeared.

The choice of social respectability as a theoretical lens casts light on the intersection of ethical cultivation and social performance in contemporary Islamic claims to piety. While there is little doubt that the performance of piety involves bodily practices ("technologies of the self," to use the Foucaultian term on which both Hirschkind and Mahmood draw) that orient the individual toward the Divine, the limitation of this lens is that it foregrounds the centrality of a diachronic Islamic tradition of ethical cultivation at the expense of analyzing the entanglement of these individual ethical projects within a broader political, social, and economic context. Social respectability, by contrast, allows one to engage with piety as a practice of ethical cultivation that intersects with broader structures of class and gender. These claims to piety, however, are only comprehensible in the context of the dueling religious projects of this period.

Conceptualizing Statism, Islamism, and Salafism

The engagement of ostensibly "secular" states in the regulation and production of religion is now a truism[43] and, in this vein, recent scholarship on state power and religion across the Middle East has examined this dynamic through the analytical lens of "Secularism."[44] While this scholarship has valuably illuminated the fundamental dynamics of Islam as it is regulated through law, it tells a story of state institutions impermeable to both bottom-up influences from within society and to Islamist contestation at the heart of state institutions. By contrast, I situate the intersection of state power, religious interpretation, and pious practice within the conceptual frame of Statism. As a global project of state power, Statism, also known as High Modernism, first arose in the mid-nineteenth century as an ideology of state-directed social and economic transformation that sought

[43] Talal Asad argues that "because the modern nation-state seeks to regulate all aspects of individual life – even the most intimate, such as birth and death – no one, whether religious or otherwise, can avoid encountering its ambitious powers" (Talal Asad, *Formations of the Secular: Christianity, Islam, Modernity* [Stanford: Stanford University Press, 2003], 199).

[44] See Asad, *Formations of the Secular*, 205–56; Agrama, *Questioning Secularism*; and Saba Mahmood, *Religious Difference in a Secular Age: A Minority Report* (Princeton: Princeton University Press, 2016).

to bring about "huge, utopian changes in people's work habits, living patterns, moral conduct and worldview."[45]

The project of Statism in Egypt, however, must first be understood within a longer history of state-sponsored modernization that began in the late nineteenth century. Alongside its goal of strengthening Egypt politically and economically in the face of European encroachment, this project sought to achieve "political order" and to cultivate national identity through the creation of institutions (most notably, the army, the school, and the factory) which would produce "the modern individual ... as an isolated, disciplined, receptive and industrious political subject."[46] The school, in particular, sought to model social order more broadly as "students were kept moving from task to task, with every motion and every space disciplined and put to use."[47] At the same time, though, practice frequently deviated from state planners' hopes; whether within army barracks or state factories, Egyptians often evaded the demands of supposedly inescapable disciplinary systems.[48]

This longer history of the exercise of modern state power would see an expansion in the 1950s under ʿAbd al-Nasir. In alliance with the Soviet Union, another adopter of Statism, ʿAbd al-Nasir embarked on an ambitious vision of mass social and economic transformation that used technology and state access to (and seizure of) capital both to attempt to remake Egyptian society in its mold and to sideline pre-revolutionary elites. An overlooked element of Statism in Egypt, however, is its religious ambitions: ʿAbd al-Nasir did not merely seek to repress religion (though he did clamp down violently on the Muslim Brotherhood) but to actively shape religious thought and practice in order to build an obedient national community.[49] In this study I will

45 James Scott, *Seeing Like a State: How Certain Schemes to Improve the Human Condition Have Failed* (New Haven: Yale University Press, 1998), 5.

46 Timothy Mitchell, Colonising Egypt (Berkeley: University of California Press, 1991), xi.

47 Mitchell, *Colonising Egypt*, 71.

48 See Khaled Fahmy, All the Pasha's Men*: Mehmed Ali, His Army and the Making of Modern Egypt* (Cairo: American University in Cairo Press, 2002), esp. 199–238, and Samer Shehata, *Shop Floor Culture and Politics in Egypt* (Albany: State University of New York Press, 2009), 4.

49 Scholarship on the religious role of state institutions under ʿAbd al-Nasir is limited. A crucial exception to this rule is Malika Zeghal's study of Azhar's *ʿulama* during the second half of the twentieth century. See Malika Zeghal, *Gardiens de l'Islam: les oulémas d'al-Azhar dans l'Egypte contemporaine* (Paris: Presses de Sciences Po, 1996). For a discussion of the politics of religious

use "Statist" to refer to the particular top-down vision of change that emerged in post-1952 Egypt, while designating concepts of order and timeliness transmitted by Egyptian state institutions from the nineteenth century on as "Modernist."

State institutions sought not only to impart a particular conception of order, but also to subordinate religious identity to political exigencies, most notably the promotion of nationalism or signature ideological campaigns. As Gregory Starrett has shown, late nineteenth-century British-led educational reforms involved a process of "objectification" that rendered Islam as a concrete set of pronouncements. This objectified religious tradition was then utilized in the service of specific political goals: the British used it to socialize the population against political revolt, ʿAbd al-Nasir to justify scientific socialism, and al-Sadat to argue that the regime (and not the Islamist opposition) possessed an authoritative claim to religious legitimacy.[50] This process of functionalization, by which religion came to be associated with particular social and political ends and practices, produced a new understanding of religion itself: "The ideas, symbols and behaviors constituting 'true' Islam came to be judged not by their adherence to contemporary popular or high traditions, but by their utility in performing social work."[51] While aspirants to piety could turn to a longer Islamic tradition of ethical cultivation, they could not escape the continued influence of the state-sponsored vision of a model citizen whose religious obligations mirrored nationalist priorities and regime interests.

Egypt's defeat in the 1967 Arab–Israeli war and changing international political winds would help to shape a different, yet not wholly discontinuous, vision of Statist transformation under al-Sadat (r. 1970–81). On the one hand, the control exercised by state institutions over traditional domains decreased: al-Sadat's 1974 *infitāḥ* increased direct foreign investment and privatized previously state-owned companies, his 1976 introduction of political platforms (*manābir*) opened up new space for limited political debate, and his comparatively open approach to the press enabled Islamists and Salafis of both Islamist and Quietist varieties to publish and even mobilize from 1976 on. On the

education under ʿAbd al-Nasir, see Starrett, *Putting Islam to Work*, 77–80. Crucially, both Statist periodicals of the al-Sadat period, *Minbar al-Islam* and *al-Azhar*, were also published under ʿAbd al-Nasir.

[50] Starrett, *Putting Islam to Work*, 77–86.

[51] Starrett, *Putting Islam to Work*, 62.

other hand, he also utilized state-based religious figures – whether scholars at the Islamic Research Academy or bureaucrats within the Supreme Council for Islamic Affairs – to facilitate a vision of regime-led religious transformation, and sought to enforce this transformation through state-controlled offices, schools, and mosques.

Mass media were central to the project of Statism, complementing the educational system's emphasis on the nation-state by creating a mass-mediated national community in which religious discourse and practice were transmitted and debated. State institutions used a variety of organs – television, radio, and print – to reinforce the "nation" as the primary frame of identity and to reaffirm the religious credentials of the ruling elite.[52] In the shadow of a mass-mediated nation in which bureaucratic order sought to organize society, and religious interpretation and practice served to affirm the legitimacy of political elites, multiple religious projects took shape.

Notwithstanding the commitment to using state power to shape religious thought and practice that defines Statism, it is not an intellectually uniform approach. While *al-Azhar* sought to uphold scholarly interpretative authority, *Minbar al-Islam* embraced an instrumental mode of religious interpretation geared toward providing religious justification for political policies. In this regard, *Minbar al-Islam*'s approach had more in common with that of the Muslim Brotherhood than with its Statist peer, while *al-Azhar*'s intellectual vision of a religious elite was similar to those of Salafi scholars within *al-I'tisam* and *al-Tawhid*.

Islamism in Egypt developed in parallel to Statist visions of political, social, and economic transformation. I follow Euben and Zaman in defining Islamism as referring to

> contemporary movements that attempt to return to the scriptural foundations of the Muslim community, excavating and reinterpreting them for application to the present-day social and political world ... Islamists may be characterized as explicitly and intentionally political and as engaging in multifaceted critiques of all those people, institutions, practices, and orientations that do not meet their standards of this divinely mandated political engagement.[53]

52 Charles Hirschkind notes this dynamic in twentieth-century Egypt more broadly: see Hirschkind, *The Ethical Soundscape*, 7. Emilio Spadola makes a similar observation regarding contemporary Morocco: see Spadola, *The Calls of Islam*, 7.

53 Roxanne Euben and Muhammad Qasim Zaman, Princeton Readings in Islamist Thought (Princeton: Princeton University Press, 2009), 4.

This relationship between Islamism and the "present-day social and political world" does not assume that Islamism developed as a mere conceptual mirror of Statist claims to religion, only that it was shaped by the extensive claims made by this project to guide the religious thought and practices of the Egyptian population.

In the specific case of the Brotherhood, the organization's rise in Egypt was directly shaped not merely by the power and challenge of the Egyptian state, but also by competition with the Palace, British colonial rule, the threat of Christian missionaries, and the expansion of state infrastructure. Most notably, the organization's historical emphasis on popular proselytization reflected both this foreign religious threat and the political restrictions of the period.[54] The ʿAbd al-Nasir period, in turn, impressed upon Egypt's Islamist movement the importance of state power,[55] and the balance between formal political participation and preaching has remained a key tension within the Muslim Brotherhood to this day. Accordingly, this project treats Statist and Islamist claims to social and political transformation as ideologically dueling visions which emerged out of and reflected similar political, social, and intellectual shifts.

[54] See Beth Baron, *The Orphan Scandal: Christian Missionaries and the Rise of the Muslim Brotherhood* (Stanford: Stanford University Press, 2014), esp. 117–34. For a discussion of Hasan al-Banna's ambivalence toward participation in national politics, see Mitchell, *The Society of the Muslim Brothers*, 27, 36–43. For a quantitative analysis of the role of economic and state infrastructure in shaping early Islamic activism, see Steven Brooke and Neil Ketchley, "Social and Institutional Origins of Political Islam," *American Political Science Review*, 112:2 (May 2018), 376–94.

[55] Nathan Brown notes that, over the course of the twentieth century, questions of the application of the shariʿa came to be increasingly focused on the state-based legal reform rather than the traditional context of juridical reasoning. Though claims that French law was culturally inappropriate first emerged in the 1930s, they did not become popular within the Islamist movement until the 1960s and 1970s when "calls for the application of the Shariʿa had moved to the center for Islamist movements of all stripes ... as a set of identifiable rules" (Nathan Brown, "Shariʿa and State in the Modern Middle East," *International Journal of Middle East Studies*, 29:3 [1997], 359–76, at 370–71). Along similar lines, Talal Asad argues: "Islamism's preoccupation with state power is the result not of its commitment to nationalist ideas but of the modern nation-state's enforced claim to constitute legitimate social identities and arenas" (Asad, *Formations of the Secular*, 200). This state-centered focus and belief in the efficacy of legal reform and state power in social transformation are thus inextricably tied to the claims of ʿAbd al-Nasir's ideological project.

Alongside and in conversation with the twentieth-century competition between Statist and Islamist visions, a project known as Salafism emerged. Henri Lauzière has traced the interconnected histories of what would become increasingly distinct categories of "Modernist" and "Purist" Salafism during the second half of the twentieth century. While the former is defined by a project of "balanced reform" (*al-islāḥ al-mu'tadil*) that could incorporate both territorial nationalism and Western intellectual categories, the latter project is distinguished by its commitment to the Hanbali doctrine of the forefathers (*madhhab al-salaf*) and to deriving law directly from the Quran and Sunna. From the 1970s on, scholars of the latter category increasingly came to enumerate Salafism as a comprehensive approach (*manhaj*) that melded creed and law and sought "purity in every aspect of life."[56] In Egypt, the Muslim Brotherhood is heir to the project of balanced reform under the banner of Islamism, and Ansar al-Sunna al-Muhammadiyya – and particular leading members of the Jam'iyya Shar'iyya – lay claim to the Purist project of neo-Hanbali theology and precise religious practice, with the latter also embracing the Brotherhood's commitment to political action. Notwithstanding the Brotherhood's ties to this heritage of moderate reform, this book will follow the organization's usage of terms such "Islamists" (*islāmiyyūn*) rather than Salafis (*salafiyyūn*).[57]

A hybrid story of Statist and Islamist contestation underscores the key sites and practices of contestation in al-Sadat's Egypt. The inclusion of Quietist Salafis in this story, in turn, reveals the internal divisions among Islamic movements in Egypt vis-à-vis the Egyptian state. Groups such as Ansar al-Sunna harbored no formal political aspirations and thus, in their engagement with both the regime and the state institutions under its

[56] Henri Lauzière, *The Making of Salafism: Islamic Reform in the Twentieth Century* (New York: Columbia University Press, 2016), 224. Lauzière's (and my) usage of Purist as distinguished by a particular approach to theology and law is distinct from that of Quintan Wiktorowicz, who uses this term to distinguish those Salafis who "emphasize a focus on nonviolent methods of propagation, purification, and education ... view[ing] politics as a diversion that encourages deviancy." Those whom Wiktorowicz terms "Politicos" are, in my terminology, "Salafi–Islamists." See Quintan Wiktorowicz, "Anatomy of the Salafi Movement," *Studies in Conflict and Terrorism*, 29 (2006), 207–39.

[57] This is distinct from acknowledging that, while he was the Brotherhood's leader, Hasan al-Banna famously described the organization as "a Salafiyya message, a Sunni way, a Sufi truth, a political organization, an athletic group, a cultural–educational union, economic company, and a social idea" (Mitchell, *The Society of the Muslim Brothers*, 14).

control, did not necessarily seek to upset the political status quo. At the same time, though, such groups lived within a shared ecosystem of mosques and educational institutions that had long facilitated intellectual cross-pollination with the Muslim Brotherhood.[58] Just as the turn of leading figures within the Jam'iyya Shar'iyya to Islamist visions of political and social transformation speaks to the rising influence of the Brotherhood within Egyptian society, so too does the persistence of a Quietist approach to politics within Ansar al-Sunna underscore the limits of conflating Islamic movements with an Islamist opposition and the latter's signature focus on directly challenging state authority. As Statist and Islamist projects clashed and collaborated – and scholars and laymen of varying priorities negotiated the balance within particular institutions – they would produce a particular set of practices that were recognizable to all, yet belonged to none.

Chapter Overview

A methodological commitment to melding social and intellectual history structures this in-depth study of Islamic magazines. Across thousands of pages of sometimes glossy and other times faded print, editors and writers sought to make competing projects of piety legible to an audience that traversed bus lines and train cars and as they made their way through public education and bureaucratic employment. In turn, the middle-class readers who participated in these projects laid claim to religious respectability while shaping these projects from the ground up.

Chapter 1 sets the stage for the study of the distinct projects of the Islamic Revival by sketching a conceptual history of ideas of religious revival in post-colonial Egypt. Opening in 1952 with the Brotherhood's early alliance with the Free Officers and their concurrent hopes of Islamic Revival in Egypt, it tells a story of how religious elites between 1952 and 1973 continually voiced their anticipation of a revival that

[58] For example, student activist and later Brotherhood leader 'Abd al-Mun'im Abu-l-Futuh noted in a recent memoir that he frequently attended mosques affiliated with both the Jam'iyya Shar'iyya and Ansar al-Sunna, which also included key Brotherhood thinkers such as Second General Guide Hasan al-Hudaybi and Muhammad al-Ghazali. See 'Abd al-Mun'im Abu-l-Futuh, *'Abd al-Mun'im Abu-l-Futuh: Shahid 'ala Tarikh al-Haraka al-Islamiyya fi Misr, 1970–1984*, ed. Hussam Tammam (Cairo: Dar al-Shuruq, 2012), 35–36.

had not yet arrived. While early stirrings of revival surfaced following the 1973 Arab–Israeli war, what such a revival entailed and whom it involved remained unclear. Centering on the period between 1978 and 1981, this chapter traces how leading figures within the Brotherhood and Jamʿiyya Sharʿiyya looked abroad, not only at sister movements throughout the Middle East and South Asia, but also to parallel stirrings in Israel and the United States, as they sought to understand the religious changes in their midst. At the intersection of local activism, regional Islamist movements, and a new awareness of ideological competitors around the world, Islamist elites constructed a future-oriented vision that would sway their state-aligned competitors and shape Egypt's religious trajectory.

Who were the literate readers, Egyptian and non-Egyptian, who participated in the competing projects of religious mobilization at the dawn of the Islamic Revival? Chapter 2 takes advantage of the information offered in the author line of letters to the editor and fatwa requests to construct a geographic and socioeconomic profile of readers who participated in the pages of *al-Daʿwa*, *al-Iʿtisam*, and *Minbar al-Islam*. Due to limited information in *al-Azhar* and *al-Tawhid*, this chapter excludes these readers. The geographic profile of participants in Islamic magazines underscores the role of middle-class participants from across Egypt well as from the Persian Gulf and North Africa in the negotiation of key issues of the Islamic Revival. Having established the spatial and socioeconomic position of these readers, though, the question remains: what were the projects in which they engaged, and how did these new models of religious practice shape Egyptian state and society alike?

Chapters 3 through 5 then trace the emergence of three key projects of the Islamic Revival as they were transmitted by and negotiated in Islamic magazines: education, prayer, and gender relations. Chapter 3 explores the rise of competing projects and conceptions of Islamic education in Egypt between 1976 and 1981. While previous scholarship suggests implicitly that Islamist and state-sponsored educational projects reflected diametrically opposed visions of religious change, this chapter shows how Islamist elites, inspired by the example of their peers in Pakistan and Saudi Arabia, first sought to affect religious educational reform through Ministry of Education-controlled public schools, before turning to the creation of independent sites of religious transmission. In parallel, middle-class participants in the Islamic

Revival asserted their prerogative to acquire the religious literacy necessary to apply Islam to their daily lives. Yet the turn away from this state institution was easier than a clear break from its guiding assumptions: both Islamist elites and their readers reproduced the Modernist claim that education could transform society, even as they sought to craft alternative social visions.

Living a pious life involved not only religious education but also ritual devotion. Chapter 4 examines the transformation of the early afternoon *ẓuhr* prayer into a key practice of political contestation within schools and government offices. Previous studies focus on the Friday (*jumʿa*) prayer, its accompanying sermon, and the battle between the Ministry of Endowments and Islamist opposition to control mosques across Egypt. By contrast, this chapter foregrounds afternoon prayer as a site of daily Islamist challenge in al-Sadat's Egypt. Specifically, by asserting rights to perform prayer publicly and in timely fashion, Egyptian Muslims laid claim to both time and space within state institutions. Yet this was not solely a story of Islamist influence: while Islamists successfully gained access to state institutions, equally significant were the ways in which state-sponsored conceptions of order, discipline, and subject formation transformed the temporal assumptions at the core of this daily ritual.

If prayer was to be performed five times daily in public fashion, a socially conservative project of gender relations was to structure social interactions outside prayer. Previous studies have highlighted calls for gender segregation among the Muslim Brotherhood and Salafism of both Islamist and Quietist varieties, and this model remains an ideal today. Indeed, efforts to both regulate and facilitate particular models of gender relations in public at this time were hardly exceptional: during this period; Iran instituted and Saudi Arabia expanded previous policies of state-sponsored gender segregation in schools and workplaces, while in Israel the Tel Aviv and Haifa municipalities introduced the first gender-segregated beaches.[59] In the Egyptian

[59] For the Iranian case, see Hamideh Sedghi, *Women and Politics in Iran: Veiling, Unveiling, Reveiling* (New York: Cambridge University Press, 2007), 221–27. For the Saudi case, see Steffen Hertog, *Princes, Brokers, and Bureaucrats: Oil and the State in Saudi Arabia* (London: Cornell University Press, 2010), 92. For the Israeli case, see Shayna Weiss, "A Beach of Their Own: The Creation of the Gender-Segregated Beach in Tel Aviv," *Journal of Israeli History*, 35 (2016), 39–56, at 39.

case, however, the central question was neither veiling nor gender segregation, but rather the emergence of a project of Islamic norms of comportment (*ādāb islāmiyya*) that legislated not merely how men and women were to avoid each other, but also how they were to interact, whether by sight, sound, or touch.

These projects are significant because they enabled Islamist organizations to reorder state institutions and public life alike without access to either a broad-based infrastructure or to the coercive power of the state. Education stands at the heart of state efforts to build the nation by forming individual citizens; it is a realm in which state power is highly tangible yet, as a project that seeks to shape behavior outside the classroom, it is also vulnerable to alternative projects of religious transmission. Prayer, in turn, represents a practice that is traditionally private, with particular public exceptions, such as the Friday prayer. Contestation over prayer within state institutions involved an effort to de-privatize prayer and, in doing so, to challenge the relegation of non-Statist religious visions to the private realm. Finally, the promotion of a socially conservative model of gender relations cuts to the question of how citizens relate to one another in daily life.

The success of the Islamic Revival lies not only in its initial inroads in 1970s Egypt, but in its striking consolidation across Egyptian state and society over the subsequent four decades. This consolidation was often expressed in a de-politicization of particular practices of the Revival; while both the pursuit of alternative religious education (Chapter 3) and the performance of the daily *ẓuhr* prayer (Chapter 4) may index particular religious commitments, neither represents a central point of contention for Egypt's diverse religious movements or a key concern for the ruling regime.

Norms of comportment, by contrast, remain a key site of contestation. Yet, if the story of the Revival's genesis appears as a straightforward one of Islamist organizations successfully capturing space within state institutions by melding modernist notions of order and longstanding practices of transmission, ritual practice, and comportment, the consolidation of this shift over the past four decades complicates the directionality of this narrative. Chapter 6, which tackles continued debates over women's public presence under Hosni Mubarak (r. 1981–2011), traces the process by which Muslim Brothers and both Islamist and Quietist Salafis, who had once feared women's public presence, came to present women as a central marker of public morality. In the process, these groups, which had so successfully used Modernist notions as a means to disrupt the status quo of state institutions in the second half of the 1970s, came to adopt the Secular Nationalist vision of women as objects and agents of national progress as an end unto itself in maintaining Egypt's Islamic Revival. It is to the intellectual architecture of this shift – a conceptual history of revival in 1970s Egypt – that we now turn.

1 *Mind before Matter*

Visions of Religious Change in Postcolonial Egypt

It does not bother me that external enemies lurk and seek to obstruct the contemporary Islamic Revival (*al-ṣaḥwa al-islāmiyya al-muʿāṣira*), as this is a logical matter dictated by the principles of mutual opposition between Truth and Falsehood ... Rather, what bothers, haunts, and afflicts my heart is the sorrow of the Revival's internal conflict (*taʿadī al-ṣaḥwa nafsuhā*), as its enemy resides within it.

-Yusuf al-Qaradawi, 1989[1]

Needless to say, we must connect the "return of the hijab" (*ʿawdat al-ḥijāb*) on the faces of Muslim women to the Islamic Revival that has arisen (*al-ṣaḥwa al-islāmiyya al-nāhiḍa*) and whose light has illuminated many Islamic countries, including Egypt.

-Muhammad b. Ismaʿil al-Muqaddam, 2002[2]

Yusuf al-Qaradawi and Muhammad b. Ismaʿil al-Muqaddam are two of Egypt's most prominent religious scholars, the former a longtime Muslim Brother and pioneer of the Centrist approach (known as *al-wasaṭiyya*) and the latter the founder of the Salafi Call (al-Daʿwa al-Salafiyya), an Islamist–Salafi movement that forms the basis of Egypt's leading Salafi party, Hizb al-Nur. While al-Qaradawi summons the "objectives of the shariʿa" (*maqāṣid al-sharīʿa*) to argue for women's participation in public life, al-Muqaddam argues that women must cover their faces and avoid appearing in public whenever possible.[3]

1 Yusuf al-Qaradawi, *al-Sahwa al-Islamiyya bayna al-Ikhtilaf al-Mashruʿ wa-l-Tafarruq al-Madhmum* (Cairo: Dar al-Shuruq, 2001), 5. This book was first published by Maktabat Wahba in 1989.

2 Muhammad b. Ismaʿil al-Muqaddam, *Adillat al-Hijab: Bahth Jamiʿ li-Fadaʾil al-Hijab wa Adillat Wujubihi wa-l-Radd ʿala Man Abaha bi-l-Sufur* (Alexandria: Dar al-Iman, 2002), 5.

3 For al-Qaradawi, see Yusuf al-Qaradawi, *Min Fiqh al-Dawla* (Cairo: Dar al-Shuruq, 1997), 67, 161–77. For al-Muqaddam, see al-Muqaddam, *Adillat al-Hijab*, esp. 28–29.

Divided by policy positions, these two intellectual giants of contemporary Egypt are united by a belief that Egypt has been living through an Islamic Revival (*ṣaḥwa islāmiyya*) since the 1970s.

Despite widespread agreement that an Islamic Revival has arisen in Egypt, however, we know little about how this religious shift came to exist as a concept defined by particular practices. Put differently, when and why did Statist and Islamist elites embrace the assumption that Egyptians were living in a time of religious transformation, and how did this diagnosis come to be paired with particular social practices? While subsequent chapters will trace the genesis of the practices that have driven religious change in Egypt over the past forty years, the following pages examine the process by which leading voices within Islamist organizations and state institutions came to conceive of themselves as enmeshed in a period of religious change, variously termed *ṣaḥwa*, *yaqaẓa*, *baʿth*, and *al-mudd al-islāmī*.[4] Far from being a latent force that suddenly arose, the intellectual project of Islamic change was driven by a vanguard of religious elites, the ideological tumult of two wars, the emergence of global piety movements over the course of the 1970s, and particular projects of religious mobilization within Egypt. This shift, in turn, reveals the intellectual architecture that has undergirded a reconfiguration of the relationship between religion and politics in Egypt over the past four decades.

Historiographies of Islamic Change

What are the intellectual roots of Islamic change in Egypt? Contemporary academic studies refer to an "Islamic Revival" that

[4] For purposes of clarity, I will translate *ṣaḥwa* and *baʿth* as "revival," while rendering *yaqaẓa* as "awakening," and *al-mudd al-islāmi* as "the Islamic wave." As Samuli Schielke explains regarding the "free translation" of *ṣaḥwa* as revival rather than awakening, "there is a dynamic and creative moment implied in *revival*, and the Islamic revival is best understood as a historic event characterized by a turn to a specific kind of religiosity associated with strong hopes and anxieties, intimately linked to a shift in the shape of the world at large" (Samuli Schielke, *Egypt in the Future Tense: Hope, Frustration and Ambivalence before and after 2011* [Bloomington: Indiana University Press, 2015], *loc.* 399). Furthermore, I will capitalize these terms in English when they refer specifically to a project of Islamic revival in 1970s Egypt, but not when they are used to refer to religious change more broadly.

arose during the 1970s,[5] yet do not specify whether they are using it as an endogenous term that reflects the self-conception of Egyptians during this period or as an exogenous analytical construct.[6] Nor is this ambiguity regarding endogenous origins unique to the study of religious change in Egypt during this period, extending to studies of Syria, the Indian subcontinent, and West Africa.[7] Yet, without establishing the internal origins of concepts of revival, one cannot chronicle its roots or process of emergence.

This question of conceptual origins intersects with a broader debate over the value of revival as an analytic category in the study of the Islamic past and present. Historians of Islam in the eighteenth and nineteenth centuries have argued that claims to *iṣlāḥ* (reform), *tajdīd* (renewal), and *iḥyā* (revival) reveal the intellectual unity of Islamic visions across time and place.[8] In conjunction, leading scholars of

5 A particularly striking example of this slippage is Charles Hirschkind's statement that "the centripetal consolidation of religious authority and knowledge by the Egyptian state from the 1950s onward occurred simultaneously with a vast centrifugal movement, what both observers and participants often refer to as the Islamic Revival movement, al-Sahwa al-Islamiyya" (Hirschkind, *The Ethical Soundscape*, 55). Also see Mittermaier, *Dreams That Matter*, 4; Wickham, *Mobilizing Islam*, 136; Mahmood, *The Politics of Piety*, 3; and Yvonne Haddad, "Islamists and the 'Problem of Israel': The 1967 Awakening," *Middle East Journal*, 46:2 (1992), 266–85, at 266.

6 A partial exception to this trend is Ellen Anne McLarney, who notes the usage of *al-yaqaẓa al-islāmiyya* by the Islamist intellectual Muhammad ʿImara in 1982. See Ellen Anne McLarney, *Soft Force: Women in Egypt's Islamic Awakening* (Princeton: Princeton University Press, 2015), at 102.

7 For examples that span the Arab world, South Asia, and Africa, see Line Khatib, *Islamic Revivalism in Syria: The Rise and Fall of Baʿthist Secularism* (New York: Routledge, 2011), 6; Nasr, *Mawdudi and the Making of Islamic Revivalism*; Ali Rahnema (ed.), *Pioneers of Islamic Revival* (London: Zed Books, 1994); Adeline Masquelier, *Women and Islamic Revival in a West African Town* (Bloomington: Indiana University Press, 2009); Daniel W. Brown, *Rethinking Tradition in Modern Islamic Thought* (Cambridge: Cambridge University Press, 1999), esp. 108–32. Indeed, Khatib's definition of Islamic Revival in Syria specifically cites Mahmood's definition of Islamic Revival in Egypt, implicitly suggesting yet not proving a joint transnational project of religious change. See Khatib, *Islamic Revivalism in Syria*, 3.

8 For example, see John Esposito, "Tradition and Modernization in Islam," in Charles Wei-hsun Fu and Gerhard E. Spiegler (eds.), *Movements and Issues in World Religions* (New York: Greenwood Press, 1987), 92; and John O. Voll, "Muḥammad Ḥayyā' al-Sindī and Muḥammad ibn ʿAbd al-Wahhāb: An Analysis of an Intellectual Group in Eighteenth-Century Madīna," *Bulletin of the School of Oriental and African Studies*, 38:1 (1975), 32–39. By contrast, Ahmed Dallal surveys five cases of "the fundamentalist tradition" and finds little

modern Islam, including of the Islamic Revival in 1970s Egypt, argue that one must consider twentieth-century practices of Revival as part of a diachronic tradition capable of offering distinctly Islamic responses to changing external conditions.[9]

Collectively, these *scholars* use revival primarily as a means of denoting either an intellectual methodology employed by scholars or a set of ethical practices employed by laymen and women to adapt Islam to new challenges. In competition with an open-ended temporal vision of Secular Nationalist fulfillment inspired by Romantic German nationalism, both proponents and scholars of Egypt's Islamic Revival implicitly offer an alternative temporality: every century a renewer (*mujaddid*) will return the Islamic community to its core foundations, and the religious changes in late twentieth-century Egypt are but one manifestation of this cyclical process.[10] At the core of this methodological approach is the assumption that twentieth-century religious change is most fundamentally understood with reference to an Islamic tradition (inclusive of its distinct temporal and intellectual assumptions) rather than to a non-Islamic present.

Conceptual history offers the tools to trace the formation of the distinct understanding of Islamic Revival in post-1952 Egypt. While the remainder of this book will examine particular practices that undergirded a changing relationship between religion and politics and reveal the ties that bind projects of Statism and Islamism, respectively, this chapter explores how increasingly well-defined concepts of religious change in Egypt both created the "conditions of possibility" for alternative religious projects and were then used to "signify" developments on the ground.[11] Put differently, religious elites offered the Islamic

to connect them as a group. See Ahmed Dallal, "The Origins and Objectives of Islamic Revivalist Thought, 1750–1850," *Journal of the American Oriental Society*, 113:3 (Jul.–Sept. 1993), 341–59, at 341–42.

9 See Asad, *Formations of the Secular*, esp. 205–56, and Samira Haj, *Reconfiguring the Islamic Tradition: Reform, Rationality, and Modernity* (Stanford: Stanford University Press, 2009), esp. 5–13, 28. For Egypt, see Hirschkind, *The Ethical Soundscape*, 117–18; Mahmood, *The Politics of Piety*, 113–17.

10 A significant exception to this trend is McLarney's study of women's role in Egypt's Islamic Revival, which situates ideas of *ṣaḥwa* and *yaqaẓa* within locally mediated contestations over political and cultural reform, specifically the early twentieth-century *nahḍa* (renaissance) and the mid-twentieth-century secular–nationalist *ba'th* (awakening) movements. See McLarney, *Soft Force*, 13–14.

11 See David Scott, *Conscripts of Modernity: The Tragedy of Cultural Enlightenment* (Durham, NC: Duke University Press, 2004), 107–19.

Revival as an apparent *fait accompli* and then used this frame both to spearhead new projects and to incorporate local developments that, in a previous period, would have been seen as a matter of individual religiosity. At first, though, this was a limited undertaking, as early calls for revival came from an intellectually diverse religious vanguard that had yet to set forth key projects to shape society.

A narrow focus on how concepts of religious change emerged in post-1952 Egypt cuts to the heart of the "big idea"[12] that altered Egypt's religio-political trajectory. The process by which the frame of revival became the norm rather than the exception in Egyptian religious debate, in turn, reveals that the Islamic Revival in Egypt differed from its premodern and modern predecessors for three central reasons: it oriented its participants to an open-ended rather than a cyclical future; it foregrounded embodied social practice over intellectual methodology; and its self-definition was shaped directly by the perception of parallel religious revivals, both Islamic and non-Islamic. In contrast to scholarship that foregrounds the centrality of diachronic Islamic intellectual and ethical traditions to religious change in Muslim-majority countries, this chapter argues that, in Egypt, the concept of the Islamic Revival emerged secondarily out of a diachronic Islamic tradition and primarily out of local and global contestations of communal identity and piety over the course of the 1970s.

A conceptual history of Egypt's Islamic Revival also enables us to examine how it emerged as a mass project. A focus on the ideological bases of mobilization – rather than on textual methodology or ethical cultivation – reveals the process by which the Islamic Revival came to be defined by particular practices and was then trumpeted not only by its Islamist pioneers, but also by their Statist competitors. Just as importantly, this approach facilitates a distinction between the particular ruptures of this period and those ideas and practices that preceded it and persisted throughout the 1970s. At the intersection of

[12] In the European context, Reinhart Koselleck argues that since the 1770s "old words such as *democracy, freedom*, and *the state* have indicated a new horizon of the future, which delimits the concepts in a different way; traditional topoi gained an anticipatory content that they did not have before" (Reinhart Koselleck, *The Practices of Conceptual History: Timing History, Spacing Concepts*, trans. Todd Samuel Presner et al. [Stanford: Stanford University Press, 2002], 5). Also see Reinhart Koselleck, *Futures Past: On the Semantics of Historical Time*, trans. Keith Tribe (New York: Columbia University Press, 2004), 75–92.

a particular idea and specific social practices, a "big tent" of Islamic Revival arose.

This chapter begins by examining when and how *ṣaḥwa, yaqaẓa, ba'th*, and *al-mudd al-islāmī* came to be used as catchall phrases for religious change in Egypt. By establishing the specific usage of these terms prior to and during the 1952 rise of the Free Officers, it identifies both precursors to later visions of revival and the temporal assumptions employed by state-aligned and Islamist religious elites alike to describe the prospect of mass religious change.[13] The next section, in turn, examines the interval between 1967 and 1978, during which religious elites across the political spectrum sought to pinpoint the causes of defeat and success in the 1967 and 1973 Arab–Israeli wars, respectively. Charting perceptions of crisis and stirrings of renewal alike, it shows that both Islamist and Statist elites first saw a religious void, and that claims to revival only began to emerge tentatively following the 1973 war.

What such a revival entailed, and whom it involved, however, was still unclear. As they searched for ways to define themselves and their project between 1978 and 1981, leading figures within the Brotherhood and Jam'iyya Shar'iyya looked abroad, not only at sister movements throughout the Middle East and South Asia, but also at parallel stirrings in Israel and the United States.[14] At the intersection of local activism, regional Islamist movements, and a new awareness of ideological competitors around the world, Islamist elites constructed a future-oriented vision that would sway their state-aligned competitors and shape Egypt's religious trajectory.

The Roots of Islamic Revival

In June 1952 a group within the military, known as the Free Officers, toppled the British-backed Egyptian monarchy. Led by Muhammad Najib and Jamal 'Abd al-Nasir, they soon faced a different challenge: how to mobilize Egyptian society in the service of a nationalist vision of

[13] The centrality of these terms stands in contrast to Haddad's argument for the prominence of the concept of *tajdīd* until the late 1970s. See Haddad, "Islamists and the 'Problem of Israel'," 272.

[14] While Haddad argues that the 1967 war catalyzed Jewish, Christian, and Muslim "fundamentalists," she does not prove this connection, nor does she demonstrate its periodization. See Haddad, "Islamists and the 'Problem of Israel'," 271.

political, economic, and ideological independence. These men, however, were career army officers rather than politicians or social activists, and knew little about enlisting millions of Egyptians to their cause. The Free Officers, though, did not have to look far to spot a potential ally: leading figures within this faction, including the future Egyptian president Anwar al-Sadat (r. 1970–81) and a high-ranking army officer, Muhammad Labib, had maintained contact with the Muslim Brotherhood's founder Hasan al-Banna (d. 1949) during the 1940s, and knew that the Muslim Brotherhood could effectively play this role. The Muslim Brotherhood, which boasted millions of members throughout Egypt, was thus an ideal partner as Egypt's new rulers sought to navigate the transition from monarchical to nationalist rule.

In turn, leading Brothers had supported the Free Officers' revolution, working in the days that followed it to maintain public order. Indeed, only three days after the toppling of King Faruk, Hasan al-Banna's father, ʿAbd al-Rahman al-Banna (d. 1957), declared to his fellow Islamists: "O ye Brothers, this day your message has come forth ... This is a new dawn for you ... and a new day for the nation ... embrace Neguib [Najib] and help him with your hearts, your blood, and your wealth."[15] The Brotherhood thus supported the new regime, working with the Free Officer-aligned Revolutionary Command Council (RCC) while they continued previous efforts to spread a vision of Islam that saw it as an all-encompassing antidote to the ills of the modern age. ʿAbd al-Nasir, on the other hand, knew little about Islam and had scant reason to quarrel with the Brotherhood's approach in particular. As the senior al-Banna had indicated, a new era had arrived, and ʿAbd al-Nasir would lead the charge to national destiny.

Prior to ʿAbd al-Nasir's rise, discourses of Islamic revival had occupied a decidedly marginal position within broader political debate. *Majallat al-Manar*, the Islamic journal edited and published by religious reformer and political activist Rashid Rida between 1898 and 1935, contained no reference to *ṣaḥwa, yaqaẓa*, or *baʿth*.[16] The same was true of the Muslim

[15] Mitchell, *The Society of the Muslim Brothers*, 105.

[16] This assertion is based on keyword searches, carried out through the Maktabat al-Shamela program, of a .bok file of this periodical. References in *al-Ikhwan al-Muslimun* are derived from a survey of the titles of this periodical's issues during the 1930s (1933–37) and 1940s (1943–46). *Al-Manar* and *al-Ikhwan al-Muslimun* are representative of an elite project of Islamic reform and a key local movement of such reform, respectively.

Brotherhood's flagship periodical, *al-Ikhwan al-Muslimun*, during the 1930s: while editors and writers periodically discussed the prospect of religious change, they did so with reference to a renaissance (*nahḍa*), a concept then dominant in Egyptian reformist circles.[17]

As the 1940s arrived, Islamist writers began to adopt a discourse of nationalist, yet not religious, awakening. By way of example, a 22 March 1946 article in *al-Ikhwan al-Muslimun* asserted that "the Arabs have awoken in solidarity" (*faqad istayqaẓ al-ʿarab mutaḍāminīn*) with one another.[18] While visions of change could be applied to a religious project – most notably, a 25 May 1946 article in *al-Ikhwan al-Muslimun* noted the "the revival of the Islamic shariʿa" (*baʿth al-sharīʿa al-islāmiyya*) – this denoted a specific legal development rather than a broad social shift.[19] By 1948, however, self-consciously Islamic projects of open-ended change had grown more common, and a 28 February 1948 article by Dr. Muhammad al-Hussayni, head of the Brotherhood's Italian branch, noted:

> The world's awakening (*yaqaẓat al-ʿālam*) has spread to 300 million [Muslim] souls ... [it is] a new revival (*baʿth jadīd*) for a high, authentic, and deeply rooted civilization ... in the Islamic world generally and in the region of the Mediterranean Sea in particular ... the driver of this Islamic renaissance (*bāʿith hādhihi al-nahḍa*) is a political movement inspired by Islam ... [by] the Muslim Brotherhood.[20]

While the author's definition of revival was coterminous with the spread of the Muslim Brotherhood, his description underscores a turn toward adopting discourses of temporally open-ended religious revival.

17 For example, see Hasan al-Banna, "La Budda li-Kull Umma Turid al-Nuhud," *al-Ikhwan al-Muslimun*, 28 February 1934/14 Dhu al-Qaʿda 1352, 1–3. As Israel Gershoni and James P. Jankowski note, "The concept of 'revival' [*nahḍa*] suffused all varieties of Egyptian Arab nationalist thought." See Israel Gershoni and James P. Jankowski, *Redefining the Egyptian Nation, 1930–1945* (Cambridge: Cambridge University Press, 1995), 133. While *nahḍa* was hardly a stand-alone concept – it was often joined by invocations of both *iḥyā* and *baʿth* – these concepts were not yet dominant. See Gershoni and Jankowski, *Redefining the Egyptian Nation*, 68.

18 Muhammad ʿAli Awiya Basha, "Qad Istayqaz al-ʿArab Mutadaminin," *al-Ikhwan al-Muslimun*, 16 April 1946/14 Jumada al-Ula 1365, 13.

19 Hasan Muhammad al-Thawni, "Baʿth al-Shariʿa al-Islamiyya," *al-Ikhwan al-Muslimun*, 25 May 1946/23 Jumada al-Thaniyya 1365, 6–7.

20 Muhammad al-Hussayni, "Baʿth Jadid li-l-Islam Sadan Daʿwat al-Ikhwan al-Muslimin fi Junub wa Wasat wa Gharb Awruba," *al-Ikhwan al-Muslimun*, 28 February 1948/18 Rabiʿ al-Thani 1398, 13.

Back in Egypt, however, other Brothers envisioned a revival that transcended this Islamist movement to embrace the national community. In September 1952 an article in the Brotherhood's new magazine, *al-Da'wa*, entitled "Dam al-Ba'th Yanba'ith min al-Damā" (The Blood of Awakening Emerges from Tears), noted that "the Egyptian people ... do not accept corruption and tyranny (*al-fasād wa-l-ṭughyān*) ... the Free Officers are an armed symbol (*ramz musallaḥ*) of this fact ... a human symbol of the hand of God (*yad allah*)."[21] Hopes were high: the previous May another Brotherhood writer had declared his anticipation that "the Islamic wave" (*al-mudd al-islāmī*) would be seen in Egypt once again.[22] In the face of this support for the ruling regime – itself based on a combination of political pragmatism and optimism regarding the religious status quo – it was little surprise that a January 1953 ban on existing political parties specifically excluded Egypt's leading Islamist organization.[23]

Indeed, a revival appeared to be imminent to the Brotherhood's leading voices. In July 1954 a literary-critic-turned-Islamist-thinker by the name of Sayyid Qutb (d. 1966) penned an article in *al-Ikhwan al-Muslimun* entitled "A Revival (*ṣaḥwa*) Which Will Not Be Followed by Lethargy." Qutb, who had not yet fully embraced a Manichean worldview that depended on a Purist vanguard (*ṭalī'a*) to effect change, expressed his faith in the capacity of the Egyptian masses to turn to Islam:

> Colonialism has done everything that it could [to stamp out Islam], to the point that people believed it had succeeded ... [They believed] that this creed had gone to sleep and would not awaken (*hādhihi al-'aqīda qad nāmat ilā ghayr yaqaẓa*) ... but it will arise in a revival free of lethargy (*fa-idha bihā tantafiḍ fī ṣaḥwa ilā ghayr subāt*). Indeed, the day of salvation is near ... light will shine on the horizon ... and this Islamic world won't sleep after its awakening (*ba'da ba'thihi*).[24]

As Qutb surveyed the religious landscape, he did not see a revival as having yet occurred; such a movement was merely an anticipated future

21 Muhammad 'Abd al-Hamid, "Dam al-Ba'th Yanba'ith min al-Dama," *al-Da'wa*, 9 September 1952/19 Dhu al-Hijja 1371, 13.
22 Sayyid Qutb, "al-Muslimun Mu'tassibun," *al-Da'wa*, 6 May 1952/12 Sha'ban 1371, 3.
23 Mitchell, *The Society of the Muslim Brothers*, 131.
24 Sayyid Qutb, "Sahwa Laysa Ba'daha Subat," *al-Ikhwan al-Muslimun*, 1 July 1954/1 Dhu al-Qa'da 1373, 3.

event. The hypothetical nature of religious change in Egypt was mirrored by the inchoate vocabulary used to describe it: while *ṣaḥwa* was prominent, so too were *yaqaẓa* and *ba'th*, the latter associated with the transnational secular nationalist party whose Iraqi and Syrian branches later took power. As both writers in *al-Da'wa* and *al-Ikhwan al-Muslimun* chronicled the position of Muslims globally during this period, they saw change on the horizon in a manner that mirrored, consciously or unconsciously, Secular Nationalism's vision of future-oriented progress.[25]

This new philosophy of open-ended Islamic history was not exclusively Islamist. In September 1954 scholars within al-Azhar's Grand Shaykh's Office (Mashyakhat al-Azhar) remarked on the need for "Islamic awakening" (*al-ba'th al-islāmī*) based on morality (*'alā usus al-akhlāq*) and guided by the Islamic Conference at al-Azhar. As the prominent Islamic publicist Muhibb al-Din al-Khatib[26] noted in the early days of October 1954: "Today, we have begun to awaken from a long sleep (*bada'anā nastayqiz min nawm ṭāla 'alaynā layluhu*) ... this Islamic Conference will be one of the Islamic bodies that can teach about the affairs of Muslims and their esteemed heritage ... and about their points of weakness and the causes for [such weakness]."[27] The revival envisioned by Qutb and al-Khatib, however, had no public manifestation. Indeed, the coming years, far from witnessing an outpouring of religiosity, would see a massive project of religious repression in Egypt following an assassination attempt by members of the Brotherhood's Secret Apparatus (*al-jihāz al-sirrī*) against 'Abd al-Nasir on 26 October 1954.[28] Whether in direct response to the assassination, or merely as a pretext to eliminate a political opponent, the Free Officers brought the might of the

[25] Leading theorists of Arab nationalism, most notably the Ottoman–Syrian writer Sati' al-Husri (d. 1968), envisioned an Arab nation that directly paralleled the German *Volk*. Forged through shared blood and soil, the nation would move to the future to fulfill its national destiny. See Roel Meijer, *Cosmopolitanism, Identity and Authenticity in the Middle East* (London: Curzon Press, 1999), 125–38, 146–47.

[26] Al-Khatib (1886–1969) was a premier Islamic publicist and most famously edited *al-Fath*, which published roughly 800 issues between 1926 and 1943.

[27] Muhibb al-Din al-Khatib, "Ma'a al-Mu'tamar al-Islami," *al-Azhar*, October 1954/ Safar 1374, 194–98, at 195–96.

[28] It has never been established whether this assassination attempt was approved by Hudaybi or whether it was a decision made independently by individual members of the Brotherhood. See Mitchell, *The Society of the Muslim Brothers*, 150–51.

state's security forces down on Egypt's premier Islamist organization, jailing thousands of Brothers in what came to be known as the ordeal (*miḥna*) of 1954.[29]

As leading and rank-and-file members of the Muslim Brotherhood sat in prison, Quietist Salafis sought to reorient the question of anticipated religious change to the policies of the existing political order. In December 1957 Abu-l-Wafa Muhammad Darwish, a leading member of Ansar al-Sunna who had established the group's branch in Sohag, attempted to draw a parallel between the Prophet's time and that of ʿAbd al-Nasir's rule, arguing that "the Prophetic migration (*hijra*) was an awakening (*baʿth*) in the path of freedom, just as our blessed revolution (*thawratunā al-mubāraka*) is an awakening (*baʿth*) in the path of freedom."[30] If the crackdown on the Brotherhood had cast a pall over hopes of revival, the next best option was to claim, however dubiously, that such change had already occurred.

While Egypt's scholarly elite at al-Azhar expressed a similar tone of political Quietism, they made one crucial distinction. In May 1965 the Shaykh of al-Azhar, Hasan Maʾmun (r. 1964–73), explained that both the Grand Shaykh's Office and ʿAbd al-Nasir were committed to facilitating the "Islamic awakening" (*al-baʿth al-islāmī*),[31] thus signaling that, contrary to the claims of Ansar al-Sunna, a revival was not yet under way. Although it is not possible to establish the motivations of this Azhari scholar, a central development separated claims to revival in 1957 and 1965: the 1964 publication of Sayyid Qutb's *Milestones* (*Maʿalim fi al-Tariq*). In this pamphlet, Qutb had journeyed far from his early days of optimism, warning his readers that Egyptian society existed in a state of pre-Islamic ignorance (*jāhiliyya*) and that its ruler applied man-made laws (*al-qawānīn al-waḍʿiyya*).[32] Implicitly, Qutb

29 Mitchell, *The Society of the Muslim Brothers*, 151–62.

30 Abu-l-Wafa Muhammad Darwish, "Inbiʿath fi Sabil al-Huriyya," *al-Hadi al-Nabawi*, August–September 1957/Safar–Jumada al-Ula 1377, 53–54, at 53.

31 Hasan Maʾmun, "Kalimat Fadilat al-Imam al-Akbar Shaykh al-Azhar," *al-Azhar*, May 1965/Muharram 1395, 9–10, at 9.

32 While the context of political repression certainly shaped Qutb's ideas, this Islamist writer had long seen the world in black-and-white fashion. For Qutb's specific explanation of action as a necessary manifestation of faith, see Sayyid Qutb, *Maʿalim fi-l-Tariq* (Cairo: Dar al-Shuruq, 1979), 83–84. For an explanation of Qutb's previous leanings toward a binary division of the world, see William E. Shephard, "Sayyid Qutb's Doctrine of Jāhiliyya," International Journal of Middle East Studies, 35:4 (Nov. 2003), 521–45.

suggested that incremental change in the service of a *ṣaḥwa* was no longer possible: Egyptian society had to be rebuilt through the coercive powers of a highly interventionist state manned by a religious vanguard. Notwithstanding Qutb's ideological turn, however, scholars and intellectuals across the religious spectrum had not lost hope that Egyptian society could turn to Islam.

What came first, however, was not a new age but a crushing defeat. In June 1967 the Israeli Air Force mounted a surprise attack on its Egyptian counterpart following ʿAbd al-Nasir's decision to close the Straits of Tiran to Israeli shipping. Though the war would continue for five more days and include Egypt's Syrian and Jordanian allies, the destruction of dozens of Egyptian planes on that first day would, in retrospect, signal the final phase of ʿAbd al-Nasir's pan-Arab nationalist ambitions and Egypt's regional political centrality.[33]

In the shadow of military defeat, impiety rather than religiosity became the dominant motif. In a September 1968 address to al-Azhar's annual Islamic Conference, the Shaykh of al-Azhar, Hasan Maʾmun, explained:

We would have loved for this meeting to occur earlier [prior to June 1967], but God wished to lengthen the trial (*amd al-miḥna*) ... the catastrophe of the setback (*nakbat al-naksa*)[34] faced by the Arab and Islamic peoples ... was less a political trial than a religious one (*miḥnat dīn*) ... [so that Muslims can learn] that faith (*al-imān*) is not demonstrated through thought alone, but is reflected in action (*al-ʿamal*) ... God has punished us that we may go back to him (*li-narjiʿ ilayhi*). He has afflicted us that we may come [back] to him (*li-naqbul ilayhi*).[35]

Neither was this concern limited to religious elites: a student from al-Azhar's Faculty of Shariʿa wrote to *al-Iʿtisam* to bemoan the "dangerous spiritual crisis" (*azma rūḥiyya khaṭīra*) that afflicted the youth.[36] Defeat was not merely a matter of technological prowess but social health.

33 Michael Oren, *Six Days of War: June 1967 and the Making of the Modern Middle East* (New York: Oxford University Press, 2002), 170–78.

34 *Nakba* is an allusion to the 1948 Arab–Israeli war, while *naksa* references its 1967 counterpart.

35 Hasan Maʾmun, "Kalimat Fadilat al-Imam al-Akbar Shaykh al-Azhar al-Shaykh Hasan Maʾmun fi Iftitah al-Muʾtamar," in *Kitab al-Muʾtamar al-Rabiʿ li-Majmaʿ al-Buhuth al-Islamiyya: al-Muslimun wa-l-ʿUdwan al-Israʾili* (Cairo: Islamic Research Academy at al-Azhar, 1968), 11–12.

36 "Barid al-Iʿtisam," *al-Iʿtisam*, May 1969/Safar 1389, inside front cover.

Religiosity, or the lack thereof, was also seen as a threat to national security. As the Azhari scholar Mahmud ʿAbd al-Wahhab Fayyad asked rhetorically in *al-Iʿtisam* several months later, "Will Muslims [finally] move after an extended period of stagnancy (*rukūd*)?"[37] Fayyad was particularly concerned with Egypt's Jewish neighbors: "[The Jews] fear an Islamic revolution in the Islamic world and thus have worked to weaken the religious and nationalist spirit (*al-ruḥ al-dīniyya wa-l-qawmiyya*) among Muslims ... [while Israel has succeeded] in igniting religious feeling in the heart of Jews (*ilhāban li-l-mashāʿir al-dīniyya fī nufus al-yahūd*)."[38] Indeed, as an excerpt in *al-Iʿtisam* two years later exhorted readers, "there is no victory without faith" (*lā naṣr bi-ghayr imān*).[39] With the arrival of the 1970s, these scholars and religious activists and others saw only stagnation and weakness as they surveyed Islam's place in Egypt and, by extension, Egypt's place in the regional and global order.

The Dawn of Revival

The early years of al-Sadat's rule would not only bring a reprieve from fears of religious apathy but would also provide key conditions for a call to religious action. Following the 1973 Arab–Israeli war – in which legends of Egyptian soldiers crossing the Bar Lev line circulated far and wide[40] – the Azhari scholar Ahmad Musa Salim noted the "Awakening of Faith" that had swept Egypt on the tenth of Ramadan (*fī al-ʿāshir min ramaḍān jaʾat ṣaḥwa*), propelling the Egyptian army to victory on the opening day of the war.[41] If 1967 had represented divine punishment and ideological disappointment, 1973 appeared to portend both divine reward and a restoration of national honor.

The fervor of war was joined by national political shifts and local activism. In the shadow of the 1967 defeat – and despite ʿAbd al-Nasir's

37 Muhammad ʿAbd al-Wahhab Fayyad, "Hal Yataharrak al-Muslimun Baʿda Tul al-Rukud?" *al-Iʿtisam*, September 1969/Rajab 1389, 4–5, at 5.
38 Ibid., 5.
39 "Min al-Suhuf," *al-Iʿtisam*, May 1971/Rabiʿ al-Awwal 1391, 12.
40 See Fadwa el-Guindi, "Veiling Infitah with a Muslim Ethic: Egypt's Contemporary Islamic Movement," *Social Problems*, 28:4 (1981), 465–85, at 476.
41 Ahmad Musa Salim, "al-Maʿraka wa Isharatuha: Haqaʾiq al-Iman," *al-Azhar*, January 1974/Dhu al-Hijja 1393, 888.

still-powerful legacy – al-Sadat sought to contrast himself with the Secular Nationalist pan-Arab vision of his predecessor by billing himself as the "Believing President" (*al-ra'īs al-mu'min*). As Muslim Brothers returned home from exile and others emerged from prison, the regime shifted from its attempts to monopolize the religious debate to a more modest (and realistic) effort of channeling it, including through the medium of magazines. Al-Sadat didn't make this decision out of a commitment to a marketplace of ideas; rather, like his experiment in political pluralism through platforms (*manābir*),[42] it was an attempt to marginalize violent groups that challenged the regime's legitimacy and to monitor Islamists of multiple stripes who had accepted peaceful accommodation with the regime (or at least the reality of its coercive power).[43] This was an "inclusive" religious policy that set the lines of legitimate debate to exclude those who explicitly challenged al-Sadat's claim to power.

Alongside a new policy of facilitating public religious debate within narrow lines, al-Sadat allowed new religious groups to flourish on university campuses. Most notably, the 1972–73 academic year saw the emergence of Jama'at Shabab al-Islam (the Muslim Youth Group, henceforth Shabab al-Islam) on Egyptian campuses, alongside a previously existing movement, al-Jama'a al-Diniyya (the Religious Group). As Shabab al-Islam worked to fend off al-Sadat's efforts to co-opt it as a tool in its battle against Leftist student organizations, it struggled with al-Jama'a al-Diniyya, and each accused the other of being a tool of the regime.[44] Notwithstanding the ideological intensity of these battles – and the eventual victory of a third faction, al-Jama'a al-Islamiyya (the Islamic Group), over both of these organizations in 1974 – these student groups lacked the resources to publish on a broad scale, let alone to sketch out a religious revival. Indeed, beyond

[42] The three platforms – Leftist, Centrist, and Rightist – were predicated on allowing limited electoral competition. In the 1976 elections the Centrist platform, to which al-Sadat belonged, won 280 seats, as compared to 12 seats on the Right, four on the Left, and 48 among independents. See Ninette S. Fahmy, *The Politics of Egypt: State–Society Relationship* (New York: RoutledgeCurzon, 2002), 62.

[43] The ambiguity of this distinction comes through in 'Abd al-Mun'im Abu-l-Futuh's memoirs, in which he recounts how 'Umar al-Tilmisani counseled leaders from al-Jama'a al-Islamiyya to eschew violence in principle as opposed to merely strategically. See Abu-l-Futuh, *'Abd al-Mun'im Abu-l-Futuh*, 65.

[44] al-Arian, *Answering the Call*, 59–70, esp. 69.

campuses, religious activism on the ground hadn't changed substantially as Muslim Brothers emerged cautiously and Quietist Salafis worked within the network of mosques and schools that they had guarded carefully under ʿAbd al-Nasir.[45]

These early manifestations of public piety and broadening of student activism, amplified by the excitement of the 1973 war, would spur Islamist elites to take stock of the changed religious landscape. As the Brotherhood and varied Salafi organizations turned toward greater public activism in the mid-1970s, they sought to transform popular outpourings of religiosity into a vision of religious revival that could be harnessed toward concrete ends. Yet, while the Brotherhood frequently cited the teachings (*taʿālīm*) of Hasan al-Banna, and Salafis situated themselves in relation to strict adherence to the Prophetic Sunna, these sources spoke only in the most general terms to the political, social, and religious realities of 1970s Egypt.

It was thus no surprise that early claims to revival were extremely vague. In this vein, an October 1975 article in *al-Iʿtisam* noted the perceived threat of "the broad movement of awakening" (*ḥarakat al-baʿth al-wāsiʿ*) in the Arab world to disrupt Communist designs.[46] Yet, even as the author of this article praised this shift as both a "blessed awakening" (*hādhihi al-yaqaẓa al-mubāraka*) and "the new Islamic awakening" (*al-baʿth al-Islāmī al-jadīd*), he gave little indication as to its scope beyond noting that it had stimulated "pan-Islamic unity" (*al-waḥda al-islāmiyya*).[47]

Along similar lines, the Muslim Brotherhood's Supreme Guide, ʿUmar al-Tilmisani, set forth the cultural threat posed by the military success of European colonialism in the Muslim world over the previous two centuries. Al-Tilmisani explained that Muslims had always been able to overcome these challenges through religious revival (*kāna li-l-muslimīn ʿalayhi ṣaḥwa*), whether in Egypt against Napoleon in 1798, in Algeria against the French beginning in 1827, or in Libya following Italian occupation in 1911.[48] In the summer of 1976

45 The JS had largely preserved its mosque network during the ʿAbd al-Nasir period, and received permission from the Ministry of Endowments in 1971 to maintain its mosque network independently. See Muhammad ʿAbd al-ʿAziz Dawud, *al-Jamʿiyyat al-Islamiyya fi Misr wa-Dawraha fi Nashr al-Daʿwa al-Islamiyya* (Cairo: al-Zahra li-l-Iʿlam al-ʿArabi 1992), 151.

46 "Yaqazat al-Shuʿub al-ʿArabiyya wa-l-Islamiyya," *al-Iʿtisam*, October 1975/Shawwal 1395, 6–8, at 6.

47 Ibid., 7.

48 "Sahwa ʿala al-Islam," *al-Daʿwa*, August 1976/Shaʿban 1396, 2–3.

Muslims in Egypt appeared to be on the verge of revival (*'alā bawādir al-ṣaḥwa*) and al-Tilmisani exhorted his followers, particularly those young men and women on university campuses, to take advantage of these previous models as they pushed Egyptian society toward Islam.[49] Yet, like his Quietist Salafi peers, al-Tilmisani could not specify the particular form that revival would take.

Islamist elites first sought to claim responsibility for preexisting practices, signaling that individual piety was now a marker of religious change. A May 1978 report in *al-Da'wa* bore witness to the rise of an "Islamic Revival" (*ṣaḥwa islāmiyya*) among male and female students,[50] while a November 1978 article in *al-I'tisam* claimed that the Middle East was in the midst of an "Islamic awakening" (*al-ba'th al-islāmī*).[51] These claims, however, rendered elites within the Brotherhood and the Jam'iyya Shar'iyya a distinct minority: it was only in April 1979 that the Islamic Research Academy acknowledged in the pages of *al-Azhar* that an "Islamic awakening has become a reality" (*al-yaqaẓa al-islāmiyya aṣbaḥat ḥaqiqatan*),[52] and the Salafis of Ansar al-Sunna al-Muhamadiyya and the state functionaries of the Supreme Council for Islamic Affairs both waited until April 1980 to note the spread of an Islamic Revival in Egypt and beyond.[53] Although Islamist elites would eventually articulate a vision of religious change that comprised specific projects, this process was incomplete in the fall of 1978. How did a full-blown concept of Revival arise and what were its primary inspirations?

Negotiating Global Religious Change

Visions of Islamic Revival, far from being *sui generis*, responded to the ideological lines that divided Egyptian Islamists from their historical

49 Ibid., 2.

50 "Akhbar al-Shabab wa-l-Jami'at," *al-Da'wa*, May 1978/Jumada al-Thaniyya 1398, 48–50, at 49.

51 Muhammad al-Husni, "al-Ba'th al-'Arabi . . . Aw al-Ba'th al-Islami?" *al-I'tisam*, November 1978/Dhu al-Hijja 1398, 14–15, at 14.

52 Zahir 'Azab al-Zaghrabi, "Nahda Islamiyya," *al-Azhar*, April 1979/Jumada al-Ula 1399, 1017–24, at 1018.

53 For Ansar al-Sunna al-Muhamadiyya, see "Kalimat al-Tahrir," *al-Tawhid*, March 1980/Jumada al-Ula 1400, 3. For the Supreme Council for Islamic Affairs, see 'Abd al-Mu'ti Bayyumi, "Li-Hadha Kanat al-Sahwa al-Islamiyya," *Minbar al-Islam*, April 1980/Jumada al-Ula 1400, 18–22.

rivals. Whether Marxists and Secular Nationalists within the Arab camp or Israel and missionary movements beyond it, internal and external "others" were in ready supply.[54] Just as importantly, the Brotherhood and to a lesser extent the Jam'iyya Shar'iyya had developed a vocabulary to describe such "foreign" challenges: whether it was the "Missionary wave" (*al-mudd al-tabshīrī*)[55] or the Secular Nationalist awakening (*ba'th*) in Iraq and Syria,[56] the lines between Islam and its competitors were seemingly clear.

As Egyptian Islamists took stock of their religious and geopolitical conditions, they turned first to fellow Islamists. The early 1970s had been a fertile period of Islamic mobilization: *al-Da'wa*'s writers noted the rise of the "Islamic wave" (*al-mudd al-islāmī*), represented by the Shabab Muslim (Muslim Youth) organization in Malaysia,[57] the turn of Turks to Islam during this same period under the leadership of Necmettin Erbakan (r. 1926–2011),[58] and the threefold growth of Islam in sub-Saharan Africa over the previous four decades.[59] Along similar lines, *al-I'tisam* reported the growth of an "Islamic wave" (*al-mudd al-islāmī*), not merely in sub-Saharan Africa,[60] but also in Japan[61] and Eastern Europe.[62]

Perhaps less obvious, however, was that these Islamist organizations would draw on this vocabulary of ideological change previously applied

[54] For Israel, see 'Abd al-Mun'im Salim, "Isra'il al-Hadir wa-l-Mustaqbal," *al-Da'wa*, November 1976/Dhu al-Hijja 1396, 52–53. For the threat of missionaries, see "al-Ikhwan al-Muslimun fi al-Sihafa al-Amrikiyya," *al-Da'wa*, December 1976/Muharram 1396, 7.

[55] For analysis of the dangers posed by the "Missionary wave" (*al-mudd al-tabshīrī*), see "al-Ikhwan al-Muslimun fi al-Sihafa al-Amrikiyya," *al-Da'wa*, December 1976/Muharram 1396, 7.

[56] This term is most closely identified with the Secular Nationalist project of Ba'thism in Iraq and Syria. For example, see Muhammad 'Abd al-Quddus, "Limadha Intasharat al-Harakat Ghayr al-Islamiyya fi Bilad al-Muslimin," *al-Da'wa*, October 1978/Dhu al-Qa'da 1398, 20–22.

[57] "Watanuna al-Islami," *al-Da'wa*, January 1977/Safar 1397, 56–57, at 56.

[58] "Akhbar al-Shabab wa-l-Jami'at," *al-Da'wa*, August 1977/Ramadan 1397, 46–47.

[59] Muhammad Mahmud Ghali, "al-Islam Din al-Mustaqbal fi Ifriqiyya," *al-Da'wa*, October 1977/Dhu al-Qa'da 1397, 20–21.

[60] "Nafidha 'ala al-'Alam al-Islami," *al-I'tisam*, March 1978/Rabi' al-Thani 1398, 12–14.

[61] "Nafidha 'ala al-'Alam al-Islami," *al-I'tisam*, May 1978/Jumada al-Thaniyya 1398, 4–5.

[62] "Nafidha 'ala al-'Alam al-Islami," *al-I'tisam*, August 1978/Ramadan 1398, 4–5.

to longtime competitors within the Arab world to understand the rise of piety globally during this period. Religious Zionism represented a particularly compelling question for the Muslim Brotherhood and Jamʿiyya Sharʿiyya. These religious elites had long considered Israel to be a Jewish state defined by its commitment to a geographically expansionist vision derived from the Hebrew Bible (*Torah*).[63] Following 1967, a new wrinkle was added to this perceived challenge with the popularization of a Messianic strain of Religious Zionism under the leadership of Rabbi Tzvi Yehuda Kook (known as "Kookism") that advocated religiously framed territorial expansion over the land captured in that year's war as part of a reconstitution of ancient Israel.[64]

For Egyptian Islamists these movements represented a novel phenomenon. Breathlessly chronicling the activism of Gush Emunim (English: Bloc of the Faithful; Arabic: Jamaʿat Amunim), *al-Daʿwa*'s editors noted the "radical Jewish origin" (*al-aṣl al-yahūdī al-mutaṭarrif*) of this movement.[65] To make sense of Religious Zionism's post-1967 manifestation, they drew on language previously used to describe Islamic, missionary, and Marxist movements: just as an "Islamic wave" (*al-mudd al-islāmī*) was currently sweeping the world, so too did this "Jewish wave" (*al-mudd al-yahūdī*) seek to expand to the east, south, and north in the face of the new opportunities afforded by the 1967 war.[66] Indeed, *al-Daʿwa* saw this movement's leaders from within the prism of Islamism, using the term "activist scholars" (*al-ʿulamā al-ʿāmilīn*) to describe Gush Emunim's religious leadership of Settler Rabbis.[67] While leading figures within the Jamʿiyya Sharʿiyya had not yet adopted the terminology of revival to describe the Religious Zionist movement, they were certainly cognizant of its ambitions, noting that it sought to settle "Judea and Samaria" (*yahūda wa shamrūn*).[68] Post-1967 Religious

63 For example, see "Watani Isra'il . . . min al-Nil ila al-Furat," *al-Ikhwan al-Muslimun*, 27 May 1954/24 Ramadan 1373, 8.

64 Islamist claims to continuity between Israel's founding essence and post-1967 movements are belied by their specific focus on leading Religious Zionist groups. For a study of the spread of territorially expansionist visions of Religious Zionism during this period, see Aran, *Kukizm*.

65 "Watanuna al-Islami," *al-Daʿwa*, December 1976/Muharram 1396, 46–47, at 47.

66 ʿAbd al-Munʿim Salim, "Israʾil al-Hadir wa-l-Mustaqbal," *al-Daʿwa*, August 1977/Ramadan 1397, 48–49, at 49.

67 "Watanuna al-Islami," *al-Daʿwa*, April 1978/Jumada al-Ula 1398, 46.

68 "Mara Ukhra Hawla Kamb Dayfid," *al-Iʿtisam*, November 1978/Dhu al-Hijja 1398, 3–5, at 3.

Zionism, though understood explicitly as a political threat, was also a likeminded religious competitor.[69]

Religious change was on the horizon in the United States too, as Americans turned to Evangelical models of Protestantism in greater numbers across the political spectrum; the October 1976 issue of *Newsweek* had declared it to be the "year of the Evangelical."[70] The United States' centrality to Egyptian politics, in turn, had grown due to al-Sadat's move away from the Soviet Union and participation in the Israeli–Egyptian peace talks that would become the Camp David Accords. It was in this context that the Muslim Brothers, while at times castigating the United States specifically and the West more generally for its moral profligacy, came to recognize a religious peer: American President James Earl "Jimmy" Carter (r. 1977–81). References to Carter's religiosity began in March 1977 with the publication of excerpts of an article in *al-Maʿrifa*, then the mouthpiece of the Tunisian Islamist movement al-Nahda (Renaissance). The article in question described Carter's open profession of faith during the 1976 presidential campaign and contrasted it with the growth of irreligious behavior in the United States.[71]

While *al-Maʿrifa* was skeptical as to whether the United States would turn to Christianity or superstition (*al-khurāfāt*),[72] by May 1978 the answer appeared clear to *al-Daʿwa*: "The American people have chosen you [Carter] … [after] swearing off [their] materialistic life (*ḥayātahu al-mādiyya*) … [and] rejecting all traditional politicians for the first time … they elected you thanks to your fervent religiosity and memorization of the New Testament and its teachings (*tadayyunak al-shadīd wa-hifẓak ʿalā mā yuqāl ʿan al-injīl wa taʿālim al-injīl*)."[73] For

69 *al-Iʿtisam*'s writers even appeared to read the National Religious press in Israel: an otherwise unrelated January 1979 discussion of the Iranian Revolution directly referred to an article in *Hatzofeh* (inaccurately rendered in Arabic as *Hatsūfīn*), the flagship paper of this camp's premier political representative, the National Religious Party (Hebrew: Mafdal). See Muhammad ʿAbd Allah al-Samman, "al-Zaʿim al-Ruhi Ayyat Allah al-Khumayni," *al-Iʿtisam*, January 1979/Safar 1399, 4–6, at 5.

70 See J. Brooks Flippen, *Jimmy Carter, the Politics of Family, and the Rise of the Religious Right* (London: University of Georgia Press, 2011), 6.

71 "al-Suhuf al-Islamiyya Taqul," *al-Daʿwa*, March 1977/Rabiʿa al-Thani 1397, 40–41, at 40.

72 Ibid.

73 Ahmad Husayn, "Risala ila al-Raʾıs al-Amriki Jimi Kartar," *al-Daʿwa*, May 1978/Jumada al-Thaniyya 1398, 8–9, at 8.

the Brotherhood, American society had not yet fully turned to Christianity; instead, it was divided among those who denied Christianity, those who called themselves Christians but lived their lives independently from it, and those who belonged to churches and performed its rituals, yet restricted religion to their "spiritual life" (*al-ḥayāt al-rūḥiyya*).[74] Notwithstanding the Brotherhood's assessment that the United States was not yet Christian in the former's understanding of the term, its writers argued that American voters had consciously chosen to elect a pious man to the presidency.

Finally, proponents of the Islamic Revival in Egypt were aware of Western journalistic and academic debates over religious change in Egypt. In February 1979 *al-Daʿwa* printed a translation of an article in the British *Sunday Telegraph* entitled "The Islamic Threat." Authored by the conservative political commentator Peregrine Worsthorne (b. 1923), the article argued that the global growth of Islam represented an existential threat to Christianity and Judaism alike. Though contemptuous of this analysis of Islam, the Brotherhood took this threat assessment as a compliment to the "effectiveness of Islam (*faʿāliyat al-Islām*) and its deep influence in the hearts of its adherents."[75] If the effectiveness of Islam was not in doubt, the normative legitimacy of an Islamic revival certainly was.

Perceptions of religious challenge and change globally pushed Islamist leaders to articulate particular projects that could define the Islamic Revival in Egypt. In January 1979 the outlines of the Islamic Revival's projects would become clear when *al-Daʿwa* claimed to have acquired a copy of the American Central Intelligence Agency's (CIA) plan to destroy the "Islamic Movement" (*al-ḥaraka al-islāmiyya*) throughout the Middle East. Specifically, the Brotherhood alleged that Richard P. Mitchell, author of a landmark study of the Egyptian Muslim Brotherhood, had produced this document in his capacity as CIA station chief in Cairo.[76] Breathlessly following the same story, *al-Iʿtisam* published a follow-up article, which recorded the denials of the

[74] Ibid.

[75] al-Tahrir, "Hadhihi al-Hamla al-Mawtura Dudd al-Islam," *al-Daʿwa*, February 1979/Rabiʿ al-Awwal 1399, 19–21, at 20.

[76] "Taqrir Khatir li-l-Mukhabarat al-Amrikiyya Yansah bi-Khita Jadida li-Tasfiyat al-Haraka al-Islamiyya," *al-Daʿwa*, January 1979/Safar 1399, 10–11.

American embassy regarding both the provenance of this document and Mitchell's alleged ties to the CIA.[77]

This document first describes the global growth of Islamist movements in recent years, whether in the Arab and Muslim worlds, Europe, or North America. Offering alternative strategies for facing Islamists in these different regions, it proposes a multi-pronged effort to limit these movements' sway in the Middle East by casting doubt on the validity of the Prophetic tradition (the Sunna), disrupting mobilization efforts in mosques, and challenging the efforts of female students to don the hijab.[78] Along similar lines, *al-I'tisam* noted that the interest of American intelligence in female piety lay not in a simple sartorial choice but rather in its status as "strong proof of the limitless nature of the Islamic Revival" (*dalīl qawī 'alā al-ṣaḥwa al-islāmiyya al-mutanāhiyya*) that would soon reorient Egyptian society to an Islamic identity.[79] Furthermore, as *al-Da'wa* explained, the CIA sought to support the efforts of ruling regimes to limit Islamist infiltration of the educational system while directing the energy of Muslim youth to the performance of (apolitical) religious rituals.[80]

Yet this document, far from being a revelation of American machinations, was most likely the work of Islamist activists themselves. Mitchell, a full-time faculty member at the University of Michigan, had only lived in Egypt intermittently during the previous years,[81] and

[77] "Hawl Wathiqat al-Mukhabarat al-Amrikiyya wa Khitat Tasfiyat al-Harakat al-Islamiyya," *al-I'tisam*, February 1979/Rabi' al-Awwal 1399, 23–24, at 23.

[78] "Taqrir Khatir li-l-Mukhabarat al-Amrikiyya Yansah bi-Khita Jadida li-Tasfiyat al-Haraka al-Islamiyya," *al-Da'wa*, January 1979/Safar 1399, 10–11, at 11.

[79] "Hawl Wathiqat al-Mukhabarat al-Amrikiyya wa Khitat Tasfiyat al-Harakat al-Islamiyya," *al-I'tisam*, February 1979/Rabi' al-Awwal 1399, 23–24, at 23.

[80] "Taqrir Khatir li-l-Mukhabarat al-Amrikiyya Yansah bi-Khita Jadida li-Tasfiyat al-Haraka al-Islamiyya," *al-Da'wa*, January 1979/Safar 1399, 10–11, at 11.

[81] After working for the United States Department of State from 1958 to 1963, Mitchell was hired as an assistant professor at Michigan, reaching the rank of full professor in 1974. Although he continued to consult for the Department of State during this period, there is no evidence that he served as an intelligence officer, let alone as the CIA station chief in Cairo. See "Richard P. Mitchell," *Faculty History Project: University of Michigan*, available at http://um2017.org/faculty-history/faculty/richard-p-mitchell/memorial, accessed 27 September 2016. Neither *al-Da'wa* nor *al-I'tisam* specify when the document was composed, so it is difficult to determine whether Mitchell was in Cairo on research leave during the period in question. For more information on this document's origin, see Abdel Azim Ramadan, "The Strategies of the Muslim Brotherhood and the Takfir

it was unclear why a CIA station chief would write an internal report in Arabic. Accordingly, this text's value lies not in its elucidation of the efforts by the United States government to weaken Islamist activists, but in what it can tell us about those who forged it. Most crucially, the alleged CIA plan perfectly mirrors the priorities of the Islamist movement in Egypt, such as its focus on ritual as a key site of political contestation, the significance of threats to the Prophetic tradition (an unlikely front for intelligence officers),[82] and the cultural battle over piety on university campuses. Read as an Islamist plan of action, this report reveals an increasingly clear vision of the key projects of the Islamic Revival and a commitment to securing the place of the Muslim Brotherhood and Jamʿiyya Sharʿiyya at their forefront.

This conviction that the time of Revival had arrived was only strengthened by a wave of religio-political tumult in the Middle East and South Asia. The Brotherhood praised the arrival of religious revolution in Iran, noting that the "Islamic movement in Iran is illuminating [both] the path (*tubaṣṣir al-ṭarīq*) … and the different facets of this [political] stage (*abʿād al-masraḥ*)."[83] Far from being an isolated event, it saw the January 1979 Islamic Revolution in Iran as but one manifestation of an "Islamic wave" (*al-mudd al-islāmī*) that had swept Afghanistan, Pakistan, and Chad among others. In contradistinction to secularist efforts to sequester Islam in the mosque, this wave had brought a particular vision of religion squarely

Groups," in Martin E. Marty and R. Scott Appleby (eds.), *Fundamentalisms and the State: Remaking Politics, Economies, and Militancy* (London: University of Chicago Press, 1993), 152–83, at 169–70.

82 It is nonetheless necessary to note that this suspicion had historical roots, as many twentieth-century Orientalist scholars whose works had been translated into Arabic were both academics and committed missionaries. As Heather J. Sharkey explains, "Missionaries [in the early twentieth century] … were leading proponents of Orientalism: a set of discourses that asserted the corruption and weakness of the Islamic world in order to justify intervention (military, economic, cultural) in its affairs" (Heather J. Sharkey, *American Evangelicals in Egypt: Missionary Encounters in an Age of Empire* [Princeton: Princeton University Press, 2008], 51). While there were certainly scholars of Islam and the Middle East who drew financial support from the CIA – most notably, Nadav Safran – the leading revisionist scholars of this period did not. For Safran's relationship to the CIA, see Zachary Lockman, *Contending Visions of the Middle East: The History and Politics of Orientalism* (New York: Cambridge University Press, 2004), 244–45.

83 ʿAbd al-Munʿim Salim, "al-Thaʾirun fi-Iran," *al-Daʿwa*, November 1978/Dhu al-Hijja 1398, 8–9.

into the public sphere.[84] Along similar lines, *al-I'tisam* praised the Iranian Revolution as the "first Islamic revolution of its type in the modern age."[85]

It was during this period that calls for an Islamic revival in both East and West began to appear in the pages of *al-Da'wa*. In Turkey Necmettin Erbakan had exhorted his followers: "O youth, you represent the new awakening" (*al-ba'th al-jadīd*),[86] and in Tunisia the "Islamic comeback" (*al-'awda al-islāmiyya*) could be seen in the newfound popularity of mosques vis-à-vis coffeehouses.[87] Meanwhile, in the United States, the fourth annual Muslim Students Association conference in Dallas focused on the "Islamic Awakening" (*al-ba'th al-islāmī*) underway in the Islamic world (*al-'ālam al-islāmī*).[88] Declarations of – rather than merely calls for – Islamic revival had become the norm, rather than the exception, and revealed how these historical actors understood their own period and their mission as activists.

The coming of the 1980s – and, more importantly, the fifteenth Islamic century – would see further clarification of the particular projects that defined Egypt's Islamic Revival. As writers from both the Muslim Brotherhood and the Jam'iyya Shar'iyya echoed the Hadith report that an "agent of renewal" (*mujaddid*) would arrive every century,[89] analysis of Egypt's Islamic Revival filled the pages of *al-Da 'wa* and *al-I'tisam*. In *al-Da'wa* a leading student activist and later Brotherhood leader, 'Issam al-'Aryan, lauded the central role of university youth in revival and spelled out the key practices that defined this shift: the spread of the hijab among women, popularization of sartorial practices such as beards and long robes (sing. *jilbāb*, pl. *jalābīb*) based on the Prophetic Sunna among men, and the performance of Eid prayers at open-air sites throughout Egypt. With the

84 'Abd al-Mun'im Jabbara, "al-Khumayni bayna Amal al-Muslimin wa-Mu 'marat al-Salibiyya ... wa-l-Shuyu'iyya," *al-Da'wa*, February 1979/Rabi' al-Awwal 1399, 8–10, at 8.
85 "al-Dama al-Muslima Hiya Arkhas al-Dama 'ala al-Itlaq," *al-I'tisam*, September 1979/Shawwal 1399, 4–5, at 5.
86 "al-Islam wa-l-Hayat," *al-Da'wa*, August 1979/Ramadan 1399, 47.
87 "Sakratirak al-Sihafi," *al-Da'wa*, October 1979/Dhu al-Qa'da 1399, 14–15, at 15.
88 "Watanuna al-Islami," *al-Da'wa*, January 1980/Safar 1400, 56–57, at 57.
89 This is based on a Hadith report attributed to the Prophet Muhammad through the narration of his Companion Abu Huraira, that Allah will send an "agent of renewal" (*mujaddid*) every one hundred years. See Imam Hafiz Abu Dawud Sulaiman, *Sunan Abu Dawud*, trans. Nasiruddin al-Khattab (Jeddah: Maktabat Dar-us-Salam, 2008), vol. IV, 512.

youth as vanguards, Islamic awakening (*al-ba'th al-islāmī*) would spread to the *umma* as a whole.[90] The Islamic Revival was quickly becoming a project of mass mobilization with signature practices. Yet the significance of these practices lay not in their emergence – all had existed, to varying degrees, prior to the 1970s – but in their decided association with the Islamic Revival.

Al-I'tisam, by complement, sought to explicate the roots of revival, highlighting the disappointment of the 1967 Arab–Israeli war and the redemption of 1973. This conflict, though, was not merely between Egypt and Israel, but a broader battle over Western attempts to shape the Middle East, the failure of the governments of Islamic countries who depended on foreign expertise, and, last but not least, the loss of Palestine. Accordingly, Muslim states must adopt a platform of "Islamic unity" (*al-waḥda al-islāmiyya*), both political and economic.[91] Nevertheless, revival was still incomplete, and a January 1981 article warned that the "Revival of the Jews" (*ṣaḥwat al-yahūd*) sought to seize the Temple Mount and build a third Temple on top of al-Aqsa mosque. Far from being fully revived, Muslims in Egypt and Palestine alike remained asleep (*nayām*).[92] Yet, if the Jam'iyya Shar'iyya's leaders were skeptical as to the scope of the Revival, they had little doubt as to the essential similarity between religious change in Egypt and developments among their Israeli neighbors.

Cognizant of religious change transnationally and focused on mass mobilization locally, the Brotherhood and elites within Jam'iyya Shar'iyya had succeeded in changing the public debate as state-aligned scholars and bureaucrats had come to accept the arrival of an Islamic Revival and, as the coming chapters will show, its distinct projects. The Supreme Council for Islamic Affairs, a premier producer and advocate of a state-sponsored religious vision of political Quietism, praised the arrival of a "blessed Islamic Revival" (*ṣaḥwa islāmiyya mubāraka*) and presented itself as the leader of this project in the pursuit of Arab and

90 'Issam al-'Aryan, "al-Mudd al-Islami fi al-Jami'at," *al-Da'wa*, November 1980/ Muharram 1400, 72–74, at 73.

91 "al-Sahwa al-Islamiyya Allati Shahadatha Nihayat al-Qarn al-Rabi' 'Ashir al-Hijri," *al-I'tisam*, December 1980/Muharram 1401, 11–13, at 12.

92 Fahmi al-Shanawi, "al-Quds fi 'Atabat al-Bayt . . . wa Bawabat al-Hirasa li-l-Makka wa-l-Madina," *al-I'tisam*, January 1981/Safar 1401, 22–25, at 22–23.

Islamic unity.[93] The Islamic Research Academy, too, sought to seize leadership of the Revival, with a December 1980 editorial calling for a "revival from our stagnancy" (*ṣaḥwa min rukūdinā*) through sincere repentance (*al-tawba al-khāliṣa*), purification of the heart (*taṭahhur qulūbinā*), and moral refinement (*taṣaqqul akhlāqinā*).[94] While Islamist elites had spearheaded a project of revival that incorporated previous practices of piety and offered new programs, it had now become part of a battle with state institutions that, while accepting its basic premises, sought to seize ownership from its Islamist creators.

Conclusion

In July 1954 Sayyid Qutb saw a society on the verge of revival. While the Westernizing ambitions of King Faruk had distanced Egyptians from Islam, the Free Officers regime promised a new era. It is impossible to know Qutb's thoughts on this question as he went to the gallows twelve years later, but based on his assessment of Egyptian society in *Milestones*, it is unlikely that his early diagnosis of Islam's place in Egypt held. Equally significant, however, is the majority opinion that reigned among Muslim Brothers, Salafi (both Islamist and Quietist), and Statist scholars in the years that followed: if an Islamic revival was pending, it certainly had yet to arrive. While the 1973 Arab–Israeli war would stimulate the first mentions of a distinct Islamic Revival in Egypt, such references were few and far between, and said little as to about what such a revival entailed.

By tracing how the Islamic Revival in its varied Arabic renderings emerged as a concept that centered on particular temporal assumptions and embodied practices, this chapter has shown how Islamist elites in Egypt, followed by their Statist competitors, came to understand themselves as engaged in a project of religious change that emerged with full awareness of both Islamist sister movements across the Middle East and South Asia and non-Islamic competitors in Israel and the United States. This analysis of the formation of an increasingly specific and coherent project of revival, in turn, challenges previous studies that situate this religious shift primarily within a longer history of discourses of Islamic

93 "al-Tashkil al-Jadid li-l-Majlis al-Aʿla li-l-Shuʾun al-Islamiyya: Sahwa Islamiyya Mubaraka," *Minbar al-Islam*, Dhu al-Qaʿda 1400, 2–19, at 3.

94 Muhammad ʿAbd al-Rahman Baysar, "Lamhat wa Nafahat min al-Hijra," *al-Azhar*, December 1980/Muharram 1401, 1–4, at 3.

renewal and practices of ethical cultivation. While proponents of the *ṣaḥwa* were certainly knowledgeable about and responded to the Islamic tradition's intellectual and ethical models, their primary concerns were shaped by the temporal vision of Romantic nationalism, the ideological challenge of parallel religious revivals, and the need to articulate a project of religious mass mobilization.

The slowly congealing concept of an Islamic Revival also clarifies the persistence of Islamic currents both during and after the 1970s outside the bounds of this shift. The Brotherhood's opposition to Secular Nationalism and advocacy of pan-Islamism persisted, their Salafi peers retained a commitment to neo-Hanbali theology and to the derivation of law exclusively from the Quran and Sunna, and state institutions continued to propagate a religious vision that instrumentalized religion in the service of politically Quietist morality. Notwithstanding the political and ideological contrasts among these competitors, however, none had the capacity to lead a mass movement in the early 1970s, while all sought to do so through the frame of Islamic Revival by the decade's end.

In the process, contestation over Islam came to center on the performance of distinct religious practices in the heart of state institutions and, ultimately, within Egyptian society at large. Before examining the popularization of distinct practices of piety, however, the identity of the participants in this religious uprising beckons. If the emergence of the Islamic Revival as an idea among Islamist organizations and state institutions reveals the shared intellectual history of religious change, so too would that of religious mobilization underscore an interconnected world of textual consumption and religious practice.

2 Currents of Religious Change

Ideological Transmission and Local Mobilization

Where does religious change happen, who participates, and how do they do so? The previous chapter traced the emergence of a concept of Islamic Revival in 1970s Egypt, particularly between 1978 and 1981, telling a story of how religious elites came to understand themselves as enmeshed in – and responsible to guide – a religious transformation that transcended the distinction between state and society. By contrast, this chapter examines a subset of their constituencies – readers whose letters and fatwa requests appeared in the pages of these periodicals – to trace the pathways of participation in competing projects of religious mobilization and what this story can, in turn, reveal about the intersection of education, urbanization, and religious rupture during a crucial period of Egyptian religious history.

To tell a story of the pathways of participation in competing projects of religious mobilization, this chapter uses the signature line of letters to the editor and fatwa requests in *al-Daʿwa, al-Iʿtisam*, and *Minbar al-Islam*, tracing the geographic contours, socioeconomic profile, and responses to religious mobilization by the readers whose correspondence appeared within Islamic magazines during the second half of al-Sadat's reign. In doing so, this chapter draws on 1,076 unique entries from 149 columns in 64 issues for *al-Daʿwa*; 278 unique entries from 73 columns in 54 issues for *al-Iʿtisam*; and 705 unique entries from 117 columns in 60 issues for *Minbar al-Islam*.[1]

[1] Columns can include either letters or fatwa requests. These entries were coded for location (at the national, governorate, and city/village level), gender, and occupation or academic discipline (for those who listed themselves as students). Instead of limiting the data by excluding correspondence outright if it did not provide all three categories of information, all the information in this chapter's graphs was created using the percentage of valid entries, i.e. those entries containing the demographic information relevant for each section. The distinction between this measure and overall percentage is that the former disregards entries that don't

Notwithstanding the limitations on the explanatory value of this information outlined in the introduction, data on this period of Egyptian religious history is scarce, and this represents by far the largest sample available not only for Egypt but for any twentieth-century religious revival.[2] This chapter thus focuses on what the participation of a select set of middle-class Egyptians in competing projects of religious mobilization and respectability can reveal about the emergence of an Islamic Revival in Egypt.

The chapter begins by contextualizing competing projects of religious change within shifting networks of textual circulation and religious education within and beyond Egypt that had developed over the course of the twentieth century. It then turns to the geographic contours of the Islamic Revival's projects, arguing that the diffusion of Islamic magazines throughout Egypt enabled middle-class Egyptians to supplement local projects and institutions and to form themselves as pious Muslims in concert with elite-led projects emanating from Cairo. The arrival of Islamic magazines, however, did not guarantee the appeal of their call; the next section of this chapter explores why middle-class Egyptians turned to distinct projects of religious respectability, with reference to questions of socioeconomic disappointment and ideological mobilization within Statist and Islamist publications alike. Finally, advertisements in these three magazines are used to tentatively reconstruct the identities of readers who either did not write or whose letters did not appear.

contain any information, whereas the latter includes these entries. For governorates, "valid" entries represented 70.3 percent for *al-Da'wa*, 58 percent for *al-I'tisam*, and 66 percent for *Minbar al-Islam*. For locale, the statistics were 64 percent for *al-Da'wa*, 58 percent for *al-I'tisam*, and 58.8 percent for *Minbar al-Islam*. For urban/rural, *al-Da'wa* included 61 percent, *al-I'tisam* 68 percent, and *Minbar al-Islam* 59.4 percent. For occupation, *al-Da'wa* included 32 percent, *al-I'tisam* 28 percent, and *Minbar al-Islam* 22.5 percent. Among university students, 85.6 percent in *al-Da'wa* listed their disciplines, 85.7 percent in *al-I'tisam* did so, and 64.8 percent of those in *Minbar al-Islam* did so.

[2] I am not aware of any studies of twentieth-century religious change that provide an extensive demographic profile of participants in competing religious projects. For the most extensive example in the Egyptian case, see Saad Eddin Ibrahim, *Egypt, Islam and Democracy: Twelve Critical Essays* (Cairo: American University in Cairo, 1996), 1–33.

Networks of Print Distribution and Ideological Mobilization

While narratives of religious revival correctly identify shifts in public debate and practice, they tend to obscure previous institutional and discursive developments that underlay these shifts. In the case of the Islamic Revival in Egypt, the projects of religious respectability and the (re)formation of subjectivities therein emerged out of a longer history of institutions and discourses within Egypt.[3] This section sets out a longer history of state-sponsored religious education in public schools, and the questions raised, but not answered, by this system. It then turns to the specific circumstances in which readers found themselves, highlighting the socioeconomic and ideological contexts, national and transnational, of the al-Sadat period.

This story first necessitates a step back in Egyptian textual history. Cairo and Alexandria[4] had long been political, cultural, and economic hubs. They first emerged as print centers in the late nineteenth century as Lebanese and Syrian émigrés fled Ottoman censorship under Abdul Hamid II (r. 1876–1908) and re-established themselves in Egypt.[5] Cairo was a seat of government and commerce, while Alexandria was a center of Mediterranean trade and, increasingly after World War II, industrial production. Though these two cities were the most populous in Egypt,[6] they were only part of the story.

Provincial cities at considerable distance from Cairo and Alexandria expanded in the early twentieth century. Though the Egyptian state had begun to assert greater control over rural areas beginning in the mid-nineteenth century, whether through schooling, architecture, sanitation, or hygiene,[7] it was only in 1922 that the state absorbed previously independent village Quranic elementary schools (*kuttāb*) into the national educational system, and by 1930 the number of students

[3] Skeggs, *Formations of Class and Gender*, 41.

[4] Egypt's administrative divisions consider fully urbanized geographical units to be both governorates and cities, whereas mixed urban/rural governorates contain a capital city and a series of "centers" (*marākiz*) around which villages are clustered. Cairo and Alexandria are considered to comprise both an entire governorate and a city.

[5] George Atiyeh, *The Book in the Islamic World: The Written Word and Communication in the Middle East* (Albany: State University of New York, Press, 1995), 241–43.

[6] Atiyeh, *The Book in the Islamic World*, 227.

[7] Omnia al-Shakry, *The Great Social Laboratory: Subjects of Knowledge in Colonial and Postcolonial Egypt* (Stanford: Stanford University Press, 2007), 116.

under state supervision had risen from 23,000 to roughly 253,000.[8] Primary and secondary education increased further under ʿAbd al-Nasir, and the student population nearly doubled between 1953 and 1963.[9] This broadening of education produced a corresponding rise in literacy: between 1947 and 1976 the number of Egyptians who could read and write increased 78 percent from 4.32 million to 7.69 million, in line with demographic growth that brought Egypt's population from 18.97 million to 36.63 million residents.[10] The bounds of literacy had opened up new opportunities for print-based mobilization.

The possibility of such mobilization also depended on access to print. During the quarter-century leading up to 1976 the proportion of Egyptians living in urban areas nearly doubled, from 22.9 percent to 43.9 percent, and the number of Egyptians living in cities grew from 6.2 million to 16.09 million, an increase of 159 percent.[11] As a result, an unprecedented number of Egyptians had regular access to print products. Population increases affected not only Greater Cairo and Alexandria but also the Delta governorates of Sharqiyya, Daqahliyya, Gharbiyya, Monufiyya, and Beheira.[12] Urbanization was complemented by expanded postal infrastructure: Egypt's postal service had originally developed during the 1860s, but received another boost between 1952 and 1974, mushrooming from 841 public post offices to 1,531 public and 2,675 private post offices.[13]

Print distribution, however, was not only dependent on the existence of infrastructure but also on its unfettered use. While both *al-Iʿtisam* and *Minbar al-Islam* offered subscriptions, domestic and international, *al-Daʿwa* consciously limited itself to international subscriptions. The reason for this was fear of political repression: as editor Badr Muhammad Badr explains, "Had we offered subscriptions, it would

[8] Starrett, *Putting Islam to Work*, 68. [9] Starrett, *Putting Islam to Work*, 78.

[10] Central Agency for Public Mobilization and Statistics (CAPMAS), 1976 *Population and Housing Census* (Cairo: Central Agency for Public Mobilization and Statistics, 1980), vol. I, 26–27.

[11] For statistics based on the successive censuses, see Ibrahim, *Egypt, Islam and Democracy*, 99.

[12] John B. Parker and James R. Coyle, Urbanization and Agricultural Policy in Egypt, Rep. no. PB92-109034, vol. 169 (Washington DC: Economic Research Service, 1981), Foreign Agricultural Economic Report, 4.

[13] Central Agency for Public Mobilization and Statistics (CAPMAS), *Statistical Yearbook: Arab Republic of Egypt 1952–1979* (Cairo: Central Agency for Public Mobilization and Statistics, 1983), 96.

have been equivalent to providing Central Security with a list of people to harass anytime they chose to question one of us at *al-Da'wa*."[14] *Al-Da'wa*'s editors were nonetheless able, alongside their peers in *al-I'tisam*, to exploit the popularity of kiosks and newspaper stands throughout Egyptian cities during this period:[15] the former distributed between 60,000 and 80,000 copies of each issue,[16] while the latter averaged roughly 20,000 copies.[17] By contrast, *Minbar al-Islam*, though it had access to these distribution points as well as to government-controlled mosques and specialized wooden kiosks in the suburbs of Cairo and other governorates,[18] distributed somewhere between 20,000 and 60,000 copies of each issue.[19]

While these increases in literacy and education shed light on how readers were able to participate, the choice to do so was inseparable from their previous experience in the Egyptian public educational system. As Starrett and Doumato note, nationalist efforts to craft "master narratives" through religious education invariably stand in tension with "students' diverse actual experiences" stratified along lines of region, gender, class, and sect.[20] Most notably, educators faced a student body with lived experience of sectarian and economic disenfranchisement in Upper Egypt and increasing socioeconomic inequality throughout the country.

14 Badr, personal interview, 24 Feb. 2013.

15 See Yves Gonzalez-Quijano, *Les gens du livre: édition et champ intellectuel dans l'Égypte républicaine* (Paris: Centre national de recherche scientifique, 1998), 191. For relevant notices in both magazines, see "Akhi al-Qari," *al-Da'wa*, August 1976/Sha'ban 1396, 1. For *al-I'tisam*, see *al-I'tisam*, December 1976/Dhu al-Qa'da 1396, 23.

16 A January 1977 accounting statement listed an initial circulation of 60,000 copies in July 1976 and, by January 1977, a circulation of 78,000. See *al-Da'wa*, January 1977/Safar 1397, 17. Badr estimated average circulation at 60,000 copies, with increases during times of political tension such as the Camp David Accords: Badr, personal interview, 24 Feb. 2013.

17 Madbuli, personal interview, 24 Feb. 2013.

18 Najah al-Zanira, *al-Majlis al-A'la li-l-Shu'un al-Islamiyya* (Cairo: Ministry of Endowments, 1995), 103–05.

19 The March 1980 issue of the magazine cited a survey of Islamic magazines by the Egyptian Union for Radio and Television, which ranked the magazine as the second most popular religious publication in Egypt. See "Kalimat al-Tahrir," *Minbar al-Islam*, March 1980/Rabi' al-Thani 1400, 1.

20 Eleanor Abdella Doumato and Gregory Starrett, "Textbook Islam, Nation Building, and the Question of Violence," in Eleanor Abdella Doumato and Gregory Starrett (eds.), *Teaching Islam: Textbooks and Religion in the Middle East* (London: Lynne Rienner Publishers, 2007), 24.

For those within Egypt's middle class who aspired to religious respectability, Islamic magazines promised answers to questions raised, but not answered, by the public educational system's continued emphasis on the applicability of Islam to daily life. These publications were ideologically connected to public religious education, embracing the same functionalist vision by which religious education centered on goals of social policy.[21] Yet, while *Minbar al-Islam* upheld the regime's vision of political obedience and social peace, *al-Da'wa* and *al-I'tisam* challenged its subordination of religious education to its own ends. It was in this setting that readers throughout Egypt's urban centers came to engage with questions of religious transformation and, in the process, took part in defining their subjectivities as pious Muslims.

Changing economic circumstances also shaped the formation of religious subjectivities. Previous studies of this period have focused on Islamist activism in isolation. Political scientists, working out of a tradition of Functionalist Social Psychology, initially characterized the turn to Islamism as a response to "exogenous structural strains" – including rapid socioeconomic transformation, rural–urban migration paired with insufficient infrastructure, increasingly expensive basic commodities, and political disappointment – which produce "psychological discomfort" that must be relieved.[22] In response, historians and political scientists used Social Movement Theory (SMT) to push beyond questions of structural mismatch to examine pathways and methods of mobilization.

SMT- based scholarship on the Islamic Revival in Egypt argues for the intersection of socioeconomic disappointment and grassroots mobilization. Wickham shows that the Egyptian Muslim Brotherhood capitalized on the socioeconomic disappointment generated by a declining social contract to appeal to recent college graduates,[23] while Bayat notes that Islamism under al-Sadat "reflected the rebellion of the impoverished and morally outraged middle class."[24] Both argue that socioeconomic outrage was channeled into a new ethic of action, and emphasize Islamist efforts to transmit alternative religious visions

21 Starrett, *Putting Islam to Work*, 62, 77–86.
22 See Quintan Wiktorowicz, *Islamic Activism: A Social Movement Theory Approach* (Bloomington: Indiana University Press, 2004), 6.
23 See Wickham, *Mobilizing Islam*, 85–92.
24 See Asef Bayat, *Making Islam Democratic: Social Movements and the Post-Islamist Turn* (Stanford: Stanford University Press, 2007), 35.

through both media and local institutions.[25] As this chapter will demonstrate, however, this argument must also be extended to Statist religious visions and their mobilization efforts.

The middle class was open to such mobilization in the face of an increasing divide between the cultural and economic components of middle-class life under al-Sadat. On the one hand, 80,000–100,000 state managerial elites (who were joined by capitalist entrepreneurs, contractors, leading doctors and lawyers, and pharmacists) still possessed the material means to purchase a home, marry, and either fully fund or partially subsidize their children's education. Nevertheless, the segment of the middle class that struggled to achieve these basic landmarks had grown: roughly 200,000 Egyptians of similar educational background found themselves in a "contradictory location" within Egypt's class structure in which their educational qualifications did not correspond with their socioeconomic position.[26] This division was a product of changing economic circumstances: due to a faltering state modernization project, the close tie between education, white-collar employment, and socioeconomic mobility had frayed, and delays between higher education and public employment could stretch nearly ten years.[27] The emergence of an *infitāḥ*-fueled private sector in Egypt further stratified this group. While those employed in the private sector earned vastly more as a result of new opportunities in petroleum, banking, construction, and commerce, the earnings of those in public-sector positions dropped in both comparative and real terms.[28]

Individual economic explanations, however, are insufficient on their own to contextualize the religious choices that would follow. Middle-class Egyptians were also enmeshed in a series of local and international ideological and economic shifts. Locally, the al-Sadat regime had sponsored religious student groups since the early 1970s in an effort to build

25 Wickham emphasizes the role of both local educational sites and mass media in transmitting religious frames, and Bayat argues that Islamists "built hegemony" both through political pressure of the regime and by engaging in "cultural production" which communicated an alternative system of values, norms, and behavior. See Wickham, *Mobilizing Islam*, 119–49; Bayat, *Making Islam Democratic*, 195–96.

26 Mahmoud Abdel-Fadil, *The Political Economy of Nasserism: A Study in Employment and Income Distribution Policies in Urban Egypt, 1952–72* (Cambridge: Cambridge University Press, 1980), 95.

27 Wickham, *Mobilizing Islam*, 36–37.

28 Wickham, *Mobilizing Islam*, 40–41.

a viable opponent to the still-powerful Egyptian Socialists and Communists, and had expelled all Russian advisors in 1972. More broadly, al-Sadat appealed to "science and faith" (*al-ʿilm wa-l-imān*) as an alternative source of legitimacy in the face of the declining value of the social contract. These local policy shifts were augmented by regional and global developments which strengthened Islamist forces within Egyptian society: the 1973 OPEC oil embargo drastically altered the economic fortunes of the Arab Gulf monarchies, enhancing both their political reach and their financial support for Brotherhood and Salafi publications.[29] Globally, al-Sadat sought to improve Egypt's economic position by striking a Cold War alliance with the United States and crushing Leftist mobilization locally, thus providing greater space for proponents of Statist and Islamist visions alike.[30]

Before exploring this ideological contest, however, we begin with a question of geography: who were the middle-class Egyptians whose letters appeared in Islamic magazines, and what can their spatial locations reveal about the diverse projects of religiosity in which members of this segment of society participated between 1976 and 1981?

The Geography of Revival

The spatial distribution of Islamic magazine readers underscores the participation of middle-class Egyptians throughout Cairo, Alexandria, the Nile Delta, and Upper Egypt in projects of religious change anchored not in their local communities (or in local government-controlled institutions) but in print networks. These projects stand in contrast to previous programs of local religious mobilization that confined their participants to interaction with either local leaders or preachers specifically dispatched from Cairo and Alexandria.[31]

29 See Abu-l-Futuh, *ʿAbd al-Munʿim Abu-l-Futuh*, 40.

30 See Ronald E. Powaski, *The Cold War: The United States and the Soviet Union, 1917–1991* (New York: Oxford University Press, 1998), 203–30.

31 As Mitchell notes, the Muslim Brotherhood drew its leadership from urban centers and its mass constituency from the Egyptian countryside, including in the Delta. See Mitchell, *The Society of the Muslim Brothers*, 329. Other scholarship has noted the importance of provincial universities of the Delta and Upper Egypt to the Jamaʿa Islamiyya. Specifically, Saad Eddin Ibrahim's study of militant Islamists in 1970s Egypt focuses on a narrow subset of thirty-four activists, some of whom were members of the Technical Military Academy (based in Cairo, Alexandria, and the Delta) and others of whom were members

The geographic distribution of participants in Islamic magazines thus reveals how readers from these areas came to participate in national projects of religious change.[32]

Challenges of access and literacy ensured that it would be middle-class Egyptian men who would predominate in these religious projects. City dwellers constituted 94.1 percent of the correspondents for *al-Da'wa*, 96.3 percent for *al-I'tisam*, and 93.8 percent for *Minbar al-Islam*. They were similarly gendered: men accounted for 97.5 percent of this group in *al-Da'wa*, 97.8 percent in *al-I'tisam*, and 93.5 percent in *Minbar al-Islam*.[33]

A survey of governorates (Figure 2.1) illustrates the extent of the emergence of the Nile Delta alongside Cairo and Alexandria. Participants from Delta governorates accounted for 49.1 percent of the letters in *al-Da'wa*, 32.1 percent of *al-I'tisam*, and 46 percent of those for *Minbar al-Islam*. By contrast, the Upper Egyptian governorates of Asyut, Luxor, Sohag, Aswan, and Qina constituted 13.5 percent of *al-Da'wa*, 13.7 percent of *al-I'tisam*, and 15.8 percent of *Minbar al-Islam*. When the data is compiled by region, it becomes clear that the Delta governorates represent the greatest area of participation, even more so than Cairo and Alexandria. The combination of expanded education, urbanization, and distribution had brought a broader class of readers into national projects of piety.

of al-Takfir wa-l-Hijra (centered in Upper Egypt). See Ibrahim, *Egypt, Islam and Democracy*, 25. Along similar lines, Gilles Kepel highlights the role of Upper Egyptian universities, particularly those of Minya and Asyut, in the intensification of both sectarian clashes and violence within the Jama'a Islamiyya. See Kepel, *The Roots of Radical Islam*, 162–70. Wickham expands this picture, noting the strength of the Brotherhood in Cairo, Alexandria, and Delta cities and the influence of more militant Islamic groups (such as those studied by Ibrahim) in the towns and villages of the Upper Egyptian governorates of Asyut, Minya, and Sohag. See Wickham, *Mobilizing Islam*, 115.

32 An important qualification to this claim is that not all letters originated in Egypt. Letters to the editor from within Egypt in both *al-Da'wa* and *al-I'tisam* topped 89 percent (89.3 percent and 91.1 percent, respectively) and were 75.8 percent of those in *Minbar al-Islam*. The existence of a foreign contingent – ranging from North Africa to the Levant to the Persian Gulf in all three cases, particularly that of *Minbar al-Islam* – underscores the diffusion of Egyptian debates beyond this ideological and demographic heavyweight.

33 In 1976, 32 percent of Egyptian men could read and write, while only 12 percent of women could do so. By a less stringent measure, 58 percent of men and 29 percent of women were classified as literate. See CAPMAS, *1976 Population and Housing Census*, 25–26.

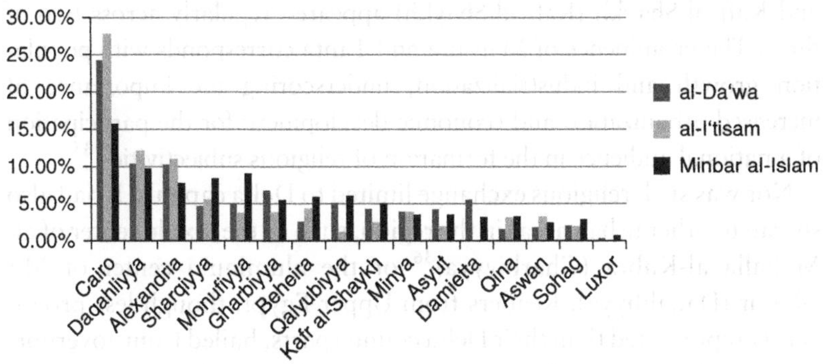

Figure 2.1: Popular participant distribution by governorate.

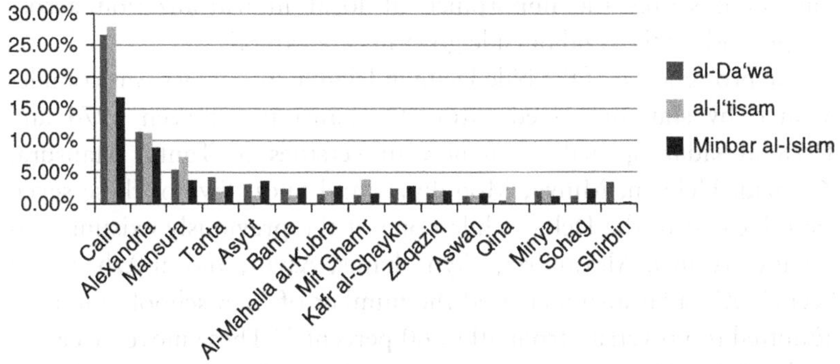

Figure 2.2: Popular participant distribution by city.

Yet this vantage point, while correctly emphasizing the centrality of the Delta, nonetheless risks obscuring those particular urban areas that were focal points of participation (see Figure 2.2).[34] Beyond the centrality of Cairo and Alexandria for all three magazines, Delta governorate capitals and even a few urban centers (*marākiz*) emerged as key sites of religious mobilization and subject formation. Participation was not concentrated in one or two Delta capitals; rather, it was dispersed, fairly evenly, among some nine cities – some capitals, others not. This distribution was largely similar among magazines: the governorate capital of Mansura (Daqahliyya) was popular in all three magazines, and Tanta (Gharbiyya)

[34] The cities listed by cumulative total are those that accounted for at least 5 percent cumulatively or over 3 percent in any one magazine, with the exception of three Upper Egypt strongholds – Minya, Qina, Sohag, and Aswan – which are included for purposes of comparison.

and Kafr al-Shaykh (Kafr al-Shaykh) appeared regularly across two of three. The prominence of Mansura and Tanta corresponds with population growth and industrialization, underscoring the importance of increased urbanization and economic development for the participation of a national audience in the formation of religious subjectivities.[35]

Nor was such religious exchange limited to Delta capitals. It had also spread to other urban areas in the region, such as the textile center of al-Mahalla al-Kubra (Gharbiyyya)[36] or the aluminum center of Mit Ghamr (Daqahliyya). Readers from Upper Egypt, though less prominently represented than their Delta counterparts, hailed from governorate capitals of Asyut, Minya, and Sohag. The profile of participants across the Delta's capitals and centers as well as pockets of Upper Egypt thus underscores the importance of local industrialization across Egypt, both within and outside governorate capitals.

The prominence of the Nile Delta in Islamic magazines was complemented by state-driven educational expansion. Between 1974 and 1978 al-Sadat opened seven new universities in Tanta, Mansura, Zaqaziq, Helwan, Minya, Monufiyya, and Suez. Five of these seven were located in the Delta, while none of the previously existing universities (Cairo, Alexandria, 'Ayn Shams, Asyut, and al-Azhar) had been.[37] Al-Sadat also increased the number of high-school graduates admitted to university from 40 to 60 percent.[38] These moves accentuated 'Abd al-Nasir-era trends, yet also signified a rupture: no longer would these youth have to travel to Cairo and Alexandria to pursue higher education. Instead, higher education – and literate culture more broadly – was to be more diffused throughout Egypt.

The significance of the participation of middle-class readers through Egypt in the formation of competing religious projects thus lies not in the sudden access of the Egyptian middle class to religious elites, but rather in the vastly expanded geographic bounds through which print-

[35] The expansion of these cities can also be attributed to forced migration of residents of Port Said and Suez following the 1956 Suez war. See Husayn Kafafi, *Ru'ya 'Asriyya li-l-Mudun al-Sana'iyya fi Misr* (Cairo: Egyptian Public Institute for Books, 1985), 56–72.

[36] The city of al-Mahalla al-Kubra, though long known for its textile production, expanded further between 1960 and 1976 from a population of 178,350 to 292,900. This was primarily thanks to a textile industry that employed 97 percent of the city's workers: Kafafi, *Ru'ya 'Asriyya li-l-Mudun al-Sana'iyya fi Misr*, 59–60.

[37] Wickham, *Mobilizing Islam*, 38. [38] Wickham, *Mobilizing Islam*, 36.

based religious mobilization could take place. Yet, as Egyptians supplemented high-school religious education and sidestepped local religious leaders, growing economic divisions within the middle class would also shape their participation.

Social Contracts and the Turn to Religion

When middle-class Egyptians sought religious respectability, how and why did they choose particular religious projects? Previous studies that rely on Functionalist Social Psychology assume a direct connection between socioeconomic disappointment and the turn to Islamism. By contrast, scholars drawing on SMT have successfully critiqued the determinist models of Islamist sympathies, arguing that economic grievances, melded with mobilization, lead to Islamist loyalties. Less theorized, however, is the distinction between "social position" (here, that of a socioeconomically frustrated middle class) and multiple "subject positions" of religious piety.[39]

The broadly similar material position of participants in Islamic magazines challenges an exclusive focus on the connection between dashed socioeconomic dreams and Islamist mobilization and subjectivities. Participants across all three magazines worked disproportionately in "clerical"[40] or "professional and technical" positions, rather than in managerial roles or in other industries (see Figure 2.3). The average among all three magazines for clerical roles within the bureaucracy was nearly 11 percent.[41] Additionally, primary and secondary educators constituted 13.9 percent in *al-Da'wa*, 11.5 percent in *al-I'tisam*, and 25.2 percent in *Minbar al-Islam*. Across all three magazines, the project of religious respectability was an undeniably middle-class affair.

The importance of considering Statist and Islamist projects side by side is further underscored by the similar socioeconomic profile of university students who read Islamic magazines (see Figure 2.4). The number of young Egyptians studying at universities had expanded

[39] While the former is determined by class and gender, the latter requires active participation even as it is organized by institutional structures, whether education or media. See Skeggs, *Formations of Class and Gender*, 12.

[40] This term refers to administrative work rather than to jobs performed by religious clerics.

[41] Percentages of clerical workers were similar among the magazines: This segment represented 10.1 percent of *al-Da'wa*, 12.5 percent of *al-I'tisam,* and 11.5 percent of *Minbar al-Islam*.

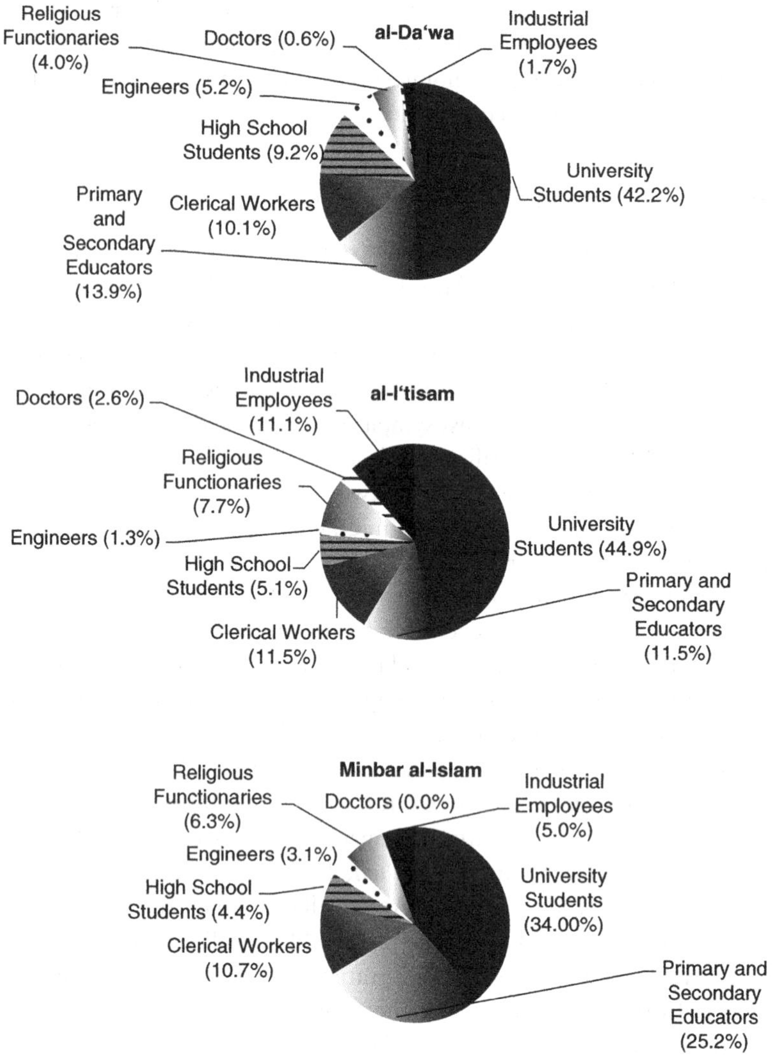

Figure 2.3: Popular participants by occupation.

first under 'Abd al-Nasir and then further under al-Sadat: the 1952–53 academic year began with 42,485 students; by 1968–69 this number had reached 142,875, and by 1980–81 it had it risen even further to 563,750.[42] These students, whose importance arose from their

[42] Haggai Erlich, *Students and University in Twentieth Century Egyptian Politics* (New York: Taylor & Francis, 2005), 175–200.

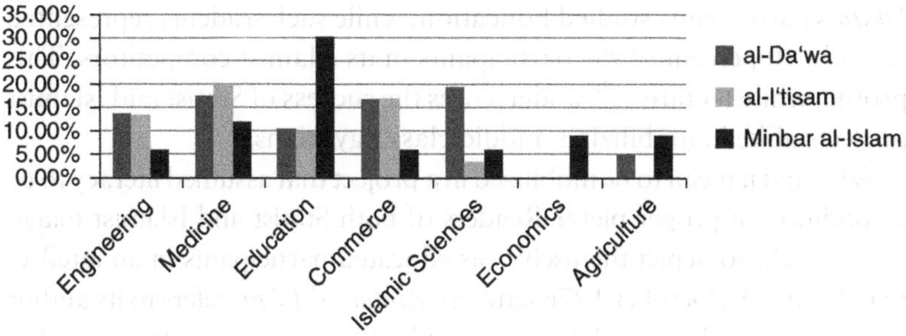

Figure 2.4: Student distribution by university faculty.

position as a bellwether for future ideological developments, represented a key target not only for Islamists but also for Nasserists, Marxists, and state-sponsored religious groups and institutions.[43]

Research on this period has often highlighted the role of students in Islamism. Ibrahim noted that militant Islamist groups such as Jamaʿat al-Muslimun (the Islamic Group, also known as al-Takfir wa-l-Hijra [Excommunication and Migration]) and al-Fanniyya al-ʿAskariyya (Military Technical Academy Group) drew primarily from the ranks of students and recent graduates.[44] Similarly, Wickham has shown how the Muslim Brotherhood succeeded in transforming prestigious faculties (such as Engineering and Medicine) into Islamist strongholds.[45] These stories highlight two components of Islamist popularity on university campuses: the elites (hailing from prestigious faculties) and the rank-and-file of more limited socioeconomic horizons.

The educational training of students whose letters appear in Islamist publications (see Figure 2.4) suggests that those student readers were no more likely than their Statist peers to study in elite departments. High-achieving students in fields such as Engineering and Medicine were featured in all three magazines, though *Minbar al-Islam*'s participants (6.1 percent) were less likely to be engineers than their counterparts in *al-Daʿwa* and *al-Iʿtisam* (13.6 percent and 13.3 percent respectively). Students who studied the Islamic Sciences participated most regularly in *al-Daʿwa*, but were marginal participants in *al-Iʿtisam* and *Minbar al-Islam*. By contrast, 30 percent of *Minbar al-*

[43] For more on the state sponsorship of Islamic student groups, see al-Arian, *Answering the Call*, 49–74.
[44] See Ibrahim, *Egypt, Islam and Democracy*, 30.
[45] Wickham, *Mobilizing Islam*, 116.

Islam's participants studied Education, while such students represented roughly 10 percent of the participants in its Islamist competitors. This profile, while tentative,[46] underscores the success of Statist and Islamist projects alike in mobilizing middle-class Egyptians.

What did it mean to be mobilized in a project that assumed literacy to be a condition of proper piety? Readers of both Statist and Islamist magazines sought to depict themselves as educated participants in an intellectual debate. An October 1976 letter in *Minbar al-Islam* refers to its author as a "continued reader" (*qāri mustadīm*),[47] and a year later another reader with particular pretensions to intellectual gravitas noted that he read not only *Minbar al-Islam* but also psychological and educational magazines.[48] Some readers even took reading magazines so seriously that they regarded it as a basic religious obligation. As an anonymous letter from Cairo explained: "Your magazine contains all that is beneficial (*mufīd*) ... and reading it is one of the highest ritual practices (*min asma al-'ibādāt*)."[49] Readers of *Minbar al-Islam* whose letters appeared collectively presented themselves as an intellectual community.

Claims to intellectual rigor extended to Islamist periodicals. In *al-Da'wa*, a letter from Dr. Muhammad al-Sharif – apparently highly educated though the details of this education are ambiguous – praised *al-Da'wa* in the June 1977 issue for "speak[ing] to the mind and not to emotion" (*tukhāṭib al-'aql wa-laisa al-'āṭifa*). Accordingly, he asked for a new "scientific section" (*bāb 'ilmī*) that would equip readers to engage in a more intellectual approach to Islam.[50]

In *al-I'tisam* the claim to literacy coexisted with a more purist religious identity: a March 1978 letter from 'Abd al-Mun'im Zahir from the Delta town of Mansura was titled "*al-I'tisam* Magazine in our Conscience," and suggested a different conception of the magazine-reading experience:

I am among those addicted to reading *al-I'tisam* because it is my only breathing space (*mutanaffas*) which assures me that Egypt is still Muslim and Muslims are still noble ... and it makes me happy to let you know that *al-*

46 Such analysis is necessarily tentative because there is no way to ascertain whether this educational distribution reflected the demographics of these readerships or whether it was merely a product of editorial intervention.
47 "Ma'a al-Qurra," *Minbar al-Islam*, October 1976/Shawwal 1396, 172.
48 "Ma'a al-Qurra," *Minbar al-Islam*, October 1977/Dhu al-Qa'da 1397, 182.
49 "Ma'a al-Qurra," *Minbar al-Islam*, July 1976/Rajab 1396, 204.
50 "Qurra al-Da'wa Yatahadathun Ilayha," *al-Da'wa*, June 1977/Rajab 1397, 54.

I'tisam penetrates the hearts (*tunfidh ilā al-qulūb*) because it is the only Islamic cannon (*al-midfa' al Islāmī al-waḥīd*) which hits the enemies of Islam.[51]

Whether through a claim to literacy or intellectual rigor, participants in competing projects of piety defined themselves as a social segment distinct from the majority of Egyptians, who could neither read nor write letters in their leisure time.

Statist and Islamist mobilization efforts, however, proceeded based on contrasting appeals. The Statist approach sought to provide a moral high ground to those disadvantaged by the broken socioeconomic system: in April 1977 *Minbar al-Islam*'s Muhammad Fahmi Latif argued that the pursuit of knowledge for the sake of material gain was "bestial" (*waḥshiyya*); instead, knowledge should be pursued in the path of ethical improvement.[52] Latif and his peers, though they could criticize the status quo, could not explicitly attribute it to the failing of the state system.

Other state-aligned figures who were less involved in projects of religious mobilization sought to acknowledge the challenges that the current socioeconomic situation posed. The doctor-turned-religious-intellectual Mustafa Mahmud emphasized the importance of "equal opportunity" (*takāffu al-furaṣ*) in education, health care, and basic living standards,[53] while former Minister of Endowments and Azhar Affairs (r. 1976–79) Muhammad Mutawalli al-Sha'rawi similarly noted the importance of "equal opportunity in life" (*takafu al-furaṣ fī al-ḥayāt*).[54] For al-Sha'rawi, equal opportunity was consistent with a rigid social structure: "The lessening (*taqlīl*) of the percentage of the population that receives higher and higher educational credentials is not a reflection of opportunity but rather of ability ... society is a pyramid (*haram*) ... If the pyramid flips over, there will immediately be deterioration (*inḥiyār*)."[55] While the acknowledgment of the value of equal opportunity spoke to Egypt's socioeconomic climate, neither

[51] "Barid al-I'tisam," *al-I'tisam*, March 1978/Rabi' al-Thani 1398, 43.
[52] Muhammad Fahmi Latif, "al-Islam wa-l-Tarbiya wa-l-Ta'lim," *Minbar al-Islam*, April 1977/Jumada al-Ula 1397, 101.
[53] Mustafa Mahmud, *Hiwar ma'a Sadiqi al-Mulhid* (Cairo: Dar al-'Awda, 1974), 33.
[54] Muhammad Mutawalli al-Sha'rawi, "al-Halqa al-Thalitha: Muqaddamat al-Tafsir," *Tafsir al-Sha'rawi*, prod. 'Abd al-Mun'im Mahmud, Channel 1, Cairo, July 1980, television.
[55] Muhammad Mutawalli al-Sha'rawi, "al-Halqa al-Thamin 'Ashra: Min al-Aya 17 ila al-Aya 21 min Surat al-Baqara," *Tafsir al-Sha'rawi*, September 1980.

Mahmud nor al-Sha'rawi sought to transform this issue into a critique of al-Sadat.

By contrast, Islamist writers sought to hold al-Sadat responsible and offer an alternative vision to men and women alike. In January 1978 *al-Da'wa*'s 'Imara Najib stressed the need for an "Islamic system" (*niẓām islāmī*) which could achieve "social progress" (*al-taqaddum al-ijtimā'ī*) without reference to socioeconomic hierarchy. Najib explained: "Islam [unlike the state] does not recognize titles such as 'Doctor', 'Bashmuhandis'[56] or 'General' (*ḥaḍrat al-ḍābiṭ*)."[57] Along more restricted lines, Ahmad 'Isa 'Ashur foregrounded morality in the face of material temptation. In response to a fatwa request about whether academic dishonesty was permitted in the pursuit of economic gain, 'Ashur explained that cheating leads to corruption (*fasād*), which harms the common good (*maṣāliḥ al-nās*) and corrupts the community's livelihood (*al-shu'ūn al-ma'īshiyya*).[58]

Such alternative Islamist frames were at once powerful and incomplete. They sought to rectify the challenge that socioeconomic stagnation posed to the attainment of respectability by offering alternative paths, yet they could not alleviate the core economic problem. By contrast, *Minbar al-Islam* had access to greater resources but was hamstrung by its dependence on the al-Sadat regime. These textual interactions deepen claims by Wickham and Bayat concerning the power of Islamist frames in the face of socioeconomic disappointment and highlight the challenges inherent in Statist and Islamist frames alike.

What did students who had not yet experienced the socioeconomic stagnation of this period make of the competing visions of Statist and Islamist writers? Bayat and Wickham assume that the al-Sadat project of "science and faith" held little ideological appeal for university students. Letters within *Minbar al-Islam* problematize this claim, though they do not entirely refute it. While it is possible that magazine editors forged laudatory correspondence, letters in *Minbar al-Islam* reflect reader enthusiasm for the magazine's religious vision and

[56] This term literally means "Chief Engineer" and, at the time, signified membership in an educational elite. See Mona Russel, *Middle East in Focus (Egypt)* (Oxford: ABC-CLIO, 2013), 211.

[57] 'Imara Najib, "Nazra Islamiyya fi Mushkilat al-Ta'lim," *al-Da'wa*, January 1978/Safar 1397, 28.

[58] "Ra'i al-Din," *al-I'tisam*, July 1977/Rajab 1397, 31.

resources. Many readers looked to the magazine to guide their religious practice in educational settings: an August 1978 letter from the Delta town of Damanhur asked whether students who were ritually impure could recite the Quran in class.[59] Similarly, in a May 1979 letter a reader from the Delta city of Beheira asked for the help of the Shaykh of al-Azhar in funding a Quranic recitation program at the local charitable association (*jam'iyya khayriyya*), while another reader in the same issue asked the Ministry of Endowments to supply Qurans for study in his local mosque.[60] Correspondence such as this suggests that Statist claims retained appeal for some readers.

At the same time, critical letters hint at the contradictions that association with state institutions entailed. In September 1976 a reader from the Delta town of Zaqaziq explained: "I am a very religious student and fear that I will be punished in the world to come for studying man-made laws (*al-qawānīn al-waḍ'iyya*) in the Law Faculty. Is the burden in this matter on me or on those responsible [for the curriculum]?" *Minbar al-Islam*'s response assured this reader that he bore no blame; rather, administrators and teachers within the Faculty of Law and a regime that trumpeted the slogan of "science and faith" (*al-'ilm wa-l-imān*) were responsible.[61] Yet, despite this condemnation, the mufti could not escape his status as a state functionary, and thus could not solve the structural challenges that these youth faced.

Islamist mobilization strategies, by contrast, were untainted by political compromises yet struggled to deliver a practical alternative to the state system. In June 1977 an unnamed writer in *al-Da'wa* criticized the Faculty of Humanities at Cairo University for not providing sufficient class time for the study of the Arabic language and the Quran.[62] Yet there was little that *al-Da'wa* or *al-I'tisam* could do, as neither was in a financial or legal position to found a university. Similarly, in a letter entitled "Where Is the Free Education?" an *al-Da'wa* reader from Asyut University complained that, despite paying 38 pounds for tuition annually, the students were given neither appropriate study space nor satisfactory nutrition.[63] At this time, however, Islamists were not in a position to offer subsidized dining or university-caliber library space.

59 "Ra'i al-Din," *al-I'tisam*, August 1978/Ramadan 1398, 173.
60 "Ma'a al-Qurra," *Minbar al-Islam*, May 1979/Jumada al-Thaniyya 1399, 123.
61 "Ifta," *Minbar al-Islam*, September 1976/Ramadan 1396, 160.
62 "Akhbar al-Shabab wa-l-Jami'at," *al-Da'wa*, June 1977/Rajab 1397, 44–45.
63 "Barid al-Da'wa," *al-Da'wa*, July 1977/Sha'ban 1397, 63.

The parallel appeals of Statist and Islamist religious visions in the mobilization of university students confirm the commonality of socio-economic disappointment to both projects and shift the focus to the ideological appeals made by competing religious elites. While functionaries of the Supreme Council for Islamic Affairs possessed greater material resources, they were also burdened by association with the al-Sadat regime. By contrast, Islamist elites successfully underlined the failings of the state system, yet were hamstrung by their inability to offer a programmatic alternative to its educational institutions. The respective challenges of association with the political failings of the ruling elite and access to material resources would shape not only efforts of religious mobilization but also the competing projects of the Islamic Revival.

Silent Readers

What about the silent majority of readers whose letters did not appear in these magazines? The final section of this chapter will explore this broader audience through a critical reading of advertisements that appeared in all three magazines. Though they did not actively contribute to debates, this broader subset of readers was an audience to which editors, writers, and readers spoke. While it is impossible to recover the selection criteria of editors, advertisements in the pages of the magazines nonetheless provide clues to who the advertisers thought were reading the magazines.

All the periodicals contained a myriad of advertisements for everything from books to banking and furniture to fashion. These advertisements, like letters, were filtered to some degree; editors presumably had the option of rejecting advertisements that didn't suit their magazine's message. Some advertisements were placed as gifts or exhibitions of religious piety,[64] while others might have been placed to provide the advertiser financial leverage if the magazine deviated from his or her ideological preferences.

Still other advertisements were included because the companies concerned perceived the magazine's audience as one that would consider buying their products, though the prominence of such advertisements

[64] This was confirmed by both Badr and Madbuli: Badr, personal interview, 24 Feb. 2013; Madbuli, personal interview, 24 Feb. 2013.

could also reflect the disproportionate resources of a small segment of readers. Neither were advertisements necessarily a direct reflection of consumer practice, as many readers looked without being able to buy.[65]

In order to disentangle these different possible motivations for advertising, this section examines advertisements from identified Muslim Brotherhood supporters, on the one hand, and public sector companies, on the other. As Kepel notes, *al-Da'wa* was replete with advertisements from Brotherhood supporters who had made their fortunes in Saudi Arabia during the preceding quarter-century, most notably al-Sharif Plastic, Masarra Real Estate, and Modern Motors.[66] Yet public-sector companies also purchased nearly one-fifth of the advertising throughout the period.[67] Crucially, such companies are unlikely to have purchased advertising space in these magazines except for economic reasons, because companies owned by the state were unlikely to support an Islamist voice in times of conflict with the regime. Finally, there were advertisements from companies of unknown political allegiance.

This section tentatively reconstructs the silent portions of the readership through attention to advertising motive, consumer practice, and political position. It then compares the picture drawn by advertisements with two other key sources of information: the "popular participant" profile of the previous section and the 1976 Egyptian census. This participant profile provides us with a guide, albeit an edited one, to readership, while the census highlights divergences between this profile and demographic trends.

Islamic magazines included advertisements aimed at *infitāḥ* elites who did business with banks, investment firms, and contractors. In *al-Da'wa*, Salim Ibn Hasan al-Ansari and Sons offered contracting opportunities[68] and the Dubai Islamic Bank sought investors.[69] In *al-I'tisam* one could enter into commercial and contracting agreements

[65] Walter Armbrust, Mass Culture and Modernism in Egypt (Cambridge: Cambridge University Press, 1994), 83–84.
[66] Kepel, *The Roots of Radical Islam*, 110.
[67] Such advertisers could conceivably have placed pressure on Islamist magazines to moderate their opposition to the al-Sadat regime, but, based on continued advertisement throughout al-Sadat's rule, it does not appear that this was the case.
[68] *al-Da'wa*, September 1976/Ramadan 1396, inside back cover.
[69] *al-Da'wa*, April 1977/Jumada al-Ula 1397, 58–59.

with the Islamic Opening Company (Shirkat al-Fath al-Islami)[70] or invest in private medical services at the Ibn Sina Medical Clinic.[71] *Minbar al-Islam*, too, featured advertisements for transnational Islamic banking with the Islamic Company for Gulf Investments,[72] and even offered life in the "City of Dreams" (*madīnat al-aḥlām*).[73] The advertisements confirm the presence of a business elite within all three readerships, though they give no indication as to its proportional role. Given the professional background of participants, businessmen were likely a minuscule component of the readership.

To what extent did advertisers also speak to middle-class readers? Both *al-Da'wa* and *al-I'tisam* were full of advertisements from Islamist supporters and from companies of unclear political allegiance. Readers could purchase household durables, whether furniture from Hawi Furniture[74] or cups, lighting appliances, and plastic plates from Sharif Plastic Factories.[75] Readers of *al-I'tisam* had fewer options on display when it came to household wares, though many ads for Sharif Plastic Company still appeared in the magazine.[76] Yet this evidence is inconclusive, because it is difficult to know whether these advertisements appeared primarily for reasons of commercial competition, vanity, or economic leverage. In *al-Da'wa* it appears that household wares were targeted at a specific audience: former editor Badr Muhammad Badr confirms the variety of potential motives listed above, while suggesting that "household appliances and clothing" (*al-adawāt al-manzaliyya wa-l-malābis*) were targeted at married couples who read the magazine.[77] In contradistinction to both of its competitors, *al-I'tisam* contained few advertisements for clothing or household goods, and thus provided few clues as to the gender composition or age of its readership.

Like the Islamist businessmen who advertised in *al-Da'wa*, Statist public-sector companies published similar advertisements directed at both men and women in *Minbar al-Islam*. Wulkas Clothing Company offered unveiled women "elegance and high taste" (*al-anāqa wa-*

70 *al-I'tisam*, January 1981/Safar 1401, 43.
71 *al-I'tisam*, March 1977/Rabi' al-Awwal 1397, back cover.
72 *Minbar al-Islam*, October 1979/Dhu al-Qa'da 1399, back cover.
73 *Minbar al-Islam*, November 1978/Dhu al-Hijja 1398, inside front cover.
74 *Minbar al-Islam*, August 1976/Sha'ban 1396, 51.
75 *Minbar al-Islam*, April 1979/Jumada al-Ula 1399, inside back cover.
76 *al-I'tisam*, December 1977/Muharram 1398, back cover.
77 Badr Muhammad Badr, message to the author, 8 May 2014, e-mail.

l-dhawq al-rafīʿ),[78] and the Egyptian Goods Sales Company marketed functional men's clothing.[79] Public-sector companies such as these could have supported this Statist magazine for reasons of either vanity or good politics; in the absence of editors who can speak to this logic of selection, this information is of limited explanatory value.

What about those situations in which advertising crossed political divisions? Islamist magazines also contained a wide variety of advertisements from public-sector companies aimed at men and women. In *al-Daʿwa* the department store ʿUmar Effendi advertised summer clothing for girls and women,[80] while the public-sector Nasr Textile and Knitwear Company (Shirkat al-Nasr li-l-Ghazl wa-l-Nasij wa-l-Triku) offered blouses and dresses for women, and pants and cologne for men.[81] Public-sector companies also advertised household wares: the Egyptian Company for Electrical Appliances (al-Shirka al-Misriyya li-l-Maʿdat al-Kahrabaʾiyya) offered everything from televisions to lamps.[82] These advertisements, targeted at those Egyptians whom advertisers believed to be readers, transcend the Statist–Islamist divide and suggest that the readership included a significant number of women. That women represented 25.1 percent and 30.4 percent, respectively,[83] of middle-class professions furthers the impression that their share of the readership exceeded 5 percent.

The specific goods offered by these companies also appealed far more to a married adult with a home than to a college student. Though students might purchase advertised clothing (assuming sufficient disposable income), furniture and electrical appliances were likely targeted at married couples.[84] Accordingly, these advertisements suggest that the correspondence in these two magazines may underrepresent the proportion of professionals within the readership. The information available from the 1976 census similarly supports a more limited role for students within the readership: already-employed middle-class

78 *Minbar al-Islam*, February 1976/Safar 1396, 169.
79 *Minbar al-Islam*, June 1977/Rajab 1397, 184.
80 *al-Daʿwa*, June 1976/Jumada al-Ukhra 1396, 58.
81 *al-Daʿwa*, May 1977/Jumada al-Ukhra 1397, 37.
82 *al-Daʿwa*, August 1976/Shaʿban 1396, 46.
83 CAPMAS, *1976 Population and Housing Census*, 60.
84 Within the twenty-to-twenty-five age group, 1.678 million had yet to marry while 149,936 were married. By contrast, in the twenty-five-to-thirty age group, the numbers are reversed: 695,000 were unmarried while 1.757 million were married: CAPMAS, *1976 Population and Housing Census*, 159.

professionals dwarfed students numerically, representing 15.7 percent of the population compared to the 1.44 percent of Egyptians who studied at universities during this period.[85] One should not assume, however, that middle-class professionals participated in Islamic magazines in proportion to their numerical weight, as the statistical profile of participants describes the dynamic within the magazine rather than broader demographic trends within Egypt.

Conclusion

Islamic magazines served as a crucial site for the transmission of competing projects of religious mobilization in the opening half-decade of Egypt's Islamic Revival. These three magazines provided religious elites with an opportunity to influence middle-class readers outside their direct supervision and, in turn, gave these readers the opportunity to participate in the formation of competing projects of religious mobilization from their homes and offices in Cairo, Alexandria, the Nile Delta, and Upper Egypt. These participants, Statist and Islamist, all faced socioeconomic frustration; their religious preferences, however, emerged out of competing programs rather than solely from the efforts of Islamist elites to challenge a religiously inert regime.

Collectively, these readers provide a window into the geographic, socioeconomic, and gender dynamics of the opening years of the Islamic Revival in Egypt. At the intersection of state educational policies, economic shifts, and mass media, religious elites and a select set of middle-class Egyptians engaged in a project of public morality from differing positions of power. Piety served as a source of social distinction premised on literacy, and aspirants to piety used their textual access to establish a place for their participation and to push religious elites to amend their prescriptions to fit local realities. It is to the specific projects of religio-political mobilization that we now turn.

[85] CAPMAS, *1976 Population and Housing Census*, 159.

3 *Could the State Serve Islam?*
The Rise and Fall of Islamist Educational Reform

In 1981 Egypt's religious landscape appeared fundamentally divided between Statist claims to Islam and Islamist movements that challenged the claims of Statist institutions to primacy. While the Ministry of Education spread state-sanctioned visions of Islam through the primary and secondary institutions under its control and the Ministry of Endowments asserted control over the contents of the Friday sermon within government mosques (*al-masājid al-ḥukumiyya*), groups such as the Muslim Brotherhood, the Jamʿiyya Sharʿiyya, and Ansar al-Sunna al-Muhammadiyya worked to spread their distinct yet complementary calls through affiliated schools, mosques, and Islamic media.

At the dawn of the 1970s, however, this bifurcated infrastructure of religious transmission was not yet set in stone as leading Brothers and Islamist–Salafis, inspired by a new emphasis on Islamic education regionally and perceptions of a continued threat to proper religious transmission globally, actively considered the possibility of state-based religious educational reform. On the surface the story is a straightforward one of how worsening relations between al-Sadat and his religious competitors shaped the lines that would structure Islamic education and knowledge in late twentieth- and early twenty-first-century Egypt.

Just as important as the competition that divided Statist and Islamist projects, however, is the shared logic of social transformation through education that bound them. Breaking away from an Islamist-centric narrative of the expansion of Islamic education within Egypt, this chapter explores the relationship between Brotherhood and Islamist–Salafi calls to Islam, the religious projects of elites within the Supreme Council for Islamic Affairs, the Islamic Research Academy at al-Azhar, and the nationalist pedagogical efforts transmitted by the Ministry of Education. A comparison among these projects, in turn, reveals both the historical circumstances that set the stage for the emergence of a parallel Islamic educational sector and the intellectual ties that bound Statist and Islamist projects of religious transmission.

How can we explain the existence of parallel Statist and Islamist educational institutions in Egypt, and the common assumption of both systems that social challenges can be solved primarily through Islam? One approach emphasizes the role of technological change in the spread of alternative Islamic education through mass media in 1970s Egypt. Eickelman and Piscatori have noted the democratic potential of new media,[1] and Salvatore and Hirschkind have highlighted the role of pamphlets, television, and audiocassettes in facilitating Islamic education outside either primary and secondary religious institutes (*ma ʿāhid azhariyya*) run by al-Azhar or their "civil" (*madanī*) counterpart schools run by the Ministry of Education.[2] The spread of mass and small media alike opened up new opportunities for scientists-turned-religious-intellectuals such as Mustafa Mahmud, oppositional preachers such as ʿAbd al-Hamid Kishk, and, more broadly, for scholars and laymen alike, to reach both literate and illiterate segments of the population. This new media complemented preexisting print products while appealing to a broader audience and introducing new voices.

A second strand of scholarship has focused more narrowly on grassroots pathways of transmission. In particular, Carrie Wickham charts the emergence of a "Parallel Islamic Sector" composed of a constellation of private mosques as well as self-consciously "Islamic" voluntary associations, publishing houses, medical clinics, banks, and investment companies.[3] This infrastructure enabled and transmitted a broad ideological project that guided its participants to personal piety and support for Islamist electoral participation. This explanation also highlights the role of Gulf capital in supporting a wide array of Islamic publishing houses that would make independent Islamic publishing a viable economic enterprise over the course of the second half of al-Sadat's rule.[4]

A third approach shifts focus from alternative sites and means of transmission to the changing role of the Egyptian state in shaping the

[1] See Dale F. Eickelman and James Piscatori, *Muslim Politics* (Princeton: Princeton University Press, 1996), 121–30.

[2] See Hirschkind, *The Ethical Soundscape*, esp. 105–42. Also see Armando Salvatore, "Social Differentiation, Moral Authority and Public Islam in Egypt: The Path of Mustafa Mahmud," *Anthropology Today*, 16:2 (April 2000), 12–15.

[3] See Wickham, *Mobilizing Islam*, 97.

[4] For example, see Kepel, *The Roots of Radical Islam*, 110. Wickham highlights the role of Gulf capital more broadly in sustaining the institutions of the parallel Islamic sector: see Wickham, *Mobilizing Islam*, 98.

population through public education. British-led educational reforms from the late nineteenth century on had presented Islam as a concrete set of pronouncements with direct applicability to daily life, a process which Gregory Starrett calls "objectification." This objectified religious tradition was then utilized in the service of concrete political goals. The British used it to socialize the population against political revolt, 'Abd al-Nasir to justify scientific socialism, and al-Sadat to argue that the state (and not the Islamist opposition) possessed an authoritative claim to religious legitimacy.[5] This process of functionalization, by which religion came to be associated with particular social and political ends, produced a new understanding of religion itself: "the ideas, symbols and behaviors constituting 'true' Islam came to be judged not by their adherence to contemporary popular or high traditions, but by their utility in performing social work."[6] In the process, what religion "taught" became increasingly incoherent as dominant interpretations changed with political winds and scholars stood on the sidelines.[7] The state thus played a primary, rather than a secondary or reactive, role in the proliferation of religious education and in changing definitions of Islamic knowledge, outside scholarly supervision.

This chapter adopts the third approach, exploring the historical circumstances in which the parallel Islamic educational infrastructures that define the Islamic Revival emerged, and adding significant empirical information to Starrett's argument for considering state-sponsored and Islamist educational efforts as two sides of the same coin. Though it acknowledges the significance of both technological change and foreign funding, it argues that the driving force behind the bifurcation of religious education in Egypt's Islamic Revival was not the incommensurability of Statist and Islamist calls for religious change, but rather their shared adoption of the Ministry of Education-sponsored Modernist vision of education as a prime motor of social change. Statist and Islamist projects diverged not because they were ideologically opposed,

5 Starrett, *Putting Islam to Work*, 77–86.
6 Starrett, *Putting Islam to Work*, 62.
7 Starrett's argument implies a teleology of functionalized religion; he describes the creation of a new Islamic "tradition" (*turāth*) which is derived from but logically distinct from the Islamic textual tradition as understood and practiced by 'ulama. This chapter accepts that state-sponsored objectification and functionalization of religious education created a new "tradition" yet views Islamist visions of social and political transformation as no less functionalized than their Statist competitors.

but rather because they were fundamentally similar in their adoption of the Modernist assumption that education could and should serve as an engine of social change. In contrast to Starrett's story of state-driven change, however, letters to the editor and fatwa requests reveal that this change emerged not only from interaction between Statist and Islamist elites, but also from the grassroots up.

Islamic Transmission prior to 1976

Islamic educators in the premodern period would have had trouble recognizing their twentieth-century counterparts. The traditional "embodied" model of Islamic education was based on human ties, in which scholars authorized students to teach particular books, and teachers formed students as pious subjects. It was premised on the assumption that such ties – and the local community that undergirded the broader enterprise of Islamic education – both guarded this knowledge against distortion and monitored the behavior of those who acquired it. This was an intellectual and moral order structured by human relationships and maintained by communal boundaries, rather than a comprehensive vision of top-down social transformation staffed by state-trained functionaries.

Yet this model of subject formation was in retreat with the spread of curricula for religious education and printing in Egypt in the late nineteenth century.[8] The diffusion of printed texts throughout society both expanded the reach of scholarly authority and broadened the knowledge that scholars sought to pass on. However, this had come at the cost of a double disembodiment, as print-mediated knowledge was not based on a personal relationship with the scholar in question, and the ability of the latter to monitor the performance of this knowledge (also known as embodiment) decreased in tandem. Meanwhile, the boundaries of the scholarly elites were challenged by an increasing number of laymen who took advantage of the shift from seminary to print as they sought to cultivate a broad audience through religiously oriented print

[8] For an overview of the *isnād* paradigm, which bases itself on this concept of embodiment within Islam, see William Graham, "Traditionalism in Islam: An Essay in Interpretation," *Journal of Interdisciplinary History*, 23:3 (1993), 495–522. For a discussion of the implications of disembodied texts in late nineteenth-century Egypt, see Mitchell, *Colonising Egypt*, 128–60.

media.[9] Though it was still possible to replicate the dynamics of face-to-face education and communal belonging through religious institutions that trained future scholars and began at the primary level, disembodied transmission became a necessary (and often convenient) concession to limited resources.

Just as importantly, the Egyptian state had entered the business of mass religious education in the late nineteenth century with efforts by British colonial officials to transform Quranic recitation schools (sing. *kuttāb*, pl. *katātīb*) into a nationwide system with a unified curriculum. Colonial administrators believed that, as in England, correct mass socialization would prevent political uprisings, battle indolence, and even increase the country's agricultural productivity.[10] The government was similarly involved in teacher training, founding the Dar al-ʿUlum teacher preparatory school, later to become part of Cairo University, in order to prepare teachers of Arabic and Islam.[11] This effort to replace one form of religious transmission (the *kuttāb*) with another (the school), however, carried with it a distinct rupture: the teachers who taught textbooks came not from scholarly genealogies or local mosques but from state institutions as they used mass-produced textbooks to affirm the existing political order.

In response, a variety of religious organizations sought to develop alternative projects, many of which mirrored the Ministry of Education's move toward disembodied transmission even as they opposed the latter's ideological goals. Most prominently, the Islamic Charitable Association (al-Jamʿiyya al-Khayriyya al-Islamiyya) began efforts to develop a parallel educational system that would meld state-mandated subjects and "Islamic values" (*al-qiyam al-islāmiyya*).[12] This project, inaugurated in 1894, was aimed at those who lacked the means

[9] The rise of *islāmiyyāt* literature in the 1930s reflected this shift. See Gershoni and Jankowski, *Redefining the Egyptian Nation*, 54–78.

[10] Starrett, *Putting Islam to Work*, 30, 45.

[11] For an extensive study of Dar al-ʿUlum's curriculum and graduates which makes use of Bourdieuan concepts of cultural capital, see Hilary Kalmbach, *Islamic Knowledge and the Making of Modern Egypt* (Cambridge: Cambridge University Press, forthcoming [2019]). Kalmbach's study reinstates the state as a key and multifaceted religious actor and shows how the hybrid religious education of Dar al-ʿUlum paved the way for projects of religious reform and changing notions of religious cultural capital.

[12] Ahmad Shalabi Hilmi and ʿAbd al-ʿAzim Muhammad Ibrahim Ramadan, *Fusul min Tarikh Harakat al-Islah al-Ijtimaʿi fi Misr: Dirasa ʿan Dawr al-Jamʿiyya al-Khayriyya al-Islamiyya* (Cairo: al-Hay'a al-Misriyya al-ʿAmma li-l-Kuttab, 1988), 108–11.

to study in government schools and began with branches in Cairo, Alexandria, Asyut, and Tanta. By 1913 it included 3,912 students.[13] As in the case of government-sponsored education, however, it was not a scholar authorized to transmit a particular set of texts, but rather a layman certified by the Ministry of Education, who was to communicate religious knowledge to students.

The Muslim Brotherhood was one contributor to this process. Egypt's leading Islamist organization had sought during the first half of the twentieth century to develop a parallel educational infrastructure, which included thirty-one educational sites spanning vocational training, female education, night classes for blue-collar workers, Quranic memorization, and literacy education.[14] Additionally, the Brotherhood organized educational activities outside an institutional setting for blue-collar workers, peasants, and women.[15]

Nevertheless, even during the first half of the twentieth century the Brotherhood was cognizant of the power of state-sponsored educational reform. Many of the organization's leaders, including its founder, Hasan al-Banna , were themselves schoolteachers,[16] and were thus intimately aware of the shortcomings of state-sponsored religious education, particularly the impiety of teachers, and the limited time dedicated to religious education.[17] Indeed, al-Banna even noted that education was the most important factor (*akbar muʾathir*) to "the life of the transnational Islamic community" (*fī ḥayāt al-umma*).[18] In contrast to the debates of the 1970s, however, the Brotherhood's founder did not yet see education as a socially transformative panacea against a wave of moral corruption.

The Brotherhood's peers, on the other hand, had given little thought to how to reform the state educational system, though a significant proportion of the young men and women who formed their rank and file had presumably attended public schools. Instead, leaders of both the Jamʿiyya Sharʿiyya and Ansar al-Sunna were focused on training imams to function outside it. The founder of the Jamʿiyya Sharʿiyya,

13 Hilmi and Ramadan, *Fusul min Tarikh Harakat al-Islah al-Ijtimaʿi fi Misr*, 151.
14 Dawud, *al-Jamʿiyyat al-Islamiyya fi Misr*, 267–68.
15 Dawud, *al-Jamʿiyyat al-Islamiyya fi Misr*, 271–72.
16 On al-Banna's familiarity with modern pedagogical theory, see Gudrun Kraemer, *Hasan al-Banna* (Oxford: Oneworld, 2010), 32–33.
17 For example, see "Fi Shuʾun al-Taʿlim," *al-Ikhwan al-Muslimin*, 28 May 1936/ 25 Safar 1354, 12–18, at 13.
18 Hasan al-Banna, "Fi Manahij al-Taʿlim," *al-Ikhwan al-Muslimin*, 25 June 1935/24 Rabiʿ al-Awwal 1354, 1–3, at 1.

Muhammad Khattab al-Subki (d. 1933), had initially taught both ʿulama and preachers from his home mosque, Masjid al-Jamiʿa, in the Khiyamiyya neighborhood of Cairo.[19] These students, in turn, fanned out to other Jamʿiyya Sharʿiyya mosques and branches (*furū*ʿ) throughout Egypt, with an elite from among them becoming leading scholars within the movement.[20] Along similar lines, Ansar al-Sunna's founder Muhammad Hamid al-Fiqi (d. 1969) taught from his local mosque, Masjid al-Hadara, in the Cairene neighborhood of Abadin, and established branches of Ansar al-Sunna al-Muhammadiyya throughout Egypt, with a particular concentration in Cairo and the Nile Delta.[21]

These two leading Islamic movements also sought to create a durable infrastructure for their particular projects. Under al-Fiqi, Ansar al-Sunna built ten preacher-training institutes, staffed by Ansar al-Sunna scholars who had graduated from al-Azhar, as well as some 203 institutes devoted to Quranic recitation.[22] Similarly, in 1964, the Jamʿiyya Sharʿiyya opened an imam-training institution in Cairo, and soon established branches in Giza, al-Matariyya, Banha, al-Mahalla al-Kubra, Mansura, Alexandria and Bani Swayf.[23] The latter's "imam institutes" (*maʿāhid al-imāma*) involved a two-year curriculum of memorization of the Quran, assorted Hadith, and training in Arabic grammar. Staffed by experienced Jamʿiyya Sharʿiyya preachers, they enabled the organization to furnish competent religious personnel to its mosques during a period in which the Ministry of Endowments suffered from a shortage of trained preachers.[24] In contrast to the Ministry of Education, the Jamʿiyya Sharʿiyya was intimately concerned with forming pious subjects through personal ties.

As Egypt entered the al-Sadat period, new opportunities to shape society through religious education beckoned, yet early efforts were limited. The Muslim Brotherhood, Jamʿiyya Sharʿiyya, and Ansar al-Sunna al-Muhammadiyya had all turned inward over the

[19] Muhammad ʿAli Masʿud, *al-Jamʿiyya al-Sharʿiyya li-Taʿawun al-ʿAmilin bi-l-Kitab wa-l-Sunna al-Muhammadiyya ʿAqidatan wa Minhajan wa Sulukan* (Cairo: al-Jamʿiyya al-Sharʿiyya, 1982), 28.

[20] Masʿud, *al-Jamʿiyya al-Sharʿiyya*, 28–29.

[21] Muhammad ʿAli al-Qadi, "Nasha al-Jamaʿa," *al-Hadi al-Nabawi*, June 1937/ Rabiʿ al-Thani 1356, 22–23.

[22] Tahir, *Jamaʿat Ansar al-Sunna al-Muhamadiyya*, 98.

[23] The foundation of this institute, however, was done under the direct supervision of a military officer. See Masʿud, *al-Jamʿiyya al-Sharʿiyya*, 151.

[24] Masʿud, *al-Jamʿiyya al-Sharʿiyya*, 151.

previous twenty years; the question of how to compose and transmit an educational project to the masses was hardly relevant in the face of continued torture, jailing, and even executions. As Khalid ʿAbd al-Qadir ʿAwda, an Islamist student activist in Asyut, noted with regard to the Muslim Brotherhood, "there was no organization (*tanẓīm*)," there was merely the "idea of the Brotherhood" (*fikrat al-ikhwān*).[25]

The Jamʿiyya Sharʿiyya and Ansar al-Sunna, on the other hand, had maintained their educational networks, yet the institutions under their control were focused on local, rather than national, religious change.[26] While each could still express concerns regarding the state of public education – a July 1973 article in *al-Tawhid* noted the abysmal performance of teachers and faulty curriculum of Islamic education within the state system[27] – such concerns were decidedly marginal within these organizations' broader educational mission. Indeed, to the extent that either group sought to lobby the Ministry of Education, this contact involved local efforts to increase the emphasis on Quranic memorization in Egyptian schools.[28]

Neither were those who sought to revive Islamist education, most notably the Jamaʿa Islamiyya, equipped to do so on a mass scale. Jamaʿa Islamiyya activist and later Brotherhood leader ʿAbd al-Munʿim Abu-l-Futuh recounts his experience during the 1971–72 academic year:

> At that time, mentioning the Muslim Brotherhood was prohibited, as was [possessing] their books. During this period the [only] books which were widespread were those of Ansar al-Sunna al-Muhammadiyya and the Jamʿiyya Sharʿiyya, and the books of Abu-l-Aʿla al-Mawdudi ... books of the Salafi orientation (*al-ittijāh al-salafī*) were distributed free of charge at

25 *Hadith Dhikrayat Maʿa Khalid ʿAbd al-Qadir ʿAwda, al-Juzʾa al-Awwal*, perf. Khalid ʿAbd al-Qadir ʿAwda, Ikhwantube, 2010.

26 These two organizations' reemergence was far from assured; ʿAbd al-Nasir's 1967 decision to merge the two and to place an ally, ʿAbd al-Rahman Amin, as president, represented an effort to limit the activities of both. See Tahir, *Jamaʿat Ansar al-Sunna al-Muhamadiyya*, 148. In 1973, however, the two reemerged as independent organizations: Tahir, *Jamaʿat Ansar al-Sunna al-Muhamadiyya*, 241.

27 al-Sayyid Sabiq, "Mazahir al-Tarbiyya al-Islamiyya," *al-Tawhid*, July 1973/Jumada al-Thani 1393, 17–21.

28 For a description of this type of activity in the governorate of Giza, which is considered part of greater Cairo, see "Akhbar al-Jamaʿa," *al-Tawhid*, June 1973/Jumada al-Ula 1393, 57.

universities ... and [we also had access to some] books from the noble al-Azhar.[29]

Within these restrictions, student activists formulated the kernels of an alternative educational project that melded Islamist, Quietist Salafi, and Statist authors. The 1973 recommended reading list for first-year students included a comparatively narrow selection of leading scholars, notably writing by Hasan al-Banna and Sayyid Qutb, alongside books by Statist preacher Muhammad Mutawalli al-Sha'rawi, Mawdudi (d. 1979), and the Quietist Salafi scholar Muhammad Nasir al-Din al-Albani (d. 1999).[30] Other Jama'a Islamiyya curricula, however, excluded Statist authors: At Alexandria University the movement's reading list included works by Ibn Taymiyya (d. 1328), Ibn Qayyim al-Jawziyya (d. 1350), Muhammad Ibn 'Abd al-Wahhab (d. 1792), Sayyid Qutb (d. 1966), and Abu-l-A'la al-Mawdudi (d. 1979).[31] Though the position of the Jama'a Islamiyya improved in 1975, when the organization's success in the General Union of Egyptian Students elections provided it with access to printing facilities with which it could produce pamphlets,[32] it still was limited to university campuses.

Prior to 1976 religious education outside the bounds of state institutions was limited by political repression, economic challenges, and a commitment among Quietist Salafis, the dominant strain in Egypt at this time, to a mosque-centered model of religious transmission. Nonetheless, the Brotherhood and, increasingly, the Jam'iyya Shar'iyya and Jama'a Islamiyya, grasped the potential power of

29 Abu-l-Futuh, *'Abd al-Mun'im Abu-l-Futuh*, 40.

30 Abu-l-Futuh, *'Abd al-Mun'im Abu-l-Futuh*, 45. The included texts, part of a series produced by the Jama'a Islamiyya called The Voice of Truth (Sawt al-Haqq), included Hasan al-Banna's *Risalat al-Mu'tamar al-Khamis* and *al-Mustalahat al-Arba'a* as well as Mawdudi's *Nazariyyat al-Islam al-Siyasiyya*, Sayyid Qutb's *Hadha al-Din* and *al-Mustaqbal li-Hadha al-Din*, Ibn Qayyim al-Jawziyya's *Tafsir Surat al-Fatiha*, al-Albani's *Hijab al-Mar'a al-Muslima fi al-Kitab wa-l-Sunna*, and excerpts from al-Sha'rawi's *La Illa ila Allah: Minhaj Hayat* and *al-Tariq ila Allah*. Crucially, all of these books are popular works oriented toward instructing a mass audience in the details of pious living with a decided emphasis on pious models that support the religious transformation of state and society.

31 This heavy Salafi emphasis also squares with the greater strength of Salafi activists generally in Alexandria. See 'Abduh Mustafa Dasuqi and al-Sa'id Ramadan al-'Abbadi, *Tarikh al-Haraka al-Tullabiyya bi-Jama'at al-Ikhwan al-Muslimin 1933–2011* (Cairo: Mu'assasat Iqra, 2013), 127.

32 Kepel, *The Roots of Radical Islam*, 144.

education to transform society. Though the first half of al-Sadat's rule opened up limited opportunities for Egypt's Islamist opposition, the Brotherhood had yet to recover from the repression of the ʿAbd al-Nasir years, and the Jamʿiyya Sharʿiyya and Ansar al-Sunna had yet to commit themselves to moving beyond mosque-based preaching. In parallel, neither the Supreme Council for Islamic Affairs nor the Islamic Research Academy at al-Azhar had expanded beyond piecemeal efforts to publish for a broader audience throughout Egypt. To the extent that an Islamic educational project emerged during this period, it was limited to the student activists of the Jamaʿa Islamiyya.

An increasing number of literate Egyptians throughout Egypt, however, beckoned. While state institutions struggled to accommodate the growing number of men and women who flocked to their gates in search of education, Islamist and Salafi leaders confronted a new opportunity for outreach. How would Islamist elites seek to mold religious subjects and society after eighteen years of repression, and to what extent were these efforts continuous with previous models?

Reforming State Religious Education

Egypt's Islamic movements had never had the opportunity to reform state educational institutions, yet by the mid-1970s the prospect of reform of civil (*madanī*) religious education appeared open in the face of apparent rapprochement with the al-Sadat government. By contrast, due to limited financial resources and the absence of a ready-made supplementary educational infrastructure, a grassroots project of Islamist education made little sense.[33] The challenge for Egypt's Islamist opposition was how to come to terms with state-sponsored educational reform.

The principle that state-sponsored educational institutions could serve as an effective means of outreach had grown increasingly plausible, particularly with the parallel rise of the Islamic University of Medina (IUM) in Saudi Arabia. Founded in 1961, the university's attractiveness

[33] This did not mean, however, that the organization ignored the need to publicize the Brotherhood's history: issues of *al-Daʿwa* frequently contained excerpts from al-Banna's "Tuesday Talks" (*Ḥadith al-Thulatha*) as well as the stories of Brotherhood leaders who had suffered under ʿAbd al-Nasir. For example, see Hasan al-Banna, "Min Wahi al-Hijra," *al-Daʿwa*, December 1976/Muharram 1397, 8–9.

as a transnational hub for Islamic education had grown as the IUM brought together leading Islamic scholars and thinkers from across the Middle East and South Asia while offering generous scholarships to students globally.[34] Indeed, in previous years Ansar al-Sunna's leading scholars had embarked on a series of trips aimed at acquainting themselves with new models of Islamic education as well as securing scholarships for their students to study at IUM and other Saudi universities.[35] A breathless report in the November 1976 issue of *al-Daʿwa* noted that "while Arab and foreign universities seek to meet the needs of the society in their respective countries (*sadd iḥtiyajāt al-mujtamaʿ fī awṭanihā*), the Islamic University of Medina . . . [seeks] to spread the message of Islam to the world through *daʿwa* . . . [and to deepen] practical religiosity (*al-tadayyun al-ʿamalī*) . . . in the individual and society alike."[36]

Just as importantly, Muslim Brothers and Salafis saw education as a central site of political contestation, both locally and globally. In the face of the continued dominance of French models of education in Tunisia and Morocco,[37] Baʿthist repression of Islamic educational institutions in Syria,[38] and post-1967 efforts in Israel to meld Jewish religiosity and a military spirit,[39] education represented an undeniable

34 Michael Farquhar, *Circuits of Faith: Migration, Education, and the Wahhabi Mission* (Stanford: Stanford University Press, 2016), 65.

35 For a description of a 1974 Ansar al-Sunna trip to the IUM, see "al-Rihla al-Mubaraka," *al-Tawhid*, January 1974/Muharram 1394, 8: 1–3. For a description of the 1975 trip, inclusive of details regarding scholarships to IUM, the University of Riyadh, and King ʿAbd al-ʿAziz University in Jeddah, see "al-Rihla al-Mubaraka," *al-Tawhid*, January 1975/Muharram 1395, 2:1–3. During the second half of the 1970s the IUM's accessibility would grow further as the Saudi government directed a portion of its increasingly significant oil proceeds toward the university and, by extension, greatly enhanced its ability to offer scholarships. See Farquhar, *Circuits of Faith*, 82.

36 "Akhbar al-Shabab wa-l-Jamiʿat," *al-Daʿwa*, November 1976/Dhu al-Qaʿda 1396, 46–47, at 47.

37 For Tunisia, see "Sakratirak al-Sihafi," *al-Daʿwa*, April 1978/Jumada al-Ula 1398, 52–53, at 52. For Morocco, see "Mukhtarat min al-Suhuf al-ʿArabiyya wa-l-Islamiyya," *al-Iʿtisam*, September 1977/Shawwal 1397, 41–42, at 41.

38 ʿAbd al-Halim ʿUways, "Hizb al-Baʿth Yashinn Harban ʿala al-Islam," *al-Daʿwa*, June 1979/Rajab 1399, 26–27.

39 Muzaffar al-Husayni, "Manahij al-Taʿlim al-Yahudi," *al-Daʿwa*, August 1979/Ramadan 1399, 14–16, at 16. For further analysis of the ideological goals of this system, see Gideon Aran, "Jewish Zionist Fundamentalism: The Bloc of the Faithful in Israel (Gush Emunim)," in Martin E. Marty and R. Scott Appleby (eds.), *Fundamentalisms Observed* (Chicago: University of Chicago Press, 1991), 265–344, at 274–75.

axis of ideological strife that cut to the core of political authority in the post-colonial Middle East. Neither was this assumption unique to the Middle East: Evangelical Christians in the United States had begun to develop their own educational institutions in the 1940s, and the 1962 Supreme Court decision banning prayer in public schools (*Engel v. Vitale*) only underscored the necessity of such institutions to the cultivation of Christian piety.[40] At home and abroad, preaching and pamphlets could spread the call to religious change, yet such efforts were invariably piecemeal; a truly comprehensive project within the boundaries of the modern state required educational institutions.

The prospects of educational reform in Egypt even looked good. In April 1977 Minister of Education Mustafa Kamal Hilmi participated in a Council on Religious Education (Lajnat al-Tarbiya al-Diniyya) alongside the former Minister of Endowments Shaykh ʿAbd al-ʿAziz ʿIsa (d. 1994) as well as ʿAbd al-Halim Mahmud, then the Shaykh of al-Azhar. This council of scholars and laymen, mobilized by al-Sadat's efforts to coopt the Islamist opposition by positioning himself as an advocate of Islamic change, discussed how to reform the emphasis and level of the religious education curriculum to enhance its effectiveness. Collectively, the council declared that henceforth religious education would be considered a "basic component" (*mādda asāsiyya*) of the educational curriculum. Its members further decided to form an additional council that would consult with the Minister of Endowments and Azhar Affairs, Muhammad Mutawalli al-Shaʿrawi, and the State Mufti, Shaykh Muhammad Khatir.[41] Nor was such an alliance necessarily wishful thinking: all of those involved could plausibly point to the possibility that the al-Sadat regime would be open to the reform of religious education as an intermediate step to satisfy varied religious factions at a time when the application of Islamic law to the regime's political and economic policies was a far more complicated endeavor.

The stakes of such reform were high. As ʿAbd al-Hamid Kishk noted in a 10 June 1977 sermon:

> Egypt has been afflicted by three plagues (*masāʾib*): one political, one economic, and the third moral ... It has been afflicted politically by the idol

[40] Matthew Avery Sutton, *American Apocalypse: A History of Modern Evangelicalism* (Cambridge, MA: Harvard University Press, 2014), 320.

[41] "al-Tarbiya al-Diniyya Tadkhul Kull Manahij al-Taʿlim," *al-Shabab al-ʿArabi*, 4 April 1977 (issue #532), 1.

(*ṣanam*) of the socialist union (*al-ittiḥād al-ishtirākī*), economically by the idol of the public sector (*al-qitāʿ al-ʿāmm*), and morally and religiously (*akhlāqiyyan wa dīnīyyan*) by the idol of socialism. These are our problems because we proceed not according to righteousness and fear of God (*al-birr wa-l-taqwa*) but according to sin and aggression (*al-ithm wa-l-ʿudwān*).[42]

Kishk did not specify an additional factor that was clear to both the Brotherhood and the Jamʿiyya Sharʿiyya: cooperation with state institutions also exposed them to accusations of co-optation into this system.

The possibilities offered by state educational reform nonetheless motivated Statist and Islamist elites to debate not only the substantive bounds of public religious education but also the religious subjects that it could produce. On the one hand, there was substantial accord among these competitors, who all agreed that the curriculum should include a heavy emphasis on the Quran and Sunna and that it should develop the child's moral faculties and professional abilities.[43] Though the focus on individual morality may have been continuous with the logic of the Quranic recitation school- centered embodied religious education,[44] the concern with professional prospects was decidedly alien to any traditional model of moral cultivation. Most importantly, participation in this conversation suggested an acceptance of the principle that educational institutions could serve as a nationally coordinated network of socioeconomic development.

With this principle clear, the key question on the table was how each faction would spearhead mass subject formation and social reform. For the Muslim Brotherhood, correct Islamic education would produce individuals who embodied their priorities and thus *ipso facto* transformed society in their image. As Muhammad Ismaʿil ʿAbduh

42 ʿAbd al-Hamid Kishk, *Qissat Ayyub ʿAlayhi al-Salam*, rec. 10 June 1977, cassette, n.d.

43 For an example from *al-Daʿwa*, see ʿImara Najib, "Nazra Islamiyya fi Mushkilat al-Taʿlim," *al-Daʿwa*, January 1978/Safar 1397, 26–28. For *al-Iʿtisam*, see Mustafa Kamal Wasfi, "Limadha la Yuthmir al-Taʿlim al-Dini fi Misr?" *al-Iʿtisam*, September 1980/Dhu al-Qaʿda 1400, 30–33. For *Minbar al-Islam*, see Muhammad Fahmi ʿAbd al-Latif, "al-Islam wa-l-Tarbiya wa-l-Taʿlim," *Minbar al-Islam*, April 1977/Jumada al-Ula 1397, 101–02. For *al-Azhar*, see ʿAli ʿAbd al-ʿAzim, "al-Tarbiya al-Diniyya: Tasawurran li-l-Islah," *al-Azhar*, March 1981/Jumada al-Ula 1401, 930–31.

44 For more on this point, see Rudolph T. Ware, *The Walking Quran: Islamic Education, Embodied Knowledge, and History in West Africa* (Chapel Hill: University of North Carolina Press, 2014), 8–9.

explained in October 1976, "Colonialism had sought to separate religion from practical life by . . . [restricting] the application of the Sharia to individual contexts such as ritual practice and personal status laws."[45] This separation, in turn, had produced a generation of secularized Egyptians who did not know to look to Islam (and Islamists) for answers to challenges of morality, economics, and politics.[46] Though ʿAbduh left the exact implications of this call to educational reform ambiguous, ʿAbd al-ʿAzim Fuda took ʿAbduh's claim further. For Fuda, a combination of Quranic education, the Prophetic Sunna, theology (*ʿaqīda*), and the study of contemporary topics would enable Muslim youth to rebuild this connection between "knowledge and action" (*al-ʿilm wa-l-ʿamal*) and, in doing so, face the ideological challenges in their midst.[47]

Cooperation could even extend to other state institutions. In May 1977 Muhammad ʿAbd al-Quddus proposed that education reform (mediated by the Ministry of Education) could play a complementary role in the creation of an "integrated religious environment" (*manākh dīnī mutakāmil*) alongside the Ministry of Information (Wizarat al-Iʿlam).[48] A reconceptualization of the function of religious education could redefine public education and, by extension, society at large.

Writers in *Minbar al-Islam* and *al-Azhar*, by contrast, sought to reorganize society around an amorphous moral order. As Mansur al-Rifaʿi ʿUbayd declared in *Minbar al-Islam*'s March 1976 issue, "morals are religion" (*al-akhlāq hiya al-dīn*),[49] and religious education should reflect this core truth. Similarly, *al-Azhar*'s August 1976 issue featured an article by the Indian scholar Abu-l-Hasan al-Nadwi (d. 1999), in which he described the goal of religious education as the transmission of "the society's traditions and its dominant values" (*taqālīd al-mujtamaʿ wa-l-qiyam al-sāʾida*).[50] Though this appeared

45 Muhammad Ismaʿil ʿAbduh, "Mushkilat al-Taʿlim fi Misr," *al-Daʿwa*, October 1976/Shawwal 1396, 22–23.
46 Ibid.
47 ʿAbd al-ʿAzim Fuda, "al-Tarbiya al-Diniyya Laysat Masʾuliyat al-Madaris Wahdaha," *al-Daʿwa*, October 1976/Shawwal 1396, 46.
48 Muhammad ʿAbd al-Quddus, "al-Masʾulun ʿan Tatwir al-Minahij al-Taʿlimiyya Yatakalamun," *al-Daʿwa*, April 1977/Jumada al-Ula 1397, 40.
49 Mansur al-Rifaʿi ʿUbayd, "Minhaj al-Islam fi Tarbiyat al-Shabab," *Minbar al-Islam*, March 1976/Rabiʿ al-Thani 1396, 131.
50 Abu-l-Hasan al-Nadwi, "Ahamiyat al-Tarbiya wa-l-Taʿlim fi-l-Islam," *al-Azhar*, August 1976/Shaʿban 1396, 752.

to pose a conflict between religion as politics and religion as morality, these religious elites shared the Modernist assumption that their respective priorities, transmitted through mass education, could and should comprehensively structure society.

These debates within Egypt reflected and furthered the guiding assumptions of debates within Saudi Arabia, which had, following the establishment of the IUM and the early 1970s oil boom, become a regional center for Islamic education. In April 1977 a conference on Islamic education in Mecca hosted over three hundred scholars from forty Islamic countries, as it emphasized the threat of Western educational institutions (such as the American Universities in Cairo and Beirut), which had led to the "nullification of Islamic legislation" (*ilghā al-tashrī' al-islāmī*) and the enforcement of "secularism" (*al-'almāniyya*).[51] A few months later a second conference, in Medina, focused on the challenges to spreading the call to Islam (*da'wa*), hosted leading figures within the Egyptian religious hierarchy, including the previous Minister of Endowments, Shaykh Muhammad al-Dhahabi (later murdered by radical Islamists in 1978), then-Minister of Endowments, Muhammad Mutawalli al-Sha'rawi, the former Mufti of Egypt, Muhammad Hasanayn Makhluf (d. 1990), and the president of Ansar al-Sunna, Shaykh Muhammad 'Ali 'Abd al-Rahim (d. 1991).[52]

It was in this context that a prominent Egyptian Islamist–Salafi writing from the IUM sought to articulate a commitment to social transformation with attention to both theology and ritual for an Egyptian audience. For Muhammad Qutb, the younger brother of Sayyid Qutb, correct Islamic education (*tarbiya islāmiyya*) would enable Muslims to live every aspect of their existence – theology (*'aqīda*), Islamic law (*sharī'a*), ritual worship (*'ibāda*), action (*al-'amal*), feeling (*al-shu'ūr*), behavior (*al-sulūk*), politics, economics, and society – according to Islam.[53] Who would transmit these texts remained a secondary question as Qutb focused on practicalities of transmission.

[51] Jabir Rizq, "Mu'tamar Makka Adana Nuzum al-Ta'lim al-Haliya . . . wa Talib bi-Nizam Islami Sahih," *al-Da'wa*, May 1977/Jumada al-Thaniyya 1397, 24–25, at 24.

[52] Muhammad 'Ali 'Abd al-Rahim, "al-Mu'tamar al-'Alami li-Tawjih al-Da'wa wa-l-Du'at," *al-Tawhid*, July 1977/Sha'ban 1397, 35–41, at 39.

[53] "al-Mufakkir al-Islami al-Kabir Muhammad Qutb," *al-I'tisam*, June 1977/ Jumada al-Ukhra 1397, 22–25, at 22.

Efforts to reform the Ministry of Education, though, would soon fall by the wayside in the heat of political conflict between the Islamist opposition and the al-Sadat regime. Egyptian–Israeli peace negotiations, the increased success of the Jamaʿa Islamiyya in university elections, and the assassination of former Minister of Awqaf, Muhammad al-Dhahabi, in July 1977 had strained the President's relationship with the Islamist opposition.[54] In the midst of these tensions, writers in *Minbar al-Islam* and *al-Azhar* sought to gird al-Sadat against these challenges by reappropriating Islamist concerns and language. *Minbar al-Islam*'s Muhammad ʿAshur acknowledged that religious education must "deal with the real problems felt by the masses ... [so as to enable them to become] active workers in resolving issues and solving problems."[55] Six months later *al-Azhar*'s Ahmad Shalabi took a similar line, explaining that Islamic education should include the study of religious models of politics, economics, peace and war, education and society.[56]

The shifts of this period are not necessarily what they appear. On the one hand, this is a story of Islamist success in challenging Statist competitors to adopt their language. Yet, what sense should we make of the decision of Islamists from the Brotherhood and the Jamʿiyya Sharʿiyya to engage with questions of civil education reform? It is unlikely that this was "mere" politics; after all, these Islamists, like their Statist competitors, agreed that state institutions were viable vessels of reform, that employees of the Ministry of Education were qualified teachers of Islam, and that religious education should serve as a transformative public project rather than an individual moral endeavor. Seen through this lens, competition between Statist and Islamist elites over the language of social transformation pales in comparison to the conceptual leap both had taken to accept the Ministry of Education as a premier transmitter of Islam. Yet neither is this the story of the success of the Ministry of Education in co-opting Islamists. Notwithstanding acceptance of the principle of state-sponsored religious education among religious elites,

[54] During the 1976–77 academic year the Jamaʿa Islamiyya was victorious in a series of leadership contests, including those of the Cairo and Minya university student unions. By 1978–79 they had won a majority on the General Union of Egyptian Students' national board. See Wickham, *Mobilizing Islam*, 116.

[55] Muhammad ʿAshur, "Tarbiyat al-Shabab," *Minbar al-Islam*, May 1978/ Jumada al-Ula wa-l-Thaniyya 1398, 135.

[56] Ahmad Shalabi, "Manahij al-Taʿlim al-Islami," *al-Azhar*, October–November 1978/Shawwal–Dhu al-Qaʿda 1398, 1577.

the student constituencies of Islamic magazines struggled to live as pious Muslims, and pushed religious elites to reconsider cooperation.

The Insufficiency of Curricular Change

As Statist and Islamist elites sought to reform the civil educational system, their readers critiqued this system from within, and pushed elites, particularly Islamists, to articulate a programmatic alternative. In doing so, these middle-class Egyptians authoritatively deployed Islamic knowledge acquired through civil education and mass media to question the efficacy of religious subjectivities formed through Egypt's premier site of mass religious transmission. Yet, like religious elites, they accepted the premise that the Ministry of Education was a legitimate arbiter of the religious tradition and a guide to religiously based social change.

Reader letters most commonly sought a greater emphasis on religious knowledge within Egyptian public schools. An August 1976 letter in *al-Daʿwa*, authored by a secondary-school student, raises this issue clearly: "How is it the case that the youth can study Religion (*al-dīn*) without learning anything about Islam? The [core] issue is that study of the Quran and shariʿa are not counted as part of the overall average (*al-majmūʿ al-ʿāmm*)." The *al-Daʿwa* editorial staff concurred, stating: "Quranic material is more important than other subjects such as History, Geography, and the English language [which are counted]."[57] Through modest curricular adjustment, Islam would regain its rightful role not merely within the school system but within Egyptian society at large.

It appears that calls to amend the curricular balance were effective: a May 1977 letter in *al-Iʿtisam* praised al-Sadat for decreeing that religious education must be a "core component" (*mādda asāsiyya*) of primary and secondary education, and thus calculated in a student's overall average.[58] This change was greeted by Statist readers with

[57] "Akhbar al-Shabab wa-l-Jamiʿat," *al-Daʿwa*, August 1976/Shaʿban 1396, 43.

[58] "Barid al-Iʿtisam," *al-Iʿtisam*, May 1977/Jumada al-Ula 1397, 43. This reader's complaint, however, blurs a distinction between the status of religious education as obligatory and its incorporation into the student's overall average. The former was obligatory according to article 19 of the 1971 constitution, while the latter was only implemented near the end of al-Sadat's rule. For external verification of the latter shift, see "al-Tarbiya al-Diniyya Tadkhul Kull Manahij al-Taʿlim," *al-Shabab al-ʿArabi*, 4 April 1977 (issue #532), 1.

excitement: in March 1980 a reader from the Delta governorate of Damietta praised the President's decision to require religious instruction (*tarbiya dīniyya*) at all levels of education in response to "the feelings of the masses" (*aḥāsis al-jamāhīr wa mashā'irihā*).[59] These were readers who saw the Ministry of Education as an authoritative transmitter of Islamic knowledge and sought to work within the system to effect educational reform and, implicitly, social change.

At the same time, other readers within *al-Da'wa* and *al-I'tisam* spearheaded a broader claim to the transformation of education more generally. In doing so, these middle-class Egyptians asserted their capacity not only to guide their own educational choices but to challenge contradictions between knowledge and action within state institutions. This began through a critique of the state's claims to the greatness of science and its relationship to Islam. In February 1977 a secondary-school student, Kamal Fahmi Muhammad Ahmad, noted his dilemma of studying natural history (*al-tārikh al-tabī'ī*): "How can I study disbelief (*kufr*) and then take an exam to answer questions which negate religion (*yatanafī 'an al-dīn*)?" *Al-Da'wa*, unable to effect change directly, responded that the Ministry of Education must face its responsibility to all Muslims for this state of affairs.[60]

The issue, however, was not just scientific development, but also literature and world history. A January 1978 letter in *al-Da'wa* noted that the textbooks in primary and secondary literature courses were not merely of poor quality, but were also morally inappropriate. The story in question, apparently a translated version of British author A. J. Cronin's *The Citadel* (1937), "contained expressions that arouse the youth" (*tuthīr al-shabāb*).[61] History was similarly problematic: a September 1978 letter in *al-I'tisam* complained that a ninth-grade textbook emphasized the European Renaissance, the history of Western revolutions, and the role of Martin Luther, while ignoring Islamic history.[62] Reform required the exclusion of inappropriate non-Islamic material that could corrupt the desired process of moral cultivation.

Other challenges to the public education curriculum, however, also struck at the core of the regime's claims to broader religious legitimacy. A December 1977 letter complained about a tenth-grade textbook,

[59] "Ma'a al-Qurra," *Minbar al-Islam*, March 1980/Rabi' al-Thani 1400, 140.
[60] "Barid al-Da'wa," *al-Da'wa*, February 1977/Rabi' al-Awwal 1397, 71.
[61] "Barid al-Da'wa," *al-Da'wa*, January 1978/Safar 1398, 62.
[62] "Barid al-I'tisam," *al-I'tisam*, September 1978/Shawwal 1398, 43.

The Modern State in Light of the October Paper.[63] This reader asked rhetorically why Egypt, as a state that upheld Islamic law, did not publish a book titled *The Modern State in Light of the Quran* (*al-dawla al-ḥadītha fī ḍaw' al-qur'ān*).[64] The reader rejected the nationalist and religious credentials of the Ministry of Education's curriculum and, by extension, of the al-Sadat government.

Readers were also concerned with the broader moral environment within schools. A December 1977 letter in *al-Da'wa* described the plight of a secondary student who had been beaten by the teacher for quoting from the Quran, Hadith reports, and the sayings of Muslim Brotherhood founder Hasan al-Banna in an exam.[65] Similarly, Anwar 'Abd al-Salam Ghulam, a secondary-school student in the Delta coastal town of Beheira, complained in a March 1977 letter to *al-I'tisam* that the Arabic-language teacher in his school had forbidden students from posting (Islamist-themed) religious wall fliers,[66] while also sanctioning co-ed dances on school grounds.[67] These students feared that the broader school environment obstructed the formation of religious subjects who could carry out the Islamist project.

For some Quietist Salafi readers and writers, however, the focus on state educational reform was misplaced at best and disastrous at worst. Muhammad al-Sharqawi, a Religious Education teacher and the local head of the Ansar al-Sunna branch in the Delta town of Banha (within the Qalyubiyya governorate) wrote in to call on the Ansar al-Sunna to establish an institute to train imams and *khaṭībs* (*ma'had imāma wa khiṭāba*) as well as to provide free lectures and lessons to students from

63 Al-Sadat's October Paper sought to use the legitimacy gained from early military success in the 1973 Arab–Israeli war to argue for a revision of the 1952 revolution, which included the open-door economic policy of the *infitāḥ* and the development of platforms (*manābir*) within the Arab Socialist Union. See Steven Cook, *The Struggle for Egypt: From Nasser to Tahrir Square* (New York: Oxford University Press, 2012), 136–41.

64 "Barid al-Da'wa," *al-Da'wa*, December 1977/Muharram 1397, 60.

65 "Barid al-Da'wa," *al-Da'wa*, December 1977/Muharram 1397, 62.

66 Such wall fliers, literally "wall magazines" (*majallāt al-ḥā'iṭ*), contained articles on key "Islamic" issues of the day, generally from an Islamist perspective. For a depiction in film, see Hasan Imam (dir.), *Khāllī Bālak min Zūzū* (Pay Attention to Zuzu, 1972). For more information on this film and its depiction of Islamists on Egyptian university campuses in the 1970s, see Armbrust, *Mass Culture and Modernism in Egypt*, 117–25.

67 "Barid al-I'tisam," *al-I'tisam*, June 1977/Jumada al-Ukhra 1397, 42.

primary school through university.[68] Indeed, for Ibrahim Ibrahim Hilal, a professor of Islamic Studies at ʿAyn Shams University's Women's College (Kuliyyat al-Banat), these debates over the respective failures of preaching and educational institutions alike missed the point: as long as the state was not defined by Islam in all its manifestation (*ṣibgh al-dawla bi-ṣibghat al-Islām ... fī jāmiʿ maẓāhirihā wa ashkālihā*) then education reform and *daʿwa* alike were futile.[69]

By and large, however, the readers of Islamic magazines sought to reform the current system rather than to craft an alternative. As relations between the al-Sadat regime and the Islamist opposition declined, however, leaders within the Muslim Brotherhood and the Jamʿiyya Sharʿiyya recognized that both political trends and their constituencies' respective needs necessitated a turn to alternative education projects, and their counterparts in the Ministry of Endowments, Education, and the Islamic Research Academy would soon follow suit. Crucially, this shift emerged primarily out of changing political winds and out of student documentation of the existing system's limitations, rather than from intrinsic ideological differences. As Islamist elites turned to the development of new educational institutions, they would reproduce the Ministry of Education's guiding assumption that education could transform society.

A Changing Project of Transmission: From Public Educational Reform to *Daʿwa*, 1979–1981

The emergence of alternative educational projects outside the Ministry of Education was neither sudden nor absolute, yet as al-Sadat's relations with the Islamist opposition deteriorated, the urgency of an independent project of proselytization increased. Indeed, the criticism of al-Sadat's regime within *al-Daʿwa* was so heated that the magazine could not publish its May 1979 issue,[70] which would have come out two months after the signing of the Camp David Accords with Israel, while *al-Iʿtisam* could not publish between March and May of 1979.[71]

68 "Barid al-Majalla," *al-Tawhid*, September 1976/Shawwal 1396, 52–53.
69 Ibrahim Ibrahim Hillal, "Min Tamam al-Tarbiya al-Islamiyya," *al-Tawhid*, August 1978/Ramadan 1398, 20–23, at 20.
70 Kepel, *The Roots of Radical Islam*, 154.
71 A bound volume of issues from this year included a small white note, which stated: "Issues no. 6 and 7 [i.e. those that covered the March–May period] did

These tensions came to the fore in the infamous Isma'iliyya incident of August 1979, in which al-Sadat publicly assailed Brotherhood Supreme Guide and *al-Da'wa* editor-in-chief 'Umar al-Tilmisani for the Brotherhood's alleged role in conspiring to destroy Egypt.[72] Though *al-Da'wa* resumed publishing and al-Tilmisani remained free, the events of 1979 had tilted influence within the Brotherhood toward those who opposed cooperation with the regime, particularly Mustafa Mashhur.[73]

Neither was this conflict limited to the Brotherhood or the Jam'iyya Shar'iyya. The al-Sadat regime also renewed its active repression of the Jama'a Islamiyya (with which both leading figures of the Brotherhood and the Jam'iyya Shar'iyya had collaborated over the preceding three years) through decree 265/1979, which froze the assets of the General Union of Egyptian Students and limited the organizing capabilities of the university-specific student unions.[74] During the same period, confrontations on university campuses grew even more heated as Jama'a Islamiyya cadres sought to assert their control over university campuses.[75] The regime appeared increasingly intransigent, and 'Abd al-Hamid Kishk gave voice to feelings of alienation in a sermon on 28 September 1979: "[We don't want] a socialist state (*ishtirākiyya*), nor a democratic state (*dimūkratiyya*), nor a populist state (*sha'biyya*) nor a republican state (*jamāhīriyya*). Rather [we demand], a Quranic Islamic state (*dawla qur'āniyya islāmiyya*) . . . deriving its light from the One (*al-wāḥid*)."[76] This divide paved the way for alternative proposals.

not reach the market." The most likely explanation for production without publication is state censorship. Also see "Sharit al-Akhbar," *al-Mujtama'*, 8 May 1979/11 Jumada al-Ukhra 1399, 6–7, at 6.

72 al-Arian, *Answering the Call*, 148.

73 See al-Arian, *Answering the Call*, 96–102. This is not to suggest, however, that no voices of cooperation remained. For example, in the July 1979 issue *al-Da'wa*'s Mufti Shaykh 'Abd Allah al-Khatib still spoke of working with the Ministry of Education: in response to a question from a student who wished to explore "Islamic culture" (*al-thaqāfa al-Islāmiyya*) yet was met by bewildered expressions from his teachers, he called both for the reform of curriculum and teaching styles and for the media to promote the spread of correct Islamic culture. See "al-Ifta," *al-Da'wa*, July 1979/Sha'ban 1399, 16.

74 "al-Ifta," *al-Da'wa*, July 1979/Sha'ban 1399, 16.

75 Kepel, *The Roots of Radical Islam*, 155.

76 'Abd al-Hamid Kishk, *al-Shart al-Khamis min Shurut Qubul al-Salat*, rec. 28 September 1979, cassette, n.d.

Most notably, in 1978 leading Brotherhood thinker Yusuf al-Qaradawi (b. 1926) published *al-Tarbiya al-Islamiyya*, in which he declared that he had little hope of cooperation with the Ministry of Education due to the "ignorance" (*jahl*) of political elites who "lived estranged in their own countries."[77] Such ignorance had produced an educational system that unduly restricted the meaning of worship (*al-ʿibāda*) to mere ritual, instead of utilizing it to reform society, whether through group prayer or voluntary work.[78] Indeed, al-Qaradawi continued, state institutions not only failed to protect Muslims from the "remnants of intellectual invasion and cultural imperialism" (*athār al-ghazw al-fikrī wa-l-istiʿmār al-thaqāfī*), but also actively propagated these faulty understandings.[79] In the face of these challenges, al-Qaradawi sought "to make prominent the landmarks" (*ibrāz al-maʿālīm*) of a *tarbiya* project.[80]

The concluding year of the decade increasingly frustrated Statist scholars too, as they were co-opted by al-Sadat in the service of blatantly political ends. During the summer of 1979 State Mufti (and Mufti within *Minbar al-Islam*) ʿAli Jadd al-Haqq was required to defend Law 44, also called "Jihan's law," which gave a woman the right to divorce her husband if he married a second wife. The law was widely criticized by Islamists as un-Islamic.[81] In a similar move, which produced even harsher opposition, al-Haqq issued a fatwa providing religious sanction for the Camp David Accords with Israel.[82] In both cases Islamists saw al-Sadat as distorting the "correct" Islamic position on these ostensibly disparate questions to fit his political needs. These conflicts, in turn, encouraged a greater focus on initiatives independent of the Ministry of Education.

Just as importantly, technological and economic change coincided with shifting political winds. Though empirical data on the Islamic publishing industry is difficult to obtain, perusal of the advertisements within Islamic magazines during this period suggests an increasingly crowded religious publishing world. This included a variety of Islamic

77 Yusuf al-Qaradawi, al-Tarbiya al-Islamiyya *wa Madrassat Hasan al-Banna* (Cairo: Maktabat Wahba 1979), 28.
78 al-Qaradawi, *al-Tarbiya al-Islamiyya*, 15–26.
79 al-Qaradawi, *al-Tarbiya al-Islamiyya*, 26.
80 al-Qaradawi, *al-Tarbiya al-Islamiyya*, 4.
81 Skovgaard-Petersen, *Defining Islam for the Egyptian State*, 232.
82 Skovgaard-Petersen, *Defining Islam for the Egyptian State*, 233.

publishing houses – most notably Maktabat al-Wahba, Dar al-I'tisam, Dar al-Da'wa, Dar al-Tawzi' wa-l-Nashr al-Islamiyya, and Dar al-Ansar – as well as an increasingly diverse offering of texts, which ranged from Quranic commentaries and Hadith collections to ritual primers to tracts of religious–political mobilization. Just as importantly, state religious institutions, most prominently the Supreme Council for Islamic Affairs, continued to publish pamphlets. Though impressionistic, this evidence suggests that when Egyptian Muslims who aspired to piety sought additional religious knowledge, they had multiple options, both Statist and Islamist.

Finally, the move beyond state institutions was shaped by the decline of universities as a central site for Islamist activism. Though the Brotherhood had successfully incorporated leading student activists by 1979, the latter's access to free space had been curtailed both by graduation and by increased repression on university campuses.[83] The loss of this key site, however, did not drive the Muslim Brotherhood into the arms of the Ministry of Education. In January 1980 Muslim Brother Muhammad 'Abd al-Rahman 'Awad dismissed public education as mere "test material" (*māddat imtiḥān*) rather than a practical plan for behavior (*sulūk*). Instead of serving as a model of virtue, religious education had now become a source of "corrupted morals" (*al-akhlāq al-fāsida*).[84] This critique that morality stood at the center of social transformation mirrored that of Statist scholars, again underscoring the ideological convergence between Statist institutions and Islamist organizations. Yet, despite these similarities, the Brotherhood had internalized both its own experiences and reader critiques that public education was incapable of producing sound religious subjects. Faced with new material circumstances and changing political opportunities, the Brotherhood turned away from the al-Sadat regime.

The frustrated Brotherhood leadership gambled that print media (whether magazines or a broad array of pamphlets[85]) and the deployment of its recent graduates to working-class neighborhoods to develop

[83] Dasuqi and al-'Abbadi, *Tarikh al-Haraka al-Tullabiyya bi-Jama'at al-Ikhwan al-Muslimin 1933–2011*, 254–55.

[84] 'Abd al-Rahman 'Awad, "Jawla fi Maydan al-Ta'lim," *al-Da'wa*, January 1980/Safar 1400, 26.

[85] For example, the *Nahwa Jil Muslim* series includes pocketsize pamphlets on how to act piously as a "Muslim sister" (*ukht muslima*), orthodox and deviant Sufi practices, correct child-raising methods, and Islamic unity. Other pamphlets reproduce selections from Hasan al-Banna's writings, particularly his "twenty

"parallel Islamic institutions"could better produce piety. This included the transmission of key Brotherhood works: as Brotherhood activist Sayyid al-Nuzayli notes, Muslim Brothers would gather locally to discuss books as part of their local family (*usra*).[86] These neighborhoods provided a new setting for the development of practices of transmission which paralleled student practices on university campuses, whether delivering the Friday sermon (*khuṭba*), providing religious lessons (*durūs*), or organizing collective activities on religious holy days.[87] These institutions, alongside a broad array of media products, would undergird a broad expansion of the organization's preaching activities that continued throughout the Mubarak period (1981–2011).

If the Brotherhood sought to rebuild a network of grassroots educational institutions alongside mass media efforts, the Jamʿiyya Sharʿiyya focused on retooling its existing infrastructure. Like their peers in *al-Daʿwa, al-Iʿtisam*'s writers had absorbed both the lessons of previous clashes with the al-Sadat regime and their readers' reports as they lost faith in public educational reform. A September 1980 article by Mustafa Kamal Wasfi sought to move beyond the Jamʿiyya Sharʿiyya's previous cooperation: "Even if the class [Religious Education] is required, and even if there are many class periods, and even if the teacher is sincere ... [such education] still has no value (*lā qīma lahā*) because the broader religious environment corrupts faith (*al-biʾa al-ʿāmma mufsida li-l-imān*)."[88] Echoing reader complaints, Wasfi concluded that the existing system was incapable of producing pious Muslims.

The question was how best to use the Jamʿiyya Sharʿiyya's network of mosques to shape the broader environment, thus enabling education to serve its socially transformative purpose. The answer to this question, in turn, appeared in the April–May 1981 issue of *al-Iʿtisam*. Beginning immediately, the organization would develop a parallel national school system with a revamped and standardized curriculum based on the Quran and Sunna. These discrete schools, however, were not sufficient; the Jamʿiyya Sharʿiyya also promised to increase its preaching (*daʿwa*) activities and to offer Islamic books to the general

principles" (*al-uṣūl al-ʿishrīn*). For more on Brotherhood pamphlets from the 1990s, see Wickham, *Mobilizing Islam*, 137–43.

86 *Sayyid al-Nuzayli wa Hadith ʿan Dhikrayathu maʿ Jamaʿat al-Ikhwan al-Juzʾa al-Thalith*, perf. Sayyid al-Nuzayli, 2009.

87 Wickham, *Mobilizing Islam*, 124. 88 Wickham, *Mobilizing Islam*, 124.

public through both libraries and bookstores.[89] Though the Jam'iyya Shar'iyya had accepted the reality of disembodied religious transmission (and thus the necessity of composing or editing pamphlets supporting its views), its focus remained on developing its own educational institutions. Along similar lines, Ansar al-Sunna would further expand its preacher-training program while establishing new institutions to host Muslims from sub-Saharan Africa and to train Egyptian Muslims to engage in *da'wa* with English, French, German, and Spanish speakers.[90]

Egypt's Islamist opposition was not alone in its frustration with the Ministry of Education. Even the Supreme Council for Islamic Affairs, the most sympathetic of the four organizations to the al-Sadat regime, had lost patience. In March 1980 'Abd al-Fattah Ghawi authored an article in *Minbar al-Islam* entitled "Toward a Better Approach to Teaching Religion," in which he argued for a three-pronged emphasis on Quranic memorization, "the behavioral aspect" (*al-jānib al-sulūkī*) of Islam, and cooperation with the Egyptian media in the dissemination of "virtue" (*al-faḍīla*). Ghawi, though he shared his Islamist competitors' concern with the incomplete formation of religious subjects and the deleterious effect of broader immorality to this effort, was not calling for a new system of religious education parallel to that of the Ministry of Education. Nonetheless, he urged both the government and the Ministry of Education to act because "writing solutions alone achieves nothing."[91] In tandem, the Supreme Council for Islamic Affairs sought to expand its meetings (*nadawāt*), which had been previously held at the Council's headquarters in Garden City, to "Islamic centers" (*al-marākiz al-islāmiyya*) that could attract the youth (*al-shabāb*).[92]

In the face of this frustration of Statist and Islamist elites alike, the Ministry of Education reasserted its educational leadership. In October 1980 it hosted a conference which included scholars from al-Azhar University, the Minister of Endowments, the Deputy Minister

89 "Hawl al-Jama'at al-Islamiyya," *al-I'tisam*, April–May 1981/Jumadan 1401, 32–34. This statement also appears in Dawud, *al-Jam'iyyat al-Islamiyya fi Misr*, 154.

90 The precise periodization of this shift is unclear, occurring under the rule of Hosni Mubarak (1981–2011). See Ahmad Zaghlul Shalata, *al-Hala al-Salafiyya al-Mu'asira fi Misr* (Cairo: Maktabat Madbuli, 2011), 217.

91 'Abd al-Fatah al-Ghawi, "Nahwa Minhaj Afdal li-Tadris al-Tarbiya al-Diniyya," *Minbar al-Islam*, March 1980/Rabi' al-Thani 1400, 125.

92 al-Zanira, *al-Majlis al-A'la li-l-Shu'un al-Islamiyya*, 130.

of Education, and an array of university professors, Islamic thinkers, and al-Azhar graduates. Curricular reforms and new criteria for selecting and developing teachers would better shape students.

The Ministry of Education also recognized that its Islamist competitors had moved beyond the civil educational system. Accordingly, it embarked on a broader project that included the expansion of the publishing activities of the Islamic Research Academy at al-Azhar under the Ministry's guidance, the foundation of an office to issue fatwas within the Ministry, the mobilization of the media to spread Islam, the "palpable implementation of the Islamic shari'a" (*al-taṭbīq al-malmūs li-l-sharīʿa al-islāmiyya*), and cooperation between the Ministry of Education and the Ministry of Endowments to spread religious awareness (*al-waʿī al-dīnī*) through the official mosque system.[93] The Ministry of Education had doubled down on its ambitious effort to shape the Egyptian population while mounting a power play for primacy among state institutions.

Though leading members of the Islamic Research Academy shared the anxiety of disembodied transmission with their fellow scholars in *al-Iʿtisam*, they eventually joined the fray. As Academy member and former Minister of Endowments Muhammad Mutawalli al-Shaʿrawi explained in the Fall of 1980: "If people don't have an approach (*manhāj*) [to life] then the story [of Egyptian society] will remain corrupt (*al-ḥikāya tabʿa fāsida*)."[94] In turn, *al-Azhar*'s ʿAli ʿAbd al-ʿAzim detailed an expansive vision of religious education that included cooperation among al-Azhar's primary and secondary institutes, the Ministry of Education, Ministry of Endowments- affiliated mosques and preachers, religious societies (*al-jamʿiyyāt al-dīniyya*), and Sufi orders. In this vision, al-Azhar's institutions were the clear first among ostensible equals.[95]

These proposals were all aimed at broadcasting the educational priorities of their own originators outside state institutions. Though they had moved away from a focus on state-centered educational reform, they neither questioned the legitimacy of state education in theory nor abandoned the Ministry of Education's *raison d'être*: the

[93] Muhsin Radi, "Tawsiyat Muʾtamar al-Tarbiya al-Diniyya," *al-Daʿwa*, October 1980/Dhu al-Hijja 1400, 32.

[94] Muhammad Mutawalli al-Shaʿrawi, "al-Halqa al-Thaniyya min Tafsir Surat al-Fatiha," *Tafsir al-Shaʿrawi*, September 1980.

[95] ʿAli ʿAbd al-ʿAzim, "al-Tarbiya al-Islamiyya: Tasawwuran li-l-Islah," *al-Azhar*, March 1981/Jumada al-Ula 1401, 930–31.

premise that education could act as a motor of social change. The problem was not, as it would have been for early twentieth-century scholars, that mass education, mediated by laymen, was incapable of producing pious subjects; rather, current political circumstances rendered this difficult. With increased sources of funding, new media opportunities, and a growing grassroots infrastructure, Islamist elites turned to an alternative project of education. Readers, however, did not wait for the new system to emerge, and sought to form themselves as pious Muslims at new sites.

Beyond the Blueprint

As elites drew up plans to implement differing visions of religious education, readers sought to create informal structures of subject formation. This was partially a function of timing as the development of a parallel Islamic educational infrastructure was still in an inchoate phase across the religious spectrum. Just as the proliferation of cheap scholarly classics, pamphlets, and periodicals facilitated alternative Islamist projects, so too did they create new opportunities for local educational institutions and self-taught laymen.

Many readers sought to set up new institutions independent of magazine elites. A representative June 1980 letter from a student at Cairo University's teacher-training college, Dar al-ʿUlum, sought to craft an educational program which would transform doctors, engineers, teachers, and both white- and blue-collar employees into devout Muslims who could carry out the call to Islam. Accordingly, the reader called for the construction of a curriculum for graduates of secular faculties of Medicine, Engineering, and Education. Yet, unlike the public educational system, this program would be headed by ʿulama "who are on board with modern civilization" (*yarkabūn ʿalā matn al-ḥaḍāra al-ʿaṣriyya*) and were capable of motivating their students to Islamic activism (*al-ʿamal al-islāmī*). Such ʿulama would do so by teaching a curriculum that included figures as diverse as Ibn Taymiyya (d. 1328), Ibn Sina (d. 1037), al-Khwarizmi (d. 850), Ibn Hazm (d. 1064), and, of course, Hasan al-Banna (d. 1949).[96] What are we to make of this multifaceted curriculum?

The call to combine the writings of polymath scholars (Ibn Sina, al-Khwarizmi), Ibn Taymiyya and Ibn Hazm (both cited by Islamist and

[96] "Akhbar al-Shabab wa-l-Jamiʿat," *al-Daʿwa*, June 1980/Rajab 1400, 62.

Quietist Salafis alike), and the founder of the Muslim Brotherhood reflects the unclear lines of textual authority that underlay this endeavor of Islamic education. Just as importantly, it underscores the opportunity available to this Cairo University reader as he deployed the religious knowledge he had acquired in public education and, presumably, mass media, to build a new model of knowledge and action in which religiously dictated "action" (*al-ʿamal*) became "Islamic activism" (*al-ʿamal al-islāmī*). The novelty of this effort is further underscored by the blurring of historical divisions, as this proposed curriculum stretched across centuries of Islamic thought and across legal schools (*madhāhib*), while ignoring fierce intellectual conflicts between Ibn Sina and Ibn Taymiyya over Speculative Theology (*kalām*) and placing Brotherhood founder Hasan al-Banna within these scholarly ranks. That said, this was not a free-for-all: despite al-Banna's inclusion in the curriculum, the reader insisted that scholars lead this effort, echoing prior proposals within the Brotherhood.[97] This proposal thus attempted to tame the potential interpretative instabilities of this polyvocal disembodied curriculum by enlisting scholarly supervision.

The question for other readers, though, was not only how to develop a new curriculum, but also how to establish new educational sites. A fatwa request that appeared in the May–June 1980 issue of *al-Iʿtisam* inquired as to whether it was appropriate to set up institutions such as hospitals, offices, scientific laboratories, or religious institutes either above or below a mosque in order to attract Muslims to study the "rulings of Islam" (*aḥkām al-islām*) inside the mosque. In response, the president of al-Azhar's Fatwa Council explained that this question had two components. First, if it was intended to serve the interests of the mosque (*marāfiq al-masjid*)[98] or the general interests of Muslims (*manāfiʿ ʿāmmat al-muslimīn*), then it was permitted. The Fatwa Council's decision then added an additional stipulation that gave greater leniency in further building if the premises had originally been a mosque and residential housing (*masjid wa masākin*); if not, the individual was forbidden from expanding the mosque.[99] This fatwa request

[97] For example, see Yusuf al-Qaradawi, *Thaqafat al-Daʿiya* (Cairo: Maktabat Wahba, 1978).

[98] This term is ambiguous and could conceivably be translated as "to be a wing of the mosque" or "for the use of the mosque."

[99] "Ifta," *al-Iʿtisam*, May–June 1980/Jumada al-Ukhra-Rajab 1400, 37.

underscores not merely the practical exigencies of expanding the educational role of the mosque, but also the role of readers in mediating between knowledge and religiously motivated socioeconomic action.[100]

These grassroots efforts to support the transmission of religious knowledge in local institutions emerge among readers in *Minbar al-Islam* as well. In May 1979 a resident of the Delta city of Beheira asked for the help of the Shaykh of al-Azhar in funding a Quranic recitation program at the local charitable association (*jam'iyya khayriyya*), while another reader in the same issue asked the Ministry of Endowments to supply Qurans for study in his local mosque.[101] As they sought knowledge and ethical cultivation, middle-class Egyptians attempted to buttress existing religious organizations and institutions through their own informal efforts.

In other instances, the question was one of the economics of book ownership and the role of the mosque as a center of text distribution. For example, a September 1980 letter from Tariq Yahya Qabil, a native of the Mediterranean city of Port Said, noted a problem with access to books:

> At a time when the price of religious books (*al-kutub al-dīniyya*), particularly Quranic commentaries, is rising, we find libraries of mosques which hold many books in glass cases . . . [yet] one cannot borrow them because they are under the care [of the administrator of the mosque] and must be preserved . . . we direct our call to the Minister of Endowments to put a stop to what is occurring here.[102]

Editor Fu'ad Hayba responded that "the goal of founding libraries for mosques is to give all who seek to do so the opportunity to explore its books . . . as long as the readers return the books after reading."[103]

100 This combination was increasingly popular in Egypt during this period as state retrenchment in the provision of social services created an opportunity for Islamic educational institutions to step in by providing both religious education and medical services. For example, lay religious intellectual Mustafa Mahmud (d. 2009) founded an "Islamic center" which included both a mosque and a medical clinic. See Armando Salvatore, "Mustafa Mahmud: A Paradigm of Public Islamic Entrepreneurship?" in Armando Salvatore (ed.), *Muslim Traditions and Modern Techniques of Power* (Münster: Lit Verlag, 2001), 220.

101 "Ma'a al-Qurra," *Minbar al-Islam*, May 1979/Jumada al-Thaniyya 1399, 123.

102 "Ma'a al-Qurra," *Minbar al-Islam*, September 1980/Shawwal 1400, 124.

103 Ibid.

Literacy and libraries could play their part in the religious transformation of Egyptian society.

Though mosques included libraries well before the second half of al-Sadat's rule, these letters underscore not merely a desire for religious knowledge but also a commitment to pursuing this transmission outside the bounds of the mosque. Crucially, the local practices of knowledge exhibited by these middle-class Egyptians did not represent a rupture of kind, but rather one of degree. While the ʿAbd al-Nasir period had imposed costs on public religious activity (rather than merely on political activism), al-Sadat's rule enabled pious Egyptians of varying political allegiances to pursue projects of piety by seeking to acquire and promoting the transmission of Islamic knowledge.

Conclusion

As Statist and Islamist elites alike surveyed their opportunities during the second half of the al-Sadat period, civil education appeared to be a promising site of reform. At a time when neither had access to a grassroots educational infrastructure, such reform could provide a new opportunity both to realize their own educational projects and to preempt rival efforts. As they turned to the Ministry of Education, however, these diverse religious elites adopted the underlying assumption of the institution that they sought to reform: public education, staffed by laymen, could produce social change. The curricular reform presumed necessary to affect social change, however, was uneven, and readers in Statist and Islamist periodicals drew attention to the recurrent conflict between impious pockets of the Egyptian state and their own devout aspirations. With frustrations mounting and political winds shifting in 1979, elites and readers alike turned away from the Ministry of Education and toward the development of independent projects of religious education. As they pursued these projects, though, Modernist assumptions of social transformation, rather than individual moral formation, would guide both the creation of competing religious institutions and the efforts of middle-class Egyptians to form themselves and others as pious subjects.

While these programs and the related shift in the public debate over Islam and public policy were only in their infancy in 1981, the Mubarak period (1981–2011) saw the realization of this shift and its expansion to include new media forms and an enlarged grassroots infrastructure. During the 1976–81 period, however, religious elites, in conversation with their respective constituencies, made key decisions that would shape the religious networks of the following decades. The emergence of alternative educational projects was neither the necessary result of a longer Islamic scholarly tradition nor a direct response to new conditions produced by state institutions. Instead, the adoption of religious education as a motor of comprehensive social transformation reflected intellectual ties that bound Statist and Islamist elites, and a grassroots push from their ideologically diverse constituencies. At issue was not Islam's capacity to transform society, but who was best qualified to transmit it.

Piety, for those who subscribed to either Statist or Islamist visions, was a distinctly literate affair. It empowered those educated within the civil educational system, both male and female, to question key premises of the Ministry of Education's vision of the relationship between Islam and social transformation, while shifting political and technological winds facilitated both the emergence of a decentralized network of educational institutions and auto-didactic Islamic education. Just as important, however, was that this project excluded the approximately 60 percent of the Egyptian population who could not read for leisure or intellectual edification. While institutions and practices of religious education privileged literate Egyptians, practices of prompt prayer and gender relations would stratify this segment internally along lines of both class and gender.

4 Prayer and the Islamic Revival

A Timely Challenge

On 2 August 1981 a reported 250,000 Egyptians flocked to ʿAbdin Square in the center of Cairo to perform the Eid al-Fitr prayers, celebrating the end of Ramadan. This square was a central site of political authority: it stood in front of a palace of the same name, built by the Khedive Ismail between 1863 and 1874 as a replacement for Cairo's Citadel, to serve as an official home and workplace for Egypt's ruler. These prayers, by contrast, were organized by groups that sought to challenge the existing political order: In an event convened by the Jamaʿa Islamiyya, and aided by the Muslim Brotherhood, Brotherhood theorist Shaykh Yusuf al-Qaradawi (b. 1926) gave an hour-long holiday sermon (*khuṭba*) analyzing the landmark events of the previous century of the Islamic calendar. Following Qaradawi, the commander (*amīr*) of the Jamaʿa Islamiyya, Muhammad al-Rawi, questioned the recent crackdowns on the Brotherhood mouthpiece, *al-Daʿwa* magazine, and mocked calls for "national unity" (*al-waḥda al-waṭaniyya*).[1]

The gathering in ʿAbdin Square was the latest in a series of holiday-prayers-turned-political-rallies. The Jamaʿa Islamiyya had organized mass prayers for both Eid al-Fitr and Eid al-Adha[2] in this square and at an athletics stadium in Alexandria since 1976 and, in the absence of access to the ballot box, used the growing attendance to index their support within Egyptian society. The pious masses of ʿAbdin Square on Eid al-Fitr served as a visual reminder to both ruler and ruled of the contrast between the state-sponsored political order and the Islamist opposition.

Yet the central site of ritual competition in al-Sadat's Egypt was neither the annual Eid prayers, nor even the weekly Friday

[1] "Akhbar al-Shabab wa-l-Jamiʿat," *al-Daʿwa*, September 1981/Dhu al-Qaʿda 1401, 50–51.

[2] Eid al-Fitr marks the end of Ramadan while Eid al-Adha falls on the tenth day of Dhu al-Hijja and honors the Prophet Ibrahim's willingness to sacrifice Ismaʿil to God.

prayer.[3] Instead, as Egyptian men and women participated in rival projects of religious change, competition revolved around the daily early-afternoon *ẓuhr* prayer. Though ostensibly "merely" one of five daily prayers – which could be performed between roughly noon and three in the afternoon[4] – the *ẓuhr* was the only prayer to fall directly in the middle of both the official work and school days, thus offering Islamists a novel means by which to insert their vision of religious piety into the clocks and corridors of Egyptian state institutions. In parallel, readers in both Islamist periodicals took advantage of the letters to the editor and fatwa sections to assert their right to pray at certain times together with their pious peers, and to challenge the claim of bureaucratic and educational institutions to temporal and spatial primacy over religious ritual. Leading Islamists, student activists, and sympathizers within state institutions thus spearheaded a project whose legacy has endured even as the Brotherhood has been driven underground.

This chapter begins by contextualizing the Islamist transformation of the *ẓuhr* prayer within a longer history of state efforts to form industrious and loyal citizens through governmental institutions and mass media alike. In doing so, it highlights the models of spatial and temporal order by which these elites sought to organize Egyptians, and demonstrates both how state planners framed religious practice within

[3] For example, see Patrick Gaffney, *The Prophet's Pulpit: Islamic Preaching in Contemporary Egypt* (Berkeley: University of California Press, 1994), esp. 194–207, and Patrick Gaffney, "The Changing Voices of Islam: The Emergence of Professional Preachers in Contemporary Egypt," *Muslim World*, 81:1 (1991), 27–47. While Friday mosque attendance is important for its inclusion of both communal prayer and a sermon which, implicitly or explicitly, affirms or denies the ruler's political authority, it is also the most obvious example of prayer, and thus has received a disproportionate share of academic attention. This attention is not confined to studies of specific mosques but also to mosque sermons. For example, see Hirschkind, *The Ethical Soundscape*. In the work of both Gaffney and Hirschkind the "battle" over mosques is a contest to define the Friday sermon and is measured by the balance between "official" and "popular" (i.e. Islamist) mosques.

[4] Notwithstanding this range, there is also a strain within the Sunni legal tradition that emphasizes the performance of prayers at the earliest possible time. See al-Tirmidhi, *Ṣalāt* 13, in A. J. Wensinck, "Mīḳāt," *Encyclopedia of Islam*, 1st edition (1913–36), ed. M. T. Houtsma, T. W. Arnold, R. Basset, and R. Hartmann, Brill Online, 2015, reference: Princeton University, 16 July 2015, available at http://referenceworks.brillonline.com/entries/encyclopaedia-of-islam-1/mikat-SIM_4667.

nationalist political objectives and how theory and practice frequently diverged. It then turns to previous conceptions of prayer as a temporally defined act, examining the history of "religious" time in Egypt and previous twentieth-century interpretations of Surat al-Nisa 4:103, the key Quranic verse which commands prayer at defined times.[5] The second half of the chapter, in turn, shows how Egyptian Islamists reconstructed the *ẓuhr* prayer as a means of political challenge that, far from simply asserting the centrality of a longstanding Islamic temporality, melded it with a state-sponsored concept of order. On this basis, leading figures within the Muslim Brotherhood, Jamʿiyya Sharʿiyya, and Jamaʿa Islamiyya, alongside the middle-class readers of Islamic magazines, established prayer within bureaucratic schedules and claimed ritual space within state institutions to facilitate its collective performance.

The negotiation of the *ẓuhr* prayer within state offices and schools casts light on the cultivation of pious subjectivities in Egypt's Islamic Revival. While Hirschkind and Mahmood emphasize the existence of distinct Islamist and secular projects of subject building,[6] I argue that the popularization of this daily prayer represents a hybrid of bureaucratic logic and Islamist piety. Specifically, although this endeavor challenged the primacy of work over prayer time and the state's vision of the correct relationship between national and religious identity, it shared the state's basic assumptions of order, discipline, and temporal

5 Surat al-Nisa 4:103 reads: "And when you have completed the prayer, remember Allah standing, sitting, or [lying] on your sides. But when you become secure, re-establish [regular] prayer. *Indeed, prayer has been decreed upon the believers a decree of specified times*" (emphasis added). It was revealed during the Medinan period when the nascent Muslim community was first able to practice and preach Islam publicly.

6 The "secular" project of subject building, as Asad notes, seeks to lay claim to broad swaths of society, including those historically claimed as "religious." See Asad, *Formations of the Secular*, 199. For Hirschkind and Mahmood's views of the bounds of the Islamist project of subject formation, see Hirschkind, *The Ethical Soundscape*, esp. 117–18 and 137–88, and Mahmood, *The Politics of Piety*, esp. 113–17. Also see Gauvain, *Salafi Ritual Purity*. Hirschkind in particular notes that "we might say that Egypt's Islamic counterpublic is inscribed within the government rationalities and institutions of national public life but also oblique to them incorporating orientations and modes of practical reason that exceed or cut across modern normatively" (*The Ethical Soundscape*, 138–39). By contrast, this chapter situates the production of pious subjectivities within state institutions, and suggests that "government rationalities" are central, rather than peripheral, to them.

precision. Far from being the tardy cousin of the "rationalized" state schedule, this project transformed the previous rhythm of prayer into a model of prompt practice that would make state planners proud.

Prayer, Religious Subjectivities, and National Identity prior to 1976

Although the Brotherhood's move to politicize the *ẓuhr* prayer was new, the battle to define ritual practice and space in order to produce particular religious subjects was not. Most notably, the Ministry of Endowments had worked since the 1920s to regulate prayer times and since the 1940s to extend physical control over Egyptian mosques.[7] In the face of this challenge, Islamists and Salafis sought to retain their own sites of ritual practice through which they could produce alternative religious subjects.[8]

Prayer – and the ritual space in which it was performed – had also become a key symbol of religious revival across the Middle East. Campus activism by Turkish Islamist Necmettin Erbakan pivoted on the mobilization facilitated by regular campus prayer,[9] while Tunisian Islamists had built a mass movement through mosques across the country.[10] Yet what occupied Egyptian Islamists to an even greater degree was a perception of threats, physical and ideological, to mosques throughout the Muslim world: whether al-Aqsa on the Temple Mount in Jerusalem and the Ibrahimi mosque in Hebron,[11] or Ba'thist

7 Daniel A. Stolz, *The Lighthouse and the Observatory: Islam, Science and Empire in Late Ottoman Egypt* (Cambridge: Cambridge University Press, 2018), 207–42, esp. 219–21.

8 Law 157 of 1960 granted the Ministry of Endowments the authority – and responsibility – to supervise and financially support all Egyptian mosques within the following decade. These attempts, however all-encompassing, were defined by practical limitations that confronted the Ministry of Endowments: in 1961 only 17.5 percent of the 17,224 mosques in Egypt were staffed and funded by the Ministry of Endowments. In 1975 the number of mosques had increased to 28,738 but the proportion of government mosques was 17.9 percent. To put it differently, the number of mosques administered by the government had increased by 71 percent (from 3,006 to 5,163), but the government's share of mosques had hardly budged. See Gaffney, "The Changing Voices of Islam," 30–40.

9 Jabir Rizq, "Hizb al-Salama," *al-Da'wa*, August 1977/Ramadan 1397, 12–14.

10 "Sakratirak al-Sihafi," *al-Da'wa*, October 1979/Dhu al-Qa'da 1399, 14–15, at 15.

11 For al-Aqsa, see "Watanuna al-Islami," *al-Da'wa*, April 1977/Jumada al-Ula 1397, 46–47, at 46. For Hebron, see Salah 'Abd al-Rahim Muhammad,

attacks on mosques in Syria,[12] Egyptian Islamists saw a transnational Islamic community's freedom to worship under siege. Whatever the particulars of specific cases, these contestations were part and parcel of a broader competition across the Middle East and South Asia to control mosques and the activities within them during the second half of the twentieth century.[13]

The significance of battles to control ritual practice in Egypt and beyond extends to broader negotiations over national and communal identity. In his study of American nationalism, Michael Billig coins the term "banal nationalism" to describe "the ideological habits which enable the established nations of the West to be reproduced ... these habits are not removed from everyday life ... [rather, they are an] endemic condition."[14] In contrast to Billig's study, however, such practices encompass not only ideological habits (such as flying a national flag) but also the embodied practice performed on a daily basis that facilitates group solidarity.[15] Praying together on a daily basis offered an alternative site for the formation of a communal identity that subordinated national to religious allegiances.

Daily ritual practice in al-Sadat's Egypt also served as an example of and for particular models of gender within a group. In her study of time and gender in Rabbinic literature, Sarit Kattan Gribetz argues that "attention must be paid to the fact that rituals are gendered, and without taking seriously the *ways* that rituals are gendered, a full account of their societal function cannot compellingly be given."[16] As Egyptian Islamists sought to mobilize men and women alike to daily prayer, they

"Madha Fa'la al-Yahud bi-l-Harram al-Ibrahimi," *al-Da'wa*, October 1980/Dhu al-Hijja 1400, 28–29.

12 "Sakratirak al-Sihafi," *al-Da'wa*, August 1979/Ramadan 1399, 62–63, at 62.

13 For Indonesia, see Florian Pohl, *Islamic Education and the Public Sphere: Today's Pesantren in Indonesia* (Münster: Waxmann Verlag GmbH, 2009), 64. For Pakistan and Malaysia, see Nasr, *Islamic Leviathan*, 123–38.

14 Michael Billig, *Banal Nationalism* (London: Sage Publications, 1995), 8.

15 As Eviatar Zerubavel notes, observance of the Sabbath facilitates group solidarity, "highlight[s] and accentuat[es] the similitude among group members vis-a-vis others ... [helping] to solidify in-group sentiments and, thus, constitutes a most powerful basis for 'mechanical' solidarity within the group" (Eviatar Zerubavel, *Hidden Rhythms: Schedules and Calendars in Social Life* [Berkeley: University of California Press, 1985], 70).

16 Sarit Kattan Gribetz, "Conceptions of Time and Rhythms of Daily Life in Rabbinic Literature, 200–600 CE" (unpublished dissertation, Princeton University, 2013), 130.

not only echoed the Modernist vision of the mosque as a site of male and female education alike,[17] but also offered women a ritual role that stood in contrast to both women's marginal position within communal prayer[18] and to previous Muslim Brotherhood and Salafi positions regarding female public activism.[19]

How can we explain the timing of this particular effort that would recruit both men and women into a project of ritually based challenge to state order? This was certainly not the first time that the contradiction between the *ẓuhr* prayer and state timetables had arisen; the expansion of both bureaucratic employment and education in Egypt over the twentieth century suggests that this was a longstanding tension.[20] Yet the initial tension was not about the ability to pray,

17 As Marion Katz notes regarding early twentieth-century Egypt, mosques were "one of the sites for the formation of a new woman who combined knowledge of a newly reformed 'correct' Islam with scientifically advanced modern home economics and the technical skills to train and treat other women in an (ideally) segregated society" (Marion Holmes Katz, *Women in the Mosque: A History of Legal Thought and Social Practice* [New York: Columbia University Press, 2014], 263).

18 Women's optional attendance of the Friday prayer is based on a broadly accepted Hadith report that states that "Jumʿa is a duty required of every Muslim, except for four: a slave, a woman, a child, and one who is sick." See Imam Hafiz Abu Dawud Sulaiman, "Bab al-Jumʿa li-l-Mamluk wa-l-Marʾa," in *Kitab al-Sunnan: Sunnan Abi Dawud* (Mecca: Dar al-Qibla li-l-Thaqafa al-Islamiyya, 1998), vol. II, 92–93 (#1060). While all four Sunni legal schools all affirm a woman's theoretical right to attend Friday prayer if she so wishes, this consensus has coexisted uneasily with discourses over the threat of *fitna* (strife or temptation) posed by women circulating in public space, a discourse that first emerged in the third/ninth centuries. See Katz, *Women in the Mosque*, 103–04.

19 The Muslim Brotherhood's founder, Hasan al-Banna, valorized a domestically anchored woman, though he did not seek to forbid mosque attendance. See Katz, *Women in the Mosque*, 266–67. The Jamʿiyya Sharʿiyya's founder, Muhammad Khattab al-Subki, did not forbid women's attendance at mosque, but preferred that they remain within the home unless absolutely necessary. See Mahmud Muhammad Khattab al-Subki and Amin Muhammad Khattab, *al-Din al-Khalis: Irshad al-Khalq ila Din al-Haqq* (Beirut: Dar al-Kutub al-ʿIlmiyya, 2007), vol. VIII, 406–7.

20 In 1952 350,000 Egyptians worked in the public sector, while by 1969/70 the number stood at 1.2 million. This nearly 70 percent increase came during a period in which both employment generally and population growth remained below 20 percent. See Nazih M Ayubi, *Bureaucracy and Politics in Contemporary Egypt* (London: Ithaca Press, 1980), 243–44. Between the 1952/53 and 1972/73 academic years the number of Egyptians studying in higher education institutions increased from 42,485 to 334,000. See Erlich, *Students and University in Twentieth Century Egyptian Politics*, 176, 200. Similarly, primary education between 1952–53 and 1965–66 expanded from 1 to

but rather concerned whether teachers and students prayed: In January 1940 Ansar al-Sunna's journal, *al-Hadi al-Nabawi*, reprinted an article authored by the Syrian scholar and preacher Muhammad Bahjat al-Baytar (d. 1976), which noted that daily prayer was not required (*ghayr wājiba*) in primary and secondary schools. While prayer could still be performed outside class time (*fī ghayr waqt al-dars*),[21] the author was troubled by the inability of state-run schools to serve as an engine of piety.

Notwithstanding these frustrations, there is little indication that either Muslim Brothers or Salafis lobbied for government institutions to structure their schedules to accommodate this ritual practice. Instead, the options were twofold: while the comparatively paltry number of Brotherhood-run schools made time for prayer within the daily schedule,[22] those who sought to maintain ritual rectitude within the state system could avoid direct challenge by performing the prayer within its roughly three-hour window between noon and three in the afternoon, rather than as soon as the call to prayer sounded.[23]

It was only during the second half of al-Sadat's rule that the Islamist opposition came to focus on the *ẓuhr*. This decision reflected not only a tension between ritual practice and state timetables, but also available political opportunities. The Brotherhood, in particular, sought a project that would facilitate its popularity within state institutions without appearing to directly challenge al-Sadat. The attractiveness of

3.5 million. Further, between 1956 and 1961, primary (*iʿdādī*) enrollment increased from 8,000 to 42,000 and secondary enrollment jumped from 22,000 to 75,000. See Alan Richards, "Higher Education in Egypt," Policy Research Working Papers, Washington: Education and Employment Division (1992), 8.

21 Muhammad Bahjat al-Baytar, "al-Tarbiya al-ʿAsriyya Qatila li-l-Islam," *al-Hadi al-Nabawi*, 25 January 1940/15 Dhu al-Hijja 1358, 11–15, at 11. This concern was not limited to Ansar al-Sunna; the original version of the article had appeared roughly six years earlier in Rashid Rida's flagship Islamic journal, *al-Manar*. See Muhammad Bahjat Baytar, "al-Tarbiya al-Islamiyya wa-l-Taʿlim al-Islami," *al-Manar*, December 1934/Ramadan 1353, 34:544–48. This concern, however, remained central to al-Baytar: see Muhammad Bahjat al-Baytar, "Fatawa," *al-Hadi al-Nabawi*, 10 March 1940/1 Safar 1359, 26–30, at 28.

22 See "Fi Jamʿiyyat al-Ikhwan al-Muslimin," *al-Ikhwan al-Muslimun*, 13 December 1933/26 Shaʿban 1352, 19–20; "Mazhar Karim bi-Madrassat al-Bulis wa-l-Idara," *al-Ikhwan al-Muslimun*, 26 November 1935/29 Shaʿban 1354, 23.

23 The technical beginning of this period is once the sun has reached true noon as it crosses the celestial meridian. At this point, it is precisely between sunrise and sunset.

a focus on this ritual practice further increased as the Brotherhood cultivated the students of the Jama'a Islamiyya, themselves disproportionately affected by state-enforced schedules.[24] By contrast, opportunities for political mobilization at Friday prayer were more circumscribed due to the efforts by state security to monitor and even dictate the content of Friday sermons.

Egyptian Islamists were not alone in their focus on the *ẓuhr* prayer. In the late 1970s female workers in Malaysian factories lobbied the government for the right to pray during work hours and for the provision of a prayer room in which they could do so, and the government responded by providing longer lunch breaks to encompass the *ẓuhr* prayer.[25] Similarly, government employees in Pakistan have employed a variety of tactics, ranging from successfully persuading their superiors to authorize the construction of a mosque on office grounds to simply spreading "reed mats out in the little-used lobby of one of the office buildings."[26] An exception to such piecemeal accommodation is the Imam Hatip system in Turkey, which sets aside time for *ẓuhr*; but this option is available only to the minority of the student population that does not attend state public schools.[27] Abstention, however, was still an option: a study of Islam in Bosnia notes that Bosnian Muslim government employees in the 1980s postponed regular performance of the *ẓuhr* prayer until after their retirement from "the 'secular' (and 'Yugoslav') public workplace."[28] Most notable for the Egyptian Brotherhood, though, was its sister branch in Kuwait, known as the Association of Social Reform (Jam'iyyat al-Islah al-Ijtima'i), which had sought, with varied degrees of success, to facilitate the performance of this prayer in Kuwaiti schools from the early 1970s on.[29] The demands

24 For more on Muslim Brotherhood efforts to cultivate the Jama'a Islamiyya, see Dasuqi and 'Abbadi, *Tarikh al-Haraka al-Tullabiyya bi-Jama'at al-Ikhwan al-Muslimin 1933–2011*, 144–45.

25 See Aihwa Ong, Spirits of Resistance and Capitalist Discipline: Factory Women in Malaysia (Albany: State University of New York Press, 1987), 111–12, 203, 234.

26 Matthew S. Hull, *Government of Paper: The Materiality of Bureaucracy in Urban Pakistan* (Berkeley: University of California Press, 2012), 67–68.

27 See Ozgur, *Islamic Schools in Modern Turkey*, 74–75.

28 Tone Bringa, *Being Muslim the Bosnian Way: Identity and Community in a Central Bosnian Village* (Princeton: Princeton University Press, 1995), 165.

29 For example, see "Thumma Ja'a . . . Dawran al-Salat," *al-Mujtama'*, 27 October 1970/27 Sha'ban 1390, 3–4; "al-Salat fi-l-Madrasa," *al-Mujtama'*, 12 February 1974/20 Muharram 1394, 23; and "Mahaliyyat," *al-Mujtama'*, 12 October 1976/19 Shawwal 1396, 7.

of Egyptian Islamists, however, also reflected local specificity, particularly the emergence of a self-consciously "Islamic" temporality in Egypt during the first half of the twentieth century.

The Temporality of Prayer: The Construction of Religious Time and the Lag of Quranic Commentaries

The transformation of the *ẓuhr* prayer into a temporal challenge to the state's claim to define its citizens is inseparable from a longer history of British colonial efforts to institute European-style conceptions of time, and the subsequent reproduction of this project by postcolonial Egyptian rulers. If the Egyptian adoption of the Gregorian calendar in 1875 signaled acceptance of a universal project of European origin,[30] efforts by nationalist secondary students in Cairo in 1908 to celebrate the Islamic (*hijrī*) calendar year underscored how the adoption of the Gregorian calendar had set the stage for new forms of self-consciously Islamic temporal challenge.[31] Nor was this challenge limited to annual celebrations: in his study of the history of temporality in modern Egypt, On Barak traces how new means of transportation and communication produced both a "European" emphasis on "expediency and promptness" and "'countertempos' predicated on discomfort with the time of the clock and a disdain for dehumanizing European standards of efficiency, linearity, and punctuality."[32] It was in this context that "'Egyptian time' retroactively sprouted roots in the Islamic tradition and rural folklore," and the religious calendar came to represent a "sacred" or "authentic" time.[33]

Temporality also emerged as a means of political dissent. As Barak notes, the Arabic press in the 1880s used "train schedules and other technical concerns ... to broach [techno] politics without directly deploying the language most associated with illicit 'politics' – that of Egyptian nationalism."[34] Put simply, the British civilizing project claimed a colonial efficiency, which this colonial power contrasted

30 Zerubavel, *Hidden Rhythms*, 98–99.
31 Zachary Lockman, "Exploring the Field: Lost Voices and Emerging Practices in Egypt, 1882–1914," in Israel Gershoni, Hakan Erdem, and Ursula Woköck (eds.), *Histories of the Modern Middle East* (London: Lynne Rienner Publishers, 2002), 137–54, at 150.
32 On Barak, *On Time: Technology and Temporality in Modern Egypt* (Berkeley: University of California Press, 2013), 5.
33 Barak, *On Time*, 4–5. 34 Barak, *On Time*, 80.

with Egyptian indolence. Egyptians, in turn, accepted the broad importance of British-imported technology, even as they highlighted the contradictions within it – "[incorrect] timetables, train malfunctions, and the exposure of inefficiencies"[35] – to challenge colonial authority. Though British rule ended officially in 1922 and unofficially in 1952,[36] the temporal claims it had made and stimulated would march on under the postcolonial Egyptian state.

These claims, however, would also be transformed by the religious identity and ambitions of the leader. After 1952 the conflict was no longer between "European" time and "Egyptian" countertempos – or, for that matter, a European ruler and an Egyptian population – but was rather an intra-Egyptian affair. It was in this context that both ʿAbd al-Nasir and al-Sadat coopted Eid al-Fitr and Eid al-Adha as occasions of national celebration by staging this annual ritual at noted nationalist battle sites.[37] Most strikingly, al-Sadat utilized Eid al-Fitr in 1976 to enact a ceremony of *bayʿa*, used from the dawn of Islamic history to affirm the allegiance of the ruled to the ruler.[38]

While ʿAbd al-Nasir and al-Sadat both laid claim to Islamic holidays as national celebrations, the latter's self-depiction as the "Believing President" and related decision to allow limited Islamist activism meant that he could hardly deny the obligation of daily prayer for those studying or employed in state institutions. Islamist elites, on the one hand, and readers of varying stripes, on the other, would use religious temporality as a wedge issue with this constituency as they challenged the disjuncture between state claims to uphold religious law and this basic practice, and sought to produce themselves and others as pious Muslims.

As the 1970s dawned, however, Islamist elites and their readers had limited textual resources at their disposal to challenge the primacy of bureaucratic over Islamic temporality, let alone to advocate a hybrid of the two temporal approaches. Indeed, Quranic commentaries popular in

35 Barak, *On Time*, 80.

36 Egypt functioned as a British Protectorate between 1922 and 1952 even as it was officially ruled by the monarchy.

37 While King Fuad (r. 1922–36) regularly attended Eid prayers at the Citadel in Cairo, ʿAbd al-Nasir turned this public ceremony into a tool of nationalist propaganda, spending Eid al-Fitr in 1956 with Egyptian military units and Palestinian refugees in Gaza and visiting Egyptian forces in Yemen for Eid al-Adha in 1964. See Elie Podeh, *The Politics of National Celebration in the Arab Middle East* (Cambridge: Cambridge University Press, 2011), 84.

38 Podeh, *The Politics of National Celebration*, 94.

Egypt during the early and mid-twentieth century said little about this question. Most notably, Rashid Rida (d. 1935) did not treat daily prayer as a pressing question in his discussion of Surat al-Nisa 4:103,[39] even as he devoted twenty-one pages in *Tafsir al-Manar* (The Lighthouse Commentary) to questions such as requirements of prayer during travel or during periods of fear for one's life (generally in the context of war).[40] Similarly, Hasan al-Banna (d. 1949) said little about regular prayer in his commentary, *Nazarat fi Kitab Allah* (Glances in the Book of God), merely enumerating the ethical and social benefits of ritual obedience.[41]

This state of affairs did not change as the twentieth century progressed. In his Quranic commentary *Fi Zilal al-Qur'an* (The Shade of the Quran), Sayyid Qutb (d. 1966) takes a strict position regarding prayer during war – he advocates praying in shifts[42] – but does not consider the ordinary circumstances of many of his readers. Neither did the Azhari Shaykh Muhammad Mahmud Hijazi (d. 1973), author of the popular 1962 commentary *al-Tafsir al-Wadih* (The Straightforward Commentary), deal with the issue of prayer times. Instead, he devoted his discussion to the question of prayer while traveling.[43] The silence of these commentators on the question of daily prayer was not for lack of commitment to this fundamental ritual practice; rather, the obligation was so obvious that there was little need to discuss it as a legal matter, and these commentators did not consider daily prayer as a political project. During the second half of al-Sadat's rule, however, prompt performance of the *zuhr* would vault forward in textual and political prominence alike as Islamist elites, state employees, and students participated in a project that transformed previous models of religious temporality.

The Prayer Project: Statist Claims and Islamist Counterclaims

As al-Sadat drew on the state's religious and educational institutions to transmit a nationalist vision in which religious piety and political

39 The latter part of the verse reads: "For such prayers are enjoined on believers at stated times."

40 Rashid Rida, *Tafsir al-Manar* (Cairo: Dar al-Manar, 1948), vol. V, 362–83.

41 Hasan al-Banna, *Nazarat fi Kitab Allah* (Cairo: Dar al-Tawzi' wa-l-Nashr al-Islamiyya, 2002), 179.

42 Sayyid Qutb, *Fi Zilal al-Qur'an* (Riyadh: Minbar al-Tawhid wa-l-Nur, n.d.), vol. IV, 268.

43 Muhammad Mahmud Hijazi, *al-Tafsir al-Wadih* (Cairo: Dar al-Fikr al-'Arabi, 1969), 419–22.

loyalty went hand in hand, he could not simply silence Islamist voices. Instead, his claim to faith depended on allowing the opposition to speak, and even mobilize. To meet the ruler's ideological needs, *Minbar al-Islam* emphasized the centrality of prayer for the everyday lives of its readers. Each issue of the magazine contained a prayer chart setting out the times of the five daily prayers (*mawāqīt al-ṣalāt*) for the coming month.[44] Alongside this roadmap to timely prayer, the Shaykh of al-Azhar, ʿAbd al-Halim Mahmud (d. 1978), issued multiple fatwas deeming performance of the five daily prayers "the most important pillar (*rukn*) of Islam besides the declaration of faith (*al-shahāda*)."[45] Prayer was to structure the daily life of Egyptian believers.

This conception of prayer, however, was also oriented toward a broader affirmation of the existing political order. In this vein, *Minbar al-Islam* chronicled the President's January 1976 visit to al-Sayyid al-Badawi mosque in Tanta, noting how the "citizens praised and hailed the life of their leader" (*tahlīl wa-takbīr al-muwaṭinīn li-ḥayāt al-qāʾid*). Though Friday prayer had always involved an affirmation of the legitimacy of the current ruler, this iteration doubled as a political rally. Instead of reciting God's praises – the usual context in which the honorific chants of *tahlīl* and *takbīr* are used – Egyptians were to affirm the political status quo. By contrast, Egyptians appear to have attended mosque little outside the Friday sermon. As ʿAbd al-Hamid Kishk noted in a 25 March 1977 sermon, "What are we thinking of when we hear the call to prayer and we are sitting on the corner of the coffee shop (*nawāṣī al-maqhā*) or on the open roads (*qawārīʿ al-turuqāt*) ... and we do not respond?" Prayer and mosque attendance would soon vault forward in importance.

Leading voices within the Jamʿiyya Sharʿiyya were the first to explicitly challenge the subordination of religious ritual to bureaucratic schedules. In the December 1976 issue of *al-Iʿtisam*, the Jamʿiyya Sharʿiyya leader, ʿAbd al-Latif Mushtahiri (d. 1995), praised Muhammad Saʿid Ahmad, a Member of Parliament from the Delta textile center of al-Mahalla al-Kubra. Ahmad had first prayed the *ẓuhr* prayer in the midst of an afternoon parliamentary session, and then the *ʿaṣr* and *maghrib* prayers in turn, as the day of deliberations dragged on

[44] For example, see *Minbar al-Islam*, March 1976/Rabiʿ al-Awwal 1396, 97.
[45] "al-Ifta," *Minbar al-Islam*, May 1976/Jumada al-Ula 1396, 170.

into the evening. For Mushtahiri this was proof of the need for an alternative schedule:

> The true principles of the religiously committed (*mabādī al-multazimīn*) do not change based on time and place ... this is the first time in the history of parliament that the papers have noted that a Muslim man has announced the rituals of his religion at their appointed time (*sha'ā'ir dīnihi fī mawāqītihā*) in a place in which hundreds have neglected the obligation of prayer and followed their desires ... we salute the Member of Parliament Doctor Muhammad al-Sa'id, a physician and the president of the Mahalla al-Kubra branch of the Jam'iyya Shar'iyya ... and we place no one above God (*lā nuzakkī 'alā allah aḥadan*).[46]

Yet, for reasons that are unclear, this public challenge of piety receded into the background of *al-I'tisam.*

Several months later *al-Da'wa* editor and leading Muslim Brother Salih 'Ashmawi (d. 1983) revived the issue of prompt prayer. His March 1977 article "Where is Prayer Performed in the State of Science and Faith?" mocked the al-Sadat regime's claim to piety by underlining the impossibility of full ritual practice within governmental institutions. For 'Ashmawi prayer was particularly incumbent upon rulers (*al-ḥukkām wa wulāt al-umūr*) so that they could serve as a model for the people. Accordingly, it must be performed five times daily at the presidential palace as well as in the parliament, cabinet, ministries, judiciary, educational institutions, and professional offices, whether private or state owned. The obligation to pray was also a social equalizer because it applied to every level of employee, whether white or blue collar, young or old, the most senior or most junior. It was this social reach that enabled the *ẓuhr* prayer to serve as an effective challenge to the state's efforts to discipline the individual citizen.

As 'Ashmawi wielded prayer as a pointed instrument of religious challenge, he singled out Members of Parliament and the educational system alike. This Brotherhood leader asked rhetorically why the Speaker of the People's Assembly – none other than the al-Sadat regime's public proponent of the application of shari'a, Sufi Abu Talib (d. 1981) – had not decreed that parliamentary meetings would be paused for ten minutes during prayer time. Just as dangerously, state-sponsored civil education (*al-ta'līm al-madanī*) was useless without a broader moral education

[46] 'Abd al-Latif Mushtahiri, "Aqwal al-Suhuf," *al-I'tisam*, December 1976/Dhu al-Hijja 1396, 40.

(*tarbiya*). 'Ashmawi thus called on "all university administrators and deans of faculties and of primary and secondary schools to stop lessons during prayer times and to go down from their offices to the prayer hall (*muṣallā*) to join professors, teachers, white-collar workers (*muwaẓẓifūn*) and students, both male and female."[47] Neither should practical obstacles stand in the way of this project. As 'Ashmawi explained: "There are those who claim that the timing and work that has to be performed [are incompatible] ... [and thus] do not allow prayers to occur in this fashion [i.e. at the correct time] ... but this is about action (*al-'amal*) and action alone is the strongest truth and most demonstrative evidence."[48] Indeed, the implementation of the *ẓuhr* prayer in all state-controlled institutions represented no less than "the serious path to the application of the Islamic shari'a ... leading to the establishment of an Islamic society (*iqāmat al-mujtama' al-islāmī*)."[49] At stake was not only the application of Islamic law, but also the reorganization of society's temporal rhythms to accord with piety rather than productivity.

Among Ansar al-Sunna's leaders, however, caution prevailed. This is not to say that this Quietist Salafi organization's elites gave no thought to the temporality of prayer: the first five months of 1979 included an extended discussion of the specific temporal requirements of daily prayer, including the *ẓuhr*.[50] Though *al-Tawhid* did not specify to its audience that it was challenging state claims to temporality, the coincidence would have been hard to miss: following a five-year period in which the magazine had made no mention of prayer times (*mawāqīt al-ṣalāt*), it now went into extended detail in successive issues, emphasizing that it was only in cases that God specified – or in conditions of excessive heat or cold – that prayer could be postponed, and that it was praiseworthy (*mustaḥḥab*) to perform prayers immediately upon the beginning of the permissible period.

47 Salih 'Ashmawi, "Ayna al-Salat fi Dawlat al-'Ilm wa-l-Iman?" *al-Da'wa*, March 1977/Rabi' al-Thani 1397, 41.

48 Ibid. 49 Ibid.

50 See Ahmad Fahmi Ahmad, "Bab al-Fiqh," *al-Tawhid*, December 1978/ Muharram 1399, 41–43; Ahmad Fahmi Ahmad, "Bab al-Fiqh," *al-Tawhid*, January 1979/Safar 1399, 45–47; Ahmad Fahmi Ahmad, "Bab al-Fiqh," *al-Tawhid*, February 1979/Rabi' al-Awwal 1399, 45–47; Ahmad Fahmi Ahmad, "Bab al-Fiqh," *al-Tawhid*, March 1979/Rabi' al-Akhar 1399, 36–38; and Ahmad Fahmi Ahmad, "Bab al-Fiqh," *al-Tawhid*, April 1979/Jumada al-Ula 1399, 42–43.

Only divine authority and inclement weather could justify missing prayer.

Notwithstanding Ansar al-Sunna's caution, the call by Egypt's Islamist opposition for a reorganization of state schedules to accommodate timely prayer led to concrete, albeit limited, policy achievements over the summer of 1977. At this time the President's relationship with these groups was frayed, but not severed. Despite deep dissatisfaction with the trials of the youth of al-Takfir wa-l-Hijra,[51] elites within the Brotherhood and the Jam'iyya Shar'iyya had yet to dismiss cooperation with the regime. Accordingly, the Brotherhood allied with local branches of the Jama'a Islamiyya as they petitioned the Ministry of Education to provide breaks for prayer time at Egyptian universities. The July 1977 issue of the magazine included an article written by two students at Asyut University's Faculty of Agriculture. This article, entitled "A Pioneering Experiment at Asyut University's Faculty of Commerce," detailed how classes during the 1976–77 academic year had paused for the *ẓuhr* prayer.[52] Indeed, according to the two authors, the faculty's dean had issued orders for all departments to allow students and white-collar employees (*muwaẓẓifūn*) to perform prayers in timely fashion within the faculty mosque.[53] Neither was Asyut the only success story: only three months earlier Salah al-Din Hasan, the deputy of the Ministry of Education in Sharqiyya, had ordered primary and secondary principals to adjust class schedules to account for the early afternoon obligation.[54] The goal of anchoring Islamization within the daily practices – and schedules – of state-controlled institutions was clear.

With Asyut as an early model, writers and readers in *al-Da'wa* argued for a restructuring of class time within al-Azhar's nationwide network of primary and secondary religious institutes, acknowledged by the regime and Islamists alike as a key pathway for the transmission of religious knowledge in Egypt. In November 1977 'Abd al-'Azim al-Mat'ani called for the "revival" (*nuhūḍ*) of this central system of Islamic education, arguing that Azhari institutes throughout Egypt

51 For example, see Muhammad 'Abd al-Quddus, "Mawqif al-Sihafa min Qadiyyat al-Takfir," *al-Da'wa*, September 1977/Shawwal 1397, 46. Along similar lines, see Jabir Rizq, "al-Sihafa al-Misriyya fi Qafas al-Ittiham," *al-I'tisam*, September 1977/Shawwal 1397, 4.

52 "Akhbar al-Shabab wa-l-Jami'at," *al-Da'wa*, July 1977/Sha'ban 1397, 44.

53 Ibid., 45.

54 "Akhbar al-'Alam al-Islami," *al-Wa'i al-Islami*, May 1977/Jumada al-Ula 1397, 113.

should organize class time around prayer, and that teachers should join their students in this ritual practice. This reorganization, in turn, would instill "virtuous morals and praiseworthy behavior" (*al-khulq al-fāḍil wa-l-sulūk al-ḥamīd*).[55] Yet, as readers reminded Islamist elites, this problem was not limited to al-Azhar's institutes, and a letter from the same month, titled "Studying and Prayer Times," demanded that al-Azhar University's classes stop for prayer times, as the university president had promised.[56] The failure of religious institutes and al-Azhar University – let alone public schools – to stop for prayer was not merely a matter of ritual rectitude, but symbolized a sense of broader moral decay that the Brotherhood and the Jamaʿa Islamiyya would exploit.

This effort to revamp school schedules, however, would be piecemeal and incomplete, and letters streamed into *al-Daʿwa* reporting these gaps as readers sought to form themselves as pious Muslims for whom religious ritual took precedence over bureaucratic obedience. In June 1979 a reader from Damietta noted that the governorate's general director (*mudīr ʿāmm*) for the Ministry of Education had ordered primary and secondary schools to coordinate prayer and class times, yet this had not occurred in practice. The reader then urged "all those responsible for education in our country to take this faithful model" (*hadha al-namūdhaj al-mukhliṣ*) as a template for their actions.[57] Similarly, in February 1980 Ashraf ʿAbd al-Hakim Mujahid, a student at ʿAli Mubarak secondary school in Daqahliyya, complained about "students not responding to the call to prayer, whether in the afternoon (*al-ẓuhr*) or at other points of conflict with class times." This reader continued with the obvious question: "Why can't teaching pause during times of prayer and why can't teachers, in cooperation with their students, perform the prayers at this time ... as we are in a state of science and faith?"[58]

However, the teachers were not necessarily at fault. A June 1980 letter from a secondary-school teacher in Daqahliyya, titled "O Ministry of Education: What about Prayers?" complained that teachers, like their students, should have the opportunity to perform

55 ʿAbd al-ʿAzim al-Matʿani, "Min Ajl al-Nuhud bi-Risalat al-Azhar," *al-Daʿwa*, November 1977/Dhu al-Hijja 1397, 31.
56 "Barid al-Daʿwa," *al-Daʿwa*, November 1977/Dhu al-Hijja 1397, 63.
57 "Barid al-Daʿwa," *al-Daʿwa*, June 1979/Rajab 1399, 64.
58 "Barid al-Daʿwa," *al-Daʿwa*, February 1980/Rabiʿ al-Awwal 1400, 64.

prayers during the school day.[59] While al-Sadat claimed to apply the shariʿa, students and teachers reported how he had fallen short, and questioned the equation of nationalist and religious loyalty. Indeed, the best strategy at times remained avoidance. As ʿAbd al-Hamid Kishk counseled students in September 1979: "O sons, O primary school students, perform the prayers prior to going to school and ask your fathers to pray for you (*al-duʿā lakum*)."[60] Even for the most steadfast, structural limitations could be overwhelming.

Despite the clear limitations of the state's efforts, Islamist lobbying sometimes bore fruit: In the April 1981 issue a reader recounted how, since the previous month, classes at the Faculties of Theology (*uṣūl al-dīn*) and Preaching (*al-daʿwa al-islāmiyya*) at al-Azhar University ceased when the time of *ẓuhr* arrived, with teachers and students directed by loudspeaker to gather in the faculty mosque. In response, *al-Daʿwa* congratulated the professors of these two faculties and called on other Egyptian university faculties to take them as a model.[61] If Islamization could be anchored within the heart (and clocks) of state institutes, prayer could become the norm through which piety was cultivated rather than the practice of a minority.

While the leading thinkers of the Jamʿiyya Sharʿiyya hesitated to further use prayer to challenge al-Sadat's hold over state institutions, the Brotherhood worked with the Jamaʿa Islamiyya to transform the *ẓuhr*. Their success was less in educational policy – the limits to the implementation of prayer times in schools is underscored by letters from readers in state and Islamist magazines alike – than in documenting a gap in the state's religious claims which was easily observable to a mass audience, both educated and uneducated. In the process, they had cornered the al-Sadat regime, which acknowledged the daily obligation of prayer, and thus found it difficult to resist the Brotherhood's lobbying.

Just as importantly, "Islamic temporality" had taken a decisive turn. Though previously less prompt than its bureaucratic counterpart, the continued demands to pray immediately following the call to prayer now compared favorably with the habitual lethargy of government offices and schools. Nevertheless, temporal accommodation was

59 "Barid al-Daʿwa," *al-Daʿwa*, June 1980/Rajab 1400, 64.

60 ʿAbd al-Hamid Kishk, *Min Shurut Qubul al-Salat* (Part 5), rec. 28 September 1979, cassette, n.d.

61 "Barid al-Daʿwa," *al-Daʿwa*, April 1981/Jumada al-Ukhra 1401, 60.

insufficient on its own: The opposition also required access to mosques to facilitate the formation of specifically Islamist subjects.

When Time Is Not Sufficient: Making Daily Prayer Collective

When the enemies of Allah come to attack Islam, they attack the mosques ... not with the heavy cannon and its long-range shells, and not with long-range bombers ... rather, they attack the mosques by scaring people away from entering them ... They frighten the men so that they don't grow beards and they frighten the women so that they don't cover their heads. This is an explicit war (*ḥarb ṣarīḥa*) against God.

-ʿAbd al-Hamid Kishk, 28 September 1979[62]

The whole land is a mosque (*kull al-ard masjid*) ... you can meet your Lord at any time and in any place ... mosques are an airstrip (*mahbaṭ*) at which God reveals truth (*al-ḥaqq*) to the people ... there are [also] houses in which God has permitted his name to be mentioned ... people must preserve these mosques so that their connection with God remains.

-Muhammad Mutawalli al-Shaʿrawi, May 1980[63]

While Kishk warned of the challenges of attracting Egyptians to the mosque in the face of the threat of state security forces, Shaʿrawi suggested that one's focus should not be limited to the mosque. The battle was not between piety and impiety, or between prayer and abstention from it. Instead, the conflict was between an Islamist preacher who sought a site at which to mobilize his followers and a Statist preacher who sought to diffuse the importance of particular religious sites by spreading religious practice more broadly throughout society. The latter strategy could serve to diffuse the specific challenge of mosques by spreading religion more "thinly" across Egypt. Alternatively, it could merely encourage a broader transformation of social spaces along religious lines. The Muslim Brotherhood, as it teamed with the Jamaʿa Islamiyya, occupied a middle ground: by taking prayer to the state's doorstep as it argued for access to ritual space at the core of state institutions, it could be seen as diffusing the threat of mosque mobilization. At the same time, though, this project of

62 ʿAbd al-Hamid Kishk, *Min Shurut Qubul al-Salat* (Part 5), rec. 28 September 1979, cassette, n.d.

63 Muhammd Mutawalli al-Shaʿrawi, "Min al-Aya 109 ila al-Aya 115 min Surat al-Baqara," *Tafsir al-Shaʿrawi*, May 1980.

pious cultivation would soon be anchored within those spaces ostensibly controlled by the regime.

Students led the charge, as they appealed to employees within state institutions. A December 1976 letter from Cairo University's Faculty of Humanities (Kuliyyat al-Adab) detailed student negotiations with upper-level administrators to provide space for regular collective prayer: A student explained that the school's mosque could hold no more than fifteen students at a time, thus requiring students to pray in successive groups. Accordingly, this reader, a member of the Jamaʿa Islamiyya, called on the dean of the faculty to "provide a broader space for prayer ... [which also includes] space for women."[64] Yet this problem persisted: A January 1978 unsigned column from a student at Cairo University, titled "Seven Years ... and the Mosque has Yet to be Finished," noted that, while original promises for a university mosque had been made during the 1970–71 academic year, the Ministry of Endowments had apparently halted the project by refusing to pay the Arab Contractors Company to finish it. The student expressed hope that the university, headed by al-Sadat ally and Speaker of the People's Assembly, Sufi Abu Talib, would complete a spacious mosque in short order.[65] At this point the Jamaʿa Islamiyya saw a possibility of accommodation with the regime, and viewed it as a potential ally for mosque construction, rather than as a direct threat to the sanctity of ritual space.

This effort was not limited to university students. In April 1977 a group of students from the Azhari secondary institute in Alexandria explained: "We cannot find a place to pray ... [even as] the institute's mosque has become a soccer field ... Will those responsible for the institute [within the state bureaucracy] listen to us?"[66] It is unclear whether the Ministry of Education responded to this call, but *al-Daʿwa*'s ʿAbd al-ʿAzim al-Matʿani grasped its importance and, in the November 1977 issue, declared that al-Azhar's renaissance (*nuhūḍ*) depended on the coordination of class time and prayer time and also the existence of a prayer hall (*muṣallā*) in all Azhari institutes.[67] Whatever

[64] "Akhbar al-Shabab wa-l-Jamiʿat," *al-Daʿwa*, December 1976/Muharram 1397, 38.
[65] "Akhbar al-Shabab wa-l-Jamiʿat," *al-Daʿwa*, January 1978/Safar 1398, 46.
[66] "Barid al-Daʿwa," *al-Daʿwa*, April 1977/Jumada al-Ula 1397, 62.
[67] ʿAbd al-ʿAzim al-Matʿani, "Min Ajl al-Nuhud bi-Risalat al-Azhar," *al-Daʿwa*, November 1977/Dhu al-Hijja 1397, 31.

the hopes of renaissance, these young Azharis struggled to reconcile their institute's educational mission with the practical obstacles it posed to collective ritual practice.

As these readers worked to effect change within their own institutions, *al-Da'wa*'s editors and writers gave comparatively little attention to questions of access to spaces in which to perform the *ẓuhr* prayer. Instead, beginning in 1978, the shift in this debate was driven by members of the Jama'a Islamiyya writing in the Youth and University News section of the magazine and by readers in high schools across Egypt. The conflict began within these schools as students clashed with low-level administrators and state security forces alike: Hisham Mahmud, a secondary student at the National Model School in Alexandria, reported that he had been repeatedly physically assaulted by the security forces (*al-amn al-markazī*) for performing the call to prayer while at school.

This reader, however, also challenged the Muslim Brotherhood to support his efforts: "As *al-Da'wa* attacks the enemies of Islam in Somalia, Burma, Eretria, and Ethiopia, I ask it to face the enemies of Islam from those who are counted as Muslims (*mimman yantamīn ilayhi*)." In response, *al-Da'wa*'s editors did not mince their words as they criticized repression by state institutions while defending themselves:

> This [action by the security services] is terrorism (*al-irhāb*) ... they instill fear in the youth of Islam ... carrying out the plans of the enemies of Islam ... but God most high will bring victory to those who support him ... we hope that these people will remember, if only for a second, that they belong to Islam and return to it. We call on Dr. Hasan Isma'il, Minister of Education, to investigate this matter so as to determine the validity of the complaint ... and to extend the secure hand of supervision, which is keen for Islam (*yad al-ishrāf al-amīna al-ḥāriṣa 'alā al-islām*) to private schools.[68]

Whatever the subsequent investigation of the Minister of Education, the challenge of repression of the *ẓuhr* prayer did not abate as these readers entered the mosque.

Once entrenched in the mosques, students frequently used their bodies to protect their claim to ritual space. Most striking is a February 1979 letter from Amal Zayn al-'Abdin, a secondary student at a girls' school in Alexandria. She described how, on 24 November 1978, a male teacher

[68] "Barid al-Da'wa," *al-Da'wa*, December 1978/Muharram 1398, 64.

had entered the prayer hall (*muṣallā*) and expelled all the female students therein who had come to perform the *ẓuhr* prayer because it conflicted with the school schedule (*niẓām al-madrasa*). The letter writer was in the midst of prayer, and thus ignored her teacher's demand; in response, the teacher entered the mosque, wearing his shoes, and dragged her outside by her hair. When another female student came to her aid, the teacher began to assault the second student, and expelled her from the prayer hall too.

Yet this was not merely a case of faculty brutality. As this student noted, the principal of the school and her deputy were both Christians, and the teacher in question was a Muslim man touching a woman unrelated to him. In response, *al-Daʿwa* noted sarcastically:

> We had not been aware previously that the presence of female students in the school's prayer hall (*muṣallā*) could be considered a disruption of the school system (*niẓām al-madrasa*) ... This constitutes audacity against God (*al-tajarru ʿalā allah*) and an attempt to destroy the mosque ... at a time when there is no authority figure at the school who is ready to prevent such behavior. Once again, we call on the Minister of Education to investigate this new incident and to determine what occurred.[69]

Educational intermediaries, though likely also involved in more quotidian struggles over authority, were fearful of a project of piety that threatened to overturn the Ministry of Education's claim to order and the subordination of religious practice within its institutions to imperatives of nationalist education. While they could not deny the time of prayer, they could seek to regulate it within each of their schools' daily schedule. Conversely, as students pursued piety, they used their bodies to challenge the authority of their teachers and state security forces alike.

Students did not stand alone in the project of the *ẓuhr* prayer; at times, they found support from teachers too. A former teacher at Qasr al-Nil secondary school in Cairo complained in the March 1980 issue of *al-Daʿwa* that he had lost his job after leading the students in the *ẓuhr* prayer. When the school principal warned him that he was not to do so, he made it clear that "there are no limits on who can perform or supervise prayers ... the students need someone to guide them to the path of God and to protect them from deviation (*al-inḥirāf*)." In response, the principal warned him: "Don't forget that there are monitors (*ruqabā*) in our school ... [and] we want to continue earning a living in peace (*nurīd*

[69] "Barid al-Daʿwa," *al-Daʿwa*, February 1979/Rabiʿ al-Thani 1397, 64.

luqmat 'aysh bi-l-salām)." The teacher saw no solution other than to resign, and took aim at the state, asking rhetorically: "If we are living in a state whose slogan is science and faith, and if the name of the Ministry is that of Education ... and if we are supposed to guide to Truth (*al-ṣawāb*) and good (*al-khayr*), then who is making the mistake here?!"[70] High schools were a key site of state control, and the Ministry of Education sought to use the implicit threat of government surveillance to prevent the emergence of a new generation of Islamist youth. This teacher's story, however, also suggests that the state's employees often disagreed with, and even subverted, the directives of their superiors, thus opening up new (if temporary) spaces for this Islamist project.

Ultimately, the most significant clashes and repression would emerge on Egyptian university campuses, particularly at Cairo University,[71] near the end of the 1979–80 academic year. At this time the Islamist opposition had not only laid claim to ritual space, but also vocally challenged Egyptian–Israeli negotiations at Camp David. Of course, Jama'a Islamiyya organizers had previously faced restrictions: most notably, student participants in one of the Jama'a Islamiyya summer camps (*mu'askarāt*) had fled Cairo University at the end of the 1977–78 academic year following a crackdown by state security forces.[72] By the 1979–80 academic year, however, this conflict had intensified further as state security entered Cairo University's Faculty of Medicine on two different occasions. The latter occasion, which fell on 3 July 1980, involved security forces surrounding the mosque at Cairo University's Faculty of Medicine set aside for female students.[73]

The scene, as described by a member of the Jama'a Islamiyya, was mayhem, and involved the ransacking of the mosque library and the forced removal of copies of the Quran and other Islamic books. Most symbolically, security forces reportedly tore down a banner bearing Surat al-Jinn 72:18: "The mosques (*masājid*) are for Allah, so do not invoke with Allah anyone."[74] This criminal act (*'amal ijrāmī*) had

70 "Barid al-Da'wa," *al-Da'wa*, March 1980/Rabi' al-Thani 1400, 65.

71 In 1979 al-Sadat shut down summer camps at Alexandria, Cairo, and Zaqaziq Universities. Clashes also occurred in Minya and Asyut, both within and beyond university grounds. See Kepel, *The Roots of Radical Islam*, 153–61.

72 Muhammad Yahya, "Kalima La Budda Minha Hawl al-Mu'askarat al-Islamiyya fi al-Jami'at," *al-I'tisam*, July 1978/Sha'ban 1398, 19.

73 "Akhbar al-Shabab wa-l-Jami'at," *al-Da'wa*, September 1980/Shawwal 1400, 60.

74 Ibid. This verse is traditionally used to denote the exclusive sovereignty of God, rather than man, over the world.

prevented worshipers from fulfilling their religious obligations; accordingly, there could be no doubt that those who had done so had engaged in injustice (*ẓulm*). The student cited Surat al-Baqara 2:114 rhetorically: "And who are more unjust (*wa-man aẓlamu*) than those who prevent the name of Allah from being mentioned in His mosques and strive toward their destruction." Whereas the students were the emissaries of God and His party (*awliyā allah wa ḥizbihi*), their opponents awaited a great punishment in the hereafter.[75] The precise identity of these opponents, however, remained unspoken.

With students spearheading the claim to mosques, *al-Da'wa*'s mufti, Muhammad 'Abd Allah al-Khatib, elaborated the religious implications of the crackdown at Cairo University's Medical Faculty. Textually, al-Khatib took a similar line to the students, citing both Surat al-Jinn 72:18 and Surat al-Baqara 2:114. But this mufti had additional targets in mind, castigating al-Azhar for the "silence" (*sukūt*) of its scholars in the face of such "aggression" (*'udwān*). He then turned his appeal to the rank and file of the security forces: "Those troops who stand ready to defend Satan ... they should prepare to defend their *umma* and to regain Jerusalem, and to struggle against [the forces of] atheism and aggression that face every Islamic community whose inviolable sites are being violated and holy objects stomped upon."[76] Quoting the Quran in rhetorical fashion, he asked: "Have you heard the story of the soldiers of Pharaoh (*fir'awn*) and Thamud[77]? / But they who disbelieve are in [persistent] denial / While Allah encompasses them from behind / But this is an honored Quran [inscribed] in a Preserved Slate."[78] Khatib had taken the rhetoric of the Jama'a Islamiyya one step further, suggesting that the troops of the security services were those of the pagan

[75] "Akhbar al-Shabab wa-l-Jami'at," *al-Da'wa*, September 1980/Shawwal 1400, 61.

[76] "Akhbar al-Shabab wa-l-Jami'at," *al-Da'wa*, September 1980/Dhu al-Qa'da 1400, 40.

[77] Thamud were a pagan people in Arabia prior to the advent of Islam. The Quran 7:73–74 exhorts the people of Thamud to worship Allah lest they face a "painful punishment" (*'adhāb 'alīm*).

[78] This is a reference to Surat al-Buruj 85:17–22. The reference to Pharaoh therein was hardly innocuous: 'Abd al-Salam Faraj, author of *al-Farida al-Gha'iba* (The Hidden Obligation) and leader of the Jihad organization, referred to Egypt's ruler by this designation and, on 6 October 1981, al-Sadat's assassin exclaimed: "My name is Khalid Islambuli, I have killed Pharaoh, and I do not fear death." See Kepel, *The Roots of Radical Islam*, 198.

civilizations of Pharaonic Egypt and Thamud, and that their leader was equally beyond the pale.

It was left to the elites of *Minbar al-Islam* to respond to the clear inconsistencies between the state's claims to religious legitimacy and the potent opposition claim to place religious temporality and identity before their respective bureaucratic and nationalist counterparts. On the discrete question of the *ẓuhr* prayer, there was little use arguing: ʿAbd al-Fattah al-Ghawi acknowledged that prayer was a central component of Islamic education (*tarbiya islāmiyya*) and that "the most important aspect of [religious education] is the timely performance of prayers during the school day."[79] Yet al-Ghawi also sought to push back against claims that the state had failed to provide proper ritual space:

> Let us be honest: the mosques in schools or university faculties are abandoned (*maḥjūra*) or nearly so ... few students go there ... and indeed, [these] mosques sometimes serve as places for students to flee from lessons ... rather, all students should go to the prayer hall (*muṣallā*), as it is a class period (*ḥiṣṣa*) in the day like any other.[80]

That al-Ghawi sought to make prayer a "class period" like any other only underscores the success of the Islamist challenge of the previous half-decade and the attempt of this representative of the Ministry of Endowments to claim the *ẓuhr* prayer within a state-sanctioned temporal and spatial order.

Although school prayer had arrived, cooperation with the Islamist opposition was short-lived: 1981 saw the arrest of thousands of Leftists and Islamists alike and the shuttering not only of dozens of mosques in Egypt but also, in the late summer of 1981, of the offices of *al-Daʿwa* and *al-Iʿtisam*. Within this environment of mass repression, *Minbar al-Islam*'s ʿAbd al-ʿAzim Mahdi authored an October 1981 opinion piece titled "Mosques Are for God" (*al-masājid li-lla*). The piece, which appeared in this Statist publication less than a week before al-Sadat's 6 October assassination, sought to reappropriate Islamist claims to the inviolability of university mosques and to paint the religious opposition as a source of strife (*fitna*).[81] Accordingly, mosques represented the

79 ʿAbd al-Fattah al-Ghawi, "Nahwa Minhaj Afdal li-Tadris al-Tarbiya al-Diniyya," *Minbar al-Islam*, March 1980/Rabiʿ al-Thani 1400, 126.

80 Ibid.

81 ʿAbd al-ʿAlim Mahdi, "al-Masajid li-lla," *Minbar al-Islam*, October 1981/Dhu al-Hijja 1401, 50.

center of the state's focus: whereas radicals (*al-mutaṭarrifūn*) sought to use mosques to foment social discord by transforming them into "dens of Satan" (*awkāran li-l-shayṭān*), the regime deemed it essential to reassert control over them in order to "realize peace and avoid bloodshed."[82] This supposed control and the avoidance of bloodshed, however, would not last long, as al-Sadat was assassinated only a few days later by a Brotherhood splinter group.

Conclusion

The 1970s were witness to contestations between the Egyptian state and society over who was to regulate ritual practice and spaces. In the face of longstanding state efforts to control Friday prayer and to limit daily religious practice within government institutions, leading members of the Muslim Brotherhood and the Jamʿiyya Sharʿiyya transformed the *ẓuhr* prayer into a tool of temporal and spatial contestation within the heart of such institutions, while leaders from the Jamaʿa Islamiyya and Islamist readers supported this effort by reporting the contradictions between the regime's claims to religious observance and local reality.

Individual prayer, however, was insufficient and, through lobbying, protest, and bodily resistance, Egypt's Islamist opposition sought to acquire space within state institutions to support collective ritual performance. Far from being walled-off citadels, the offices, classrooms, and courtyards of state institutions were key sites of Islamist activism. State writers and institutions, in both word and action, had little choice but to concede to many of the demands arising from this project. Many schools were instructed to cease instruction during prayer times, while both schools and government offices built mosques. Yet this is not solely a story of an Islamist takeover of state institutions. Leading figures within the Muslim Brotherhood and the Jamʿiyya Sharʿiyya successfully teamed up with student activists to entrench the *ẓuhr* prayer within state institutions. At the same time, though, they also adopted their opponent's vision of order and discipline. While the temporality of this Islamist project ostensibly emerged from the "natural" rhythm of daily prayer, it ultimately constituted a striking replication of state-sponsored modernist project.

[82] Ibid., 52.

The hybrid temporality at the core of the *ẓuhr* prayer also casts light on the ways in which state institutions both shape and are shaped by those who work and study within them. The story of this project of daily prayer is neither one of straightforward resistance nor one of cooptation and compromise. It reveals how Islamist leaders, students, and professionals were shaped by state-sponsored conceptions of time and space, even as they consciously and unconsciously reappropriated these concepts and reshaped institutions to serve new ends. Just as importantly, it highlights the internal diversity of a state whose employees displayed differing preferences and priorities, and a set of institutions in which even those who agreed on ends might differ on means. The regime might not have approved of how the security forces carried out its directives, while teachers and principals often found themselves on opposite sides.

The success of this hybrid project of pious cultivation through a transformed *ẓuhr* lies in its ubiquity in contemporary Egypt. Whether at the National Archives, Parliament, or in the cavernous Mujammaʿ, the necessary time and space for the collective performance of the *ẓuhr* prayer is now the norm rather than the exception. While this project began as an Islamist endeavor to occupy state institutions in the time of al-Sadat, its diffusion has been accompanied by a comparative dilution of its Islamist undertones. Indeed, contemporary Islamists and their opponents alike flaunt their ritual piety: both jailed Muslim Brotherhood president Muhammad Mursi (b. 1951) and his successor and jailor, ʿAbd al-Fattah al-Sisi (b. 1954), proudly sport the "prayer bump" (*zabība*), and al-Sisi regularly appears on television engaged in prayer. That Egypt's first democratically elected president and his successor are both products of this shift not only points to the shared logic that binds state institutions and Islamist organizations, but also underscores why representatives of each work so hard to deny this shared history. Within a polarized political landscape, the story of how the *ẓuhr* prayer became the norm, rather than the exception, is easily forgotten. As important as prayer – and just as easily forgotten – was how Egyptian Muslims came to relate to members of the other gender.

5 *Beyond* Fitna

The Emergence of Islamic Norms of Comportment

The 1970s saw what has been commonly called "the return of the veil" (*ʿawdat al-ḥijāb*). While under ʿAbd al-Nasir Egyptian women had shed traditional practices of female modesty in pursuit of Secular Nationalist modernity, their successors under al-Sadat turned to veiling as part of a broader Islamic Revival in Egypt. As Leila Ahmed notes, "This was the time that the new veil and Islamic dress ... had begun to make its appearance on the streets of Cairo and other Egyptian cities ... Women in this style of dress ... suddenly because a very noticeable presence."[1] During this same period, Muslim Brothers and Salafis called for gender segregation as they inveighed against the dangers of gender mixing (*ikhtilāṭ al-jinsayn*).[2]

[1] Leila Ahmed, *A Quiet Revolution: The Veil's Resurgence from the Middle East to America* (London: Yale University Press, 2011), 77. Other examples include el-Guindi, "Veiling Infitah," 474–75; Earl L. Sullivan, *Women in Egyptian Public Life* (Syracuse: Syracuse University Press, 1986), 75; John Alden Williams, "A Return to the Veil in Egypt," *Middle East Review*, 11:3 (1979), 49–54; Azza Mohamed Ahmed Sallam, "The Return to the Veil among Undergraduate Females at Minya University, Egypt" (unpublished dissertation, Purdue University, 1980), esp. 21–22; Homa Hoodfar, "Return to the Veil: Personal Strategy and Public Participation in Egypt," in Nanneke Redclift and M. Thea Sinclair (eds.), *Working Women: International Perspectives on Labour and Gender Relations* (New York: Routledge, 1991), 105–26, esp. 106–07; and Sherifa Zuhur, *Revealing Reveiling: Islamist Gender Ideology in Contemporary Egypt* (Albany: State University of New York Press, 1992).

[2] For an early example, see ʿAli ʿAbd al-Jalil Radi, "Qism al-Tallaba: Fitnat al-ʿAsr," *al-Ikhwan al-Muslimun*, 22 November 1933/5 Shaʿban 1352, 18–19. For a longer discussion of this shift in Salafi discourse as an outgrowth of Salafi–Brotherhood competition, see Aaron Rock-Singer, "The Salafi Mystique: The Rise of Gender Segregation in 1970s Egypt," *Islamic Law and Society*, 23:3 (2016), 279–305. For additional studies that highlight discourses of gender segregation in 1970s Egypt, see el-Guindi, "Veiling Infitah," 476. Similarly, Valerie Hoffman-Ladd describes "the modesty and segregation of women" as an "attempt to preserve traditional values ... perceived to be Islamic." See Valerie Hoffman-Ladd, "Polemics on the Modesty and Segregation of Women in Contemporary Egypt," *International Journal of Middle East Studies*, 19:1 (1987), 23–50, at 43.

In the midst of debates over modesty and gender mixing, however, a model of pious engagement, rather than avoidance, emerged. Known as *al-ādāb al-islāmiyya*,[3] these self-consciously Islamic norms of comportment dealt with a sociological reality of gender mixing by seeking to set out proper forms of male–female interaction. This chapter, in turn, traces the process through which this guide for pious interaction arose at the intersection of the Islamic legal tradition, Statist visions of social change, religio-political competition, and the local realities of middle-class Egyptian men and women.

The chapter begins by contextualizing the Islamic Revival's project of gender relations within a longer history of Islamic norms of comportment, legal rulings regarding illicit sexual contact, and, specifically, prohibitions on looking at and speaking with unrelated members of the other gender. It then turns to the twentieth century, first laying out previous intra-Islamic debates about gender relations in public space with particular attention to the question of gender mixing, before turning to the ideological, demographic, and economic shifts that justified and expanded previously present gender-mixed spaces.

Moving to the 1970s, the chapter sets out how and why leading scholars within the Muslim Brotherhood, Jamʿiyya Sharʿiyya, and Ansar al-Sunna sought to regulate cross-gender interaction by melding Quranic proof-texts regarding aural and visual communication, a premodern Islamic tradition of norms of comportment (sing. *adab*, pl. *ādāb*), and a modernist assumption that proper gender relations would either lift up or tear down society.[4] As religious elites laid claim to an increasingly restrictive vision of public morality, however, middle-class Egyptians challenged a model of modesty inconsistent with access to education and professional employment, creating durable

3 For limited previous discussion of this shift, see el-Guindi, "Veiling Infitah," 474; and Ahmed, *A Quiet Revolution*, 79, which quotes el-Guindi. Instead, it is largely scholars of tribal practice who emphasize the importance of norms of comportment that include, but are not defined by, veiling. See Jon W. Anderson, "Social Structure and the Veil: Comportment and the Composition of Interaction in Afghanistan," *Anthropos*, 77 (1982), 397–420, at 403–04 and Lila Abu-Lughod, *Veiled Sentiments: Honor and Poetry in a Bedouin Society* (Oakland: University of California Press, 2016), 161–62. Abu-Lughod, in turn, argues that Anderson's focus on broader dynamics of deference obscures the specifically "sexual motivations" of such norms. See Abu-Lughod, *Veiled Sentiments*, 161.

4 This is not to suggest that female sexuality was never seen as a threat to public morality prior to the modern period, only that it was not perceived as a threat to the mass social organism known as society.

spaces of exception to enable these newly pious men and women to meet their economic needs and pursue professional ambitions.

The Roots of Modest Comportment: Islamic Law, Public Propriety, and State Feminism

That debates over modesty and male–female interaction intensified in the 1970s should not obscure the longer history of such questions. Within the legal literature (*fiqh*), female sartorial and behavioral modesty, which related specifically to the Quranic injunction that a woman must not reveal her pudendum (*ʿawra*),[5] was traditionally addressed in either the section on prayer (*al-ṣalāt*) or that which dealt with ritual purity (*al-ṭahāra*),[6] with particular attention to the Quranic injunction to avert one's gaze (*ghaḍḍ al-baṣar*) and to women not to "speak softly" (*al-khuḍūʿ bi-l-qawl*).[7] Yet this approach to gender relations sought to prevent illicit sexual contact, rather than to comprehensively regulate public space.[8] This is not to suggest, however, that unrestricted male–female interaction was accepted during this period or earlier. Indeed, scholars often feared popular preachers and storytellers (*quṣṣās*) because their audiences

[5] In particular, see Q 24:30–31 and 33:58–59.

[6] See Khaled Abou el Fadl, *Speaking in God's Name: Islamic Law, Authority and Women* (London: Oneworld Publications, 2014), 233 and Gauvain, *Salafi Ritual Purity*, 189.

[7] Interpretations commanding that men and women avert their gaze are based on Q 24:30–31, while those restricting "softness of the voice" are based on Q 33:32. For prominent examples of Q 24:30–31, see Muhammad b. Jarir b. Yazid b. Kathir b. Ghalib al-ʿAmali Abu Jaʿfar al-Tabari, *Jamiʿ al-Bayyan fi-Tafsir al-Qur'an*, ed. Ahmad Muhammad Shakir (Cairo: Mu'asassat al-Risala, 2000), vol. XIX, 155 and Abu-l-Fada Ismail b. ʿUmar Ibn Kathir, *Tafsir al-Qur'an al-ʿAzim* (Beirut: Dar al-Kutub al-ʿIlmiyya, 1999), vol. VI, 41. For prominent premodern interpretations of Q 33:32 along these lines, see Ismaʿil b. ʿUmar Ibn Kathir, *Tafsir al-Qur'an al-ʿAzim*, ed. Sami b. Muhammad al-Salama (Riyadh: Dar Tayba li-l-Nashr wa-l-Tawziʿ, 1999), vol. VI, 363 and Abu al-ʿAbbas Ahmad b. Muhammad b. al-Mahdi b. ʿAjiba al-Anjari al-Fasi al-Sufi, *al-Bahar al-Madid fi Tafsir al-Qur'an al-Majid*, ed. Ahmad ʿAbd Allah al-Qarshi Raslan (Cairo: Hassan ʿAbbas Zaki, 1999), vol. IV, 428.

[8] Judith Tucker, *Women, Family and Gender in Islamic Law* (New York: Cambridge University Press, 2008), 175, 199. Also see Elyse Semerdjian, *Off the Straight Path: Illicit Sex, Law, and Community in Ottoman Aleppo* (Syracuse: Syracuse University Press, 2008) and Abdel-Karim Rafeq, "Public Morality in 18th Century Damascus," *Revue du Monde Musulman et de la Méditerranée*, 55–56 (1990), 180–96.

were rarely gender segregated.[9] Similarly, the Maliki Cairene jurist Ibn al-Hajj (d. 737/1336–37) sought to restrict the circulation of Muslim women in public, particularly in settings in which they were likely to mix with unrelated men.[10]

Premodern scholars of Islam were also interested more broadly in questions of *adab*. Whether dealing with relations with one's parents and neighbors, etiquette within the mosque, or even how to engage in such quotidian acts as eating or sneezing, the Islamic scholarly tradition provided a clear template for varied daily practices.[11] Yet while this tradition of comportment offered answers to basic questions of pious living, regulating male–female interaction was a marginal concern for *fiqh* scholars.[12]

In the late nineteenth century a premodern Islamic tradition of comportment would intersect with a modernist project of state power and social transformation. In Egypt, government planners sought to impart particular ethical values – most prominently industriousness and self-discipline – in the Egyptian population, particularly through schooling.[13] The emergence of what Timothy Mitchell calls a "*siyasa* of the self" made hygiene, education, and self-discipline central to a larger project of national development.[14] In tandem, an altered discourse of *adab* arose to regulate public space and to articulate new models of

9 Jonathan Berkey, *Popular Preaching and Religious Authority in the Medieval Islamic Near East* (Seattle: University of Washington Press, 2001), 31.

10 Huda Lutfi, "Manners and Customs of Fourteenth-Century Cairene Women: Female Anarchy versus Male Shar'i Order in Muslim Prescriptive Treatises," in Nikki Keddie and Beth Baron (eds.), *Women in Middle Eastern History: Shifting Boundaries in Sex and Gender* (New Haven: Yale University Press, 1991), 99–121.

11 See Katharina Anna Ivanyi, "Virtue, Piety and Law: A Study of Birgivī Meḥmed Effendī's *al-Ṭarīqa al-Muḥamadiyya*" (unpublished dissertation, Princeton University, 2013), 70. Also see Megan Reid, *Law and Piety in Medieval Islam* (Cambridge: Cambridge University Press, 2013).

12 For example, in Ibn 'Arabi's (d. 1240) landmark ethical treatise, *Tahdhib al-Akhlaq*, the Andalusian scholar of Islam said nothing about male–female interaction in particular, and only briefly mentioned the ethical risks of men sitting in the markets and on street corners (*qawāri' al-ṭuruq*). See Abu 'Abd Allah Muhammad Ibn 'Ali Ibn Muhammad Ibn 'Arabi al-Hatimi al-Ta'i, *Tahdhib al-Akhlaq li-Ibn 'Arabi*, ed. 'Abd al-Rahman Hasan Mahmud (Cairo: 'Alam al-Fikr, 1986), 32. The Basran scholar al-Jahiz (d. 868) made similarly brief reference to this matter in his ethical treatise. See Abu 'Uthman b. Bahar al-Jahiz, *Tahdhib al-Akhlaq*, ed. Ibrahim b. Muhammad (Cairo: Maktabat al-Sahaba, 1989), 22.

13 Mitchell, *Colonising Egypt*, 101–22.

14 Mitchell, *Colonising Egypt*, 102.

public conduct.[15] While previous models of comportment focused on duties to God and virtues and vices of behavior to other individuals, this neo-traditional vision of *adab* was to serve as a means for individual citizens to discipline themselves in order to serve the national community.

In the shadow of the ambitions of a modernizing state, Islamic thinkers in Egypt came to focus on a previously marginal sub-genre of *adab*: the norms of comportment along public roads (known as *ādāb al-ṭarīq* or *ḥaqq al-ṭarīq*). As Ahmad al-Maraghi (d. 1952), a 1909 graduate of the Dar al-ʿUlum Faculty of Sharia and later professor at this teacher-training institution, explained in a November 1947 article in *al-Azhar*, the injunction to uphold these rights of the road included averting one's gaze (*ghaḍḍ al-baṣar*), properly returning greetings (*radd al-salām*), and enjoining good and forbidding evil (*al-amr bi-l-maʿrūf wa-l-nahī ʿan al-munkar*).[16] While al-Maraghi could have specified particular restrictions on men and women greeting each other, he did not. Along similar lines, an August 1962 article in *Minbar al-Islam* noted the centrality of "the norms of the road" (*ādāb al-ṭarīq*) to the norms of Islam (*ādāb al-islām*). The author of this article was particularly concerned with the "corruption" (*ifsād*) caused by men who sat on the street corners at cafés and harassed passing women, whether with their tongues, glances, or through other unspecified forms of behavior (*siwā bi-l-lisān aw al-baṣar aw ghayrhimā*).[17] While Statist scholars prior to the 1970s increasingly adopted the Modernist assumption that self-regulating individual conduct was central to the stability of the broader political order, they were most concerned with the threat posed by men's behavior, particularly their gaze and speech, to public morality.

Egyptian Salafis during the first three-quarters of the twentieth century exhibited a similar lack of focus on female behavior specifically, and the sexual dangers of male–female interaction more generally. This is not to say that Ansar al-Sunna sought to promote cross-gender interaction, whether physical, aural, or visual: A December 1939

[15] Iman Farag, "Private Lives, Public Affairs: The Uses of Adab," in Armando Salvatore (ed.), *Muslim Traditions and Modern Techniques of Power* (Münster: Lit Verlag, 2001), 93–120, at 94.

[16] Ahmad al-Maraghi, "al-Hisba fi-l-Islam," *al-Azhar* November 1937/Ramadan 1356, 693–700.

[17] Muhammad Fawi ʿAsr, "Min Adab al-Islam . . . Adab al-Tariq," *Minbar al-Islam*, August 1962/Rabiʿ al-Thani 1382, 86–88.

fatwa in *al-Hadi al-Nabawi*, authored by the leading Damascene scholar Muhammad Bahjat al-Baytar (d. 1976), offered an ethic of avoidance.[18] Specifically, al-Baytar argued that that men and women should not shake hands, that women covering their faces was praiseworthy (*mustaḥḥab*) yet not obligatory, and that men must avert their gaze from women in all situations (*fī jāmiʿ al-aḥwāl*) save for those interactions that sought to achieve a religiously legitimate goal (*gharḍ ṣaḥīḥ sharʿī*).[19] Yet this text represented only one of hundreds of fatwas handed down by muftis in *al-Hadi al-Nabawi* between 1936 and 1969.[20] Indeed, Quietist Salafi scholars were just as likely to raise concerns regarding male conduct: A November 1966 article in *al-Hadi al-Nabawi*, while noting the problem of intense crowding on public transportation (*al-izdiḥām al-shadīd fī al-muwāṣalāt)*, was specifically concerned with the problem of younger men (*shabāb*) heckling older women, whether by using profanity (*al-kalimāt al-mustaqbaḥa*), or singing immoral songs (*aghānī khalīʿa*) in their vicinity.[21]

The marginal position of this question within the flagship publication of Ansar al-Sunna reflected the broader lack of concern among Egyptian Salafis, dominated by Quietists, regarding gender mixing prior to the 1970s. This state of affairs did not shift dramatically as the twentieth century progressed: in his 1952 book *Daʿwat al-Haqq* (The Call of Truth), former Ansar al-Sunna president ʿAbd al-Rahman al-Wakil emphasized the threat of Sufism and grave visitation,[22] and the founder of Ansar al-Sunna al-Muhammadiyya branch in Sohag, Abu-l-Wafa Muhammad Darwish, echoed these concerns in *Sayhat al-Haqq* (The Shout of Truth).[23] Similarly, the Salafi luminary Muhammad Nasir al-Din al-Albani's 1951 book *Hijab al-Marʾa al-Muslima fi al-Kitab wa-l-Sunna* (The Muslim Woman's Hijab in the Quran and Sunna) does not

18 While al-Baytar ultimately associated himself with the moderate reform wing of the Salafi trend, lines of divisions within Salafism would only harden from mid-century on.

19 Muhammad Bahjat al-Baytar, "al-Fatawa," *al-Hadi al-Nabawi*, Dhu al-Qaʿda 1358, 38–43, at 41.

20 Between 1936 and 1969 a fatwa section (generally entitled "al-Fatawa" or "Asʾila wa Ajwibaʾ") appeared in *al-Hadi al-Nabawi* a total of 138 times.

21 Muhammad ʿAbd al-Karim, "al-Shabab wa Awqat al-Faragh," *al-Hadi al-Nabawi*, 11 December 1966/28 Shaʿban 1386, 16–23.

22 ʿAbd al-Rahman al-Wakil, *Daʿwat al-Haqq* (Cairo: n.p., 1952).

23 For a more extensive discussion of this point, see Rock-Singer, "The Salafi Mystique," 285–88.

discuss gender mixing, and makes only the briefest mention of the obligation to avert one's gaze.[24] Because regulating gender relations was not yet a pressing challenge, there was little need to articulate clear models that would govern such interaction.

In contrast to their Salafi peers, the Muslim Brotherhood had long sought to foreground the danger of gender mixing to public order. However, this concern did not necessarily entail the articulation of a clear model of male–female interaction. Instead, the Brotherhood was initially most concerned with how to restrict women's access to public space: following the November 1933 article in *al-Ikhwan al-Muslimun* that warned of the "sea of *fitna*" created by gender mixing,[25] an article in late November 1933 argued that women's happiness was dependent on their presence within the home.[26] The Muslim Brotherhood was particularly concerned with efforts to extend women's public presence to the workplace, arguing that Islam's opposition to gender mixing precluded women working alongside men (*ishtirāk al-mar'a ma'a al-rajul*).[27] Yet, in contrast to later debates, this leading Islamist organization argued that marriage, rather than new models of gender relations or gender segregation, could alleviate sexual temptation,[28] and said little as to how men and women should conduct themselves when inhabiting gender-mixed spaces.

The Nasserist project of State Feminism would accelerate Salafi and Statist engagement with prior models of public norms of comportment while reinforcing the Brotherhood's previous concern with gender mixing. During the 'Abd al-Nasir period, populist policies accentuated the previous educational access and professional footprint of Egyptian women,[29] rendered women's presence an unmistakable question, and

24 Muhammad Nasr al-Din al-Albani, *Hijab al-Mar'a al-Muslima fi al-Kitab wa-l-Sunna* (Cairo: al-Matba'a al-Salafiyya, 1374 H [1951]), 14.

25 'Ali 'Abd al-Jalil Radi, "Qism al-Tallaba: Fitnat al-'Asr," *al-Ikhwan al-Muslimun*, 22 November 1933/5 Sha'ban 1352, 18–19.

26 Hasannayn 'Abd Allah al-Musalami, "al-Nisa'iyat: Dustur al-Mar'a al-Muslima," *al-Ikhwan al-Muslimun*, 6 December 1933/19 Sha'ban 1352, 21–22.

27 Muhammad Hilmi Nur al-Din, "al-Nisa'iyyat: Ihtijab al-Nisa Wajib," *al-Ikhwan al-Muslimun*, 3 May 1934/19 Muharram 1353, 21–22.

28 "Bayna al-Rajul wa-l-Mar'a," *al-Ikhwan al-Muslimun*, 12 August 1944/23 Sha'ban 1363, 10–11, 16.

29 Laura Bier notes the massive expansion of female education under 'Abd al-Nasir: the number of girls studying in primary schools increased from 541,712 in 1952 to 1.4 million in 1969. See Laura Bier, *Revolutionary Womanhood* (Stanford: Stanford University Press, 2011), 51. Bier argues that the Nasserist project to

made gender segregation through domestic confinement an implausible answer. In contrast to previous visions of female modesty that centered on either the hijab or the niqab, State Feminism rejected physical veiling as a "reactionary traditionalism." In its stead, it trumpeted "veiling of conduct … as a necessary solution to the tensions engendered by women's integration into formerly homosocial work spaces,"[30] which in turn produced a "performative boundary between male and female employees."[31]

Egypt was hardly alone in both the increasing role of women in public space and in the emergence of responses to this shift. In the United States the 1960s saw not only a sexual revolution, but also a civil rights movement that brought unprecedented numbers of men and women together in public protest[32] and the growing sway of second-wave feminists who demanded greater opportunities for female employment.[33] Meanwhile, in Israel, women's share of the workforce increased from 25 to 33 percent between 1948 and 1975,[34] and in Iran from 9 percent in 1956 to 14 percent in 1978.[35] In the face of this changing public arena of the 1960s, Saudi Arabia moved to forbid mixed educational or professional spaces,[36] and an Israeli ultra-orthodox party, Agudat Yisrael, successfully secured the permission of the relevant municipalities to establish gender-segregated beaches in both Tel Aviv and Haifa.[37] Yet, unlike their peers in Israel,

expand female employment saw women's participation in the labor market as part and parcel of national progress. See Bier, *Revolutionary Womanhood*, 16.

30 Bier, *Revolutionary Womanhood*, 92.

31 Bier, *Revolutionary Womanhood*, 98.

32 Nancy Weiss Malkiel, *"Keep the Damned Women Out": The Struggle for Coeducation* (Princeton: Princeton University Press, 2016), 20–24.

33 The most prominent articulation of this movement's critique of a domestic vision of femininity appeared in 1963 with the publication of activist and writer Betty Friedan's *The Feminine Mystique*. See Betty Friedan, *The Feminine Mystique* (New York: W.W. Norton & Company, 2013).

34 For the first statistic, see Ruth Halperin-Kaddari, *Women in Israel: A State of their Own* (Philadelphia: University of Pennsylvania Press, 2004), 130. For the second statistic, see Moshe Naor, *Social Mobilization in the Arab–Israeli War of 1948: On the Israeli Home Front*, trans. Shaul Vardi (New York: Routledge, 2013), 33.

35 Hammad Shahidian, *Women in Iran: Gender Politics in the Islamic Republic* (London: Greenwood Press, 2002), 41.

36 Amélie Le Renard, *A Society of Young Women: Opportunities of Place, Power and Reform in Saudi Arabia* (Stanford: Stanford University Press, 2014), 29, 178.

37 Weiss, "A Beach of Their Own," 39.

the United States, and Saudi Arabia, Muslim Brothers and Salafis had limited room to maneuver, let alone gain access to the levers of state power. As the 1970s dawned, how would these elites in al-Sadat's Egypt regulate women's public presence?

Reckoning with a New Social Reality

During the second half of the 1970s Egyptian religious elites sought to shape society not merely through the reform of state institutions, but also through an emphasis on the embodied practices of individual believers. Sound embodied practice, however, depended on the continued production of morally upright citizens to serve Islam and the Egyptian national community alike. Yet challenges abounded: Due to both perceived the scarcity of morally upright teachers and the necessity of curricular reform, religious education was not producing individuals who could, collectively, form and maintain an "Islamic" society.[38] Indeed, the challenges of regulating male–female interaction began in the classroom: whether in the overcrowded high schools in which boys and girls could scarcely avoid one another,[39] or the persistence of co-ed Scout troops (*jawwāla*) on university campuses, including that of al-Azhar University,[40] the cracks in a project of pious male–female interaction began within the institutions central to this project.

For Statist scholars, an emphasis on individual comportment was sufficient. In January 1976 the Supreme Council for Islamic Affairs offered a narrative of Islamic history defined by the successful participation of women in governance, law, and commerce. Far from

[38] For the Brotherhood, see Ismail ʿAbduh, "Mushkilat al-Taʿlim fi Misr," *al-Daʿwa*, September 1976/Ramadan 1396, 40–41; for the leading voices of the Jamʿiyya Sharʿiyya, see "Barid al-Iʿtisam," *al-Iʿtisam*, March 1977/Rabiʿ al-Awwal 1397, 40–41; for the Supreme Council for Islamic Affairs, see Muhammad al-Nizami, "Tarbiyat al-Abna fi al-Islam," *Minbar al-Islam*, June 1977/Rajab 1397, 192–94. The debate over educational reform was initially limited to the Brotherhood, Jamʿiyya Sharʿiyya, and the Supreme Council for Islamic affairs, with the Islamic Research Academy joining belatedly, and Ansar al-Sunna showing little interest in working through the state system. For the Islamic Research Academy, see ʿAli ʿAbd al-ʿAzim, "al-Tarbiya al-Diniyya: Tasawwur li-l-Islah," *al-Azhar*, March 1981/Jumada al-Ula 1401, 929–35.

[39] "Barid al-Daʿwa," *al-Daʿwa*, September 1981/Dhu al-Qaʿda 1401, 63.

[40] Muhammad ʿAbd al-Quddus, "al-Masʾulun ʿan Tatwir al-Manahij al-Taʿlimiyya Yatakalamun," *al-Daʿwa*, April 1977/Jumada al-Ula 1397, 40–42.

conflicting with the preservation of public morality, women's full engagement coincided with the reign of "proper public comportment and high moral values" (*al-ādāb al-ʿāmma wa-l-qiyam al-khulqiyya al-rafīʿa*).[41] Proponents of the Statist vision in 1970s Egypt, like advocates of the State Feminist vision that had arisen under ʿAbd al-Nasir, saw working women as engines of national and religious development. Put simply, a combination of modest dress and individual comportment was more than sufficient to guarantee public morality.

Given the Brotherhood's previous concern with gender mixing, it would have been logical for this Islamist organization to work with leading lights of the Jamʿiyya Sharʿiyya and the Jamaʿa Islamiyya to pursue a project that melded proper comportment with structures that could facilitate gender segregation. And indeed, these movements' leaders would likely have been encouraged by efforts in 1975 to restrict co-education in the Upper Egyptian governorate of Minya.[42] But limited access to the levers of state power meant that any attempt to comprehensively restructure Egyptian public space and state institutions was bound to fail. A model of domestic confinement was similarly unfeasible, whether due to the commitment of Egyptian women to the mobility that education and employment offered or the economic necessity of female labor outside the home.[43]

In the face of these challenges, Islamist elites between 1976 and 1977 mirrored their Statist counterparts in emphasizing the importance of women veiling, on the one hand,[44] and men and women alike averting

41 Ibrahim al-Fahham, "al-Marʾa wa-l-ʿAmal fi al-Islam," *Minbar al-Islam*, January 1976/Muharram 1396, 162.

42 "Ilgha Nizam al-Ikhtilat fi Madaris Muhafazat Minya bi-Misr," *al-Mujtamaʿ*, 23 September 1975/18 Ramadan 1395, 14. There is, however, reason to assess *al-Mujtamaʿ*'s reports of gender segregation with a critical eye: a July 1974 article inaccurately claimed that Egypt had already implemented gender segregation within schools and public transportation alike. See "al-Mujtamaʿ al-Kuwayti," *al-Mujtamaʿ*, 2 July 1974/12 Jumada al-Thaniyya 1394, 9–11.

43 For a study on the relationship between modesty and employment, see Arlene Macleod, *Accommodating Protest: Working Women, the New Veiling and Change in Cairo* (New York: Columbia University Press, 1991), esp. 4–5.

44 For *al-Daʿwa*, see "Bab al-Ifta," *al-Daʿwa*, February 1977/Rabiʿ al-Awwal 1397, 49. For *al-Iʿtisam*, see "Raʾi al-Din," *al-Iʿtisam*, May 1976/Jumada al-Ula 1396, 30. For *Minbar al-Islam*, see "Bab al-Ifta," *Minbar al-Islam*, August 1977/Ramadan 1397, 167. For *al-Azhar*, see "Bab al-Fatwa," *al-Azhar*, November 1976/Dhu al-Qaʿda 1396, 1504.

their gaze, on the other.[45] Understood in isolation, these particular positions were hardly novel, deriving from longstanding interpretations of Quranic proof-texts. Indeed, on the surface, the central site of contestation appears to be whether it was merely the hijab, or also the niqab, that women must wear. While the Brotherhood defined the latter as a virtue (*faḍīla*) rather than an obligation,[46] leading figures within both the Jam'iyya Shar'iyya and Ansar al-Sunna al-Muhammadiyya – most notably Zaynab 'Awad Allah Hasan and Ni'mat Sidqi – argued that women were required to don the face veil if they had just applied makeup.[47] Notwithstanding these interpretative differences, the provision of modest dress was a comparatively straightforward endeavor: In the fall of 1978 students at Cairo University, in cooperation with the Muslim Brotherhood, spearheaded an effort to provide subsidized Islamic dress for female students, even sewing the outfits by hand.[48] The question at hand, however, was not merely whether women would dress modestly, but how they would inhabit the same social space as men.

Female modesty in isolation was not, at least initially, sufficient. Accordingly, the Muslim Brotherhood sought to provide gender segregation on public transportation, and within lecture halls. Beginning in March 1977, the Brotherhood worked with the Jama'a Islamiyya, which included students of both Brotherhood and Salafi persuasion but had adopted the Brotherhood's commitment to mobilizing in pursuit of an Islamic state, to organize gender-segregated transportation by bus between Cairo University and key areas of the city, including Imbaba, Kitkat, Mit 'Aqba, Dokki, Giza, and Qasr al-'Ayni.[49] When buses could not be segregated, other means were employed: a March 1977 letter praised the Jama'a Islamiyya activists at 'Ayn Shams University

45 See Zaynab al-Ghazali, "Min Adab al-Islam," *al-Da'wa*, November 1977/Dhu al-Hijja 1397, 43; "Ra'i al-Din," *al-I'tisam*, May 1976/Jumada al-Ula 1396, 30; "al-Ifta," *Minbar al-Islam*, January 1976/Muharram 1396, 148; and 'Antar Hashshad, "Kalimat al-Tahrir," *al-Tawhid*, September 1977/Shawwal 1397, 6–9, at 7.

46 "al-Ifta," *al-Da'wa*, July 1978/Sha'ban 1398, 40–41, at 41.

47 Zaynab 'Awad Allah Hasan, "Kayf wa Liman Tatazayyin al-Mar'a al-Muslima," *al-I'tisam*, March–April 1980/Rabi' al-Thani–Jumada al-Ula 1400, 36. For the most prominent statement of female modesty from Ansar al-Sunna, see Ni'mat Sidqi, *al-Tabarruj* (Cairo: Dar al-I'tisam, 1975), 11–13.

48 "al-Fata al-Mazluma," *al-Da'wa*, February 1979/Rabi' al-Awwal 1399, 52.

49 "Akhbar al-Shabab wa-l-Jami'at," *al-Da'wa*, March 1977/Rabi' al-Thani 1396, 45.

who patrolled public buses to prevent inappropriate male–female interaction.[50] By February 1978 the Brotherhood and the Jamaʿa Islamiyya had turned their focus to the railroad, securing gender-segregated seating on a set number of train routes, particularly between Cairo and Alexandria.[51] Notwithstanding these limited successes, an ethic of avoidance was unsustainable.

Egyptian Salafi organizations, by contrast, sought to sidestep the challenge of regulating male–female interaction entirely by enticing Egyptian women, particularly female students, to return home. In May 1977 a scholar loosely affiliated with the Jamʿiyya Sharʿiyya, ʿIsa ʿAbduh, proposed a "home university" (*jāmiʿat al-dār*) through which women could complete their university education with the aid of television and radio broadcasts. Through such a program, a woman could reach a "scientific level" while remaining in her "religious stronghold."[52] Similarly, Ansar al-Sunna's Ibrahim Ibrahim Hilal argued that, while women had the right to university education, such instruction must occur in a private setting in order to avoid gender mixing.[53] These discussions, however, were short-lived as nothing came of this program, for reasons both technological and practical. If neither comprehensive gender segregation nor domestic seclusion constituted plausible solutions, how were Egyptian men and women to live piously?

The Rocky Road of Rectitude

As Egyptian men and women and men sought to adopt this call for self-regulating separation, they struggled in the face of a model of piety that placed the burden of compliance almost entirely on practitioners. Perceiving themselves as a moral minority, the readers of Islamic magazines used fatwa requests and letters to the editor to highlight the difficulties inherent in this project of pious avoidance, and pushed elites to either offer alternative prescriptions or to develop broad-based

50 "Jawlat al-Iʿtisam," *al-Iʿtisam*, March 1977/Rabiʿ al-Awwal 1397, 40.
51 "Tajriba Yajib an Tuʿammam," *al-Daʿwa*, May 1978/Jumada al-Thaniyya 1398, 44–46.
52 ʿIsa ʿAbduh, "Unshaʾu Jamiʿat al-Dar," *al-Iʿtisam*, May 1977/Jumada al-Ula 1397, 17.
53 Ibrahim Ibrahim Hilal, "Darurat ʿAwdat al-Marʾa ila al-Bayt," *al-Tawhid*, August 1977/Ramadan 1397, 44–45.

programmatic solutions that would ease the burdens of this project of gender relations.

The challenge began from the simple reality that participants in Islamist- and Salafi-inspired projects of self-regulating modesty were a numerical minority working within state institutions that did not adhere to the religious prescriptions of Egypt's leading religious bodies. In a September 1977 letter, a male student at the Alexandria Religious Institute noted that the women around him did not adhere to Islamic dress and that they continually flaunted their charms (*mafātin*). All *al-I'tisam* could offer this reader was triumphalist encouragement, assuring him that large numbers of Muslim women in Egypt were returning to Islamic dress.[54] As the anxieties of these readers suggest, however, personal modesty was particularly challenging when the ranks of the pious were a distinct minority that sought to avoid corruption by the surrounding majority.

This marginal position often led to harassment. A letter to *al-Da'wa* from a high-school student in the Delta capital, Kafr al-Shaykh, complained that, due to having grown a beard, he had been falsely accused of being a member of Jama'at al-Muslimun (pejoratively known as al-Takfir wa-l-Hijra), and then expelled. In response, *al-Da'wa* promised to contact the Ministry of Education and to inquire whether this decision was in keeping with the state's commitment to "science and faith" (*al-'ilm wa-l-imān*).[55] The threat of embodied piety was not limited to men: in February 1978 a male reader reported that a female high-school student in another Delta city, Ashmnun, had been expelled after she had decided to veil.[56]

The challenges of marginality were no less serious for white-collar women. An October 1978 letter in *al-Da'wa* from an Egyptian woman describes the criticism she faced while employed in a private-sector company when she donned "Islamic dress": She was informed that women in the office did not dress in this fashion. The response of *al-Da'wa* was to urge her to search for alternative employment that accepted her commitment to sartorial piety.[57] Similarly, a "Muslim sister in Cairo" wrote in to the September 1979 issue to express her concerns about secretarial work at a private-sector company and the specific

[54] "Barid al-I'tisam," *al-I'tisam*, September 1977/Shawwal 1397, 43.
[55] "Barid al-Da'wa," *al-Da'wa*, July 1978/Sha'ban 1398, 62–63.
[56] "Barid al-Da'wa," *al-Da'wa*, February 1978/Rabi' al-Awwal 1398, 62.
[57] "al-Ifta," *al-Da'wa*, October 1978/Dhu al-Qa'da 1398, 51.

challenge of balancing between modesty and financial need. The response of the mufti, Shaykh Muhammad Nada, reveals a striking emphasis on comportment: while mixing with men to the "limited degree necessary" (*bi-qadr al-ḍarūra*) was permissible, it was non-negotiable for a woman to adhere to "modesty ... in dress and not [to] embellish her voice" (*ma'a mura'āt al-ḥishma fī al-malbas wa allā tazān fī al-qawl*).[58] Comportment, rather than gender mixing, had become the central concern.

The issue, however, was not merely one of maintaining female modesty, but also of disciplining male sexuality. The stakes were high, as 'Abd al-Hamid Kishk explained in a 13 October 1978 sermon:

> Masturbation (*al-inzāl al-minnī bi-l-kaff*) afflicts those who engage in it with unacceptable illnesses... it takes over the memory... it causes the servant [of God] to forgot the declaration of faith on his death bed... it afflicts the body with sluggishness and laziness (*al-khumūl wa-l-kasal*) ... it causes rheumatoid tuberculosis (*al-sill al-rihawī*) ... and it leads to an addiction to alcohol and hashish and opium.[59]

Was there any escape from this temptation?

The limits to gender segregation and the inadequacy of calls for piety and avoidance in its absence were underscored, beginning in 1979, by a flood of fatwas regarding masturbation. As an *al-Da'wa* reader from Cairo noted in a request for a fatwa in the December 1979 issue, "I am a pious youth and I love obedience to God and praying. But I'm aroused when I see an unveiled woman (*mar'a sāfira*) or hear stories of love and romance ... what should I do? Is masturbation (*al-'āda al-sirriyya*) licit?" Shaykh Muhammad 'Abd Allah al-Khatib, though he noted that this was hardly the first time he had been asked about this topic, could not grant this request to authorize masturbation; instead, he recommended that the reader fast, pray five times daily, and recite the Quran.[60]

An unsigned fatwa request in the November 1979 issue of *al-I'tisam* carried a similar concern. The reader explained: "Masturbation with the hand (*al-istimnā bi-l-yad*) is forbidden. Is masturbation with something other than the hand (*bi-ghayr al-yad*) licit [as] I often am haunted

[58] "al-Ifta," *al-Da'wa*, September 1979/Shawwal 1399, 67.
[59] 'Abd al-Hamid Kishk, *Hukm al-Islam fi al-'Ada al-Siriyya*, rec. 13 October 1978, cassette, n.d.
[60] "al-Ifta," *al-Da'wa*, December 1979/Muharram 1400, 24.

by [sexual] ideas and find myself sexually aroused and, [in this state] minimal rubbing leads to ejaculation (*al-inzāl*). What is the treatment?" Ahmad ʿIsa ʿAshur had little to offer this young man: he affirmed that masturbation through any means was forbidden, and suggested that the reader distract himself through fasting, which would lessen sexual desire and "dam the paths of Satan" (*yassid masālik al-Shayṭān*).[61] As in the case of the female employee advised to adhere to modesty of dress and voice in a mixed work environment, these men were to discipline their own bodies without the aid of structural solutions.

Challenges of sexual desire had been further exacerbated by the difficulty many young men faced in assembling the financial prerequisites of marriage. A June 1979 letter from the Middle Egypt governorate capital of Bani Swayf to *al-Daʿwa* complained that it had become difficult to marry owing to the high dowries and a population crisis that had contributed to a shortage of adequate housing.[62] This editor, however, did not provide a solution to social norms, nor could the Mufti Muhammad ʿAbd Allah al-Khatib; the latter merely counseled that the shariʿa did not require more than a metal ring or a cup of dates as a dowry if both sides agreed.[63] Though al-Khatib may have sanctioned a comparatively modest dowry, this solution ignored the simple fact that marriage did not eliminate sexual desire.

Islamist elites were particularly sensitive to the possibility that their constituencies could turn away from society in order to live according to their pious prescriptions. Most notably, members of the radical Islamist organization Jamaʿat al-Muslimun/al-Takfir wa-l-Hijra distinguished themselves by marrying internally and, upon the orders of their leader, Shukri Mustafa, many rejected employment in state institutions.[64] By contrast, in the February 1980 issue, *al-Daʿwa*'s

61 "Raʾi al-Din," *al-Iʿtisam*, November 1979/Dhu al-Hijja 1399, 29.

62 "al-Ifta," *al-Daʿwa*, June 1979/Rajab 1399, 62. Egypt had experienced a shortage of adequate housing since the 1960s, owing both to population growth and to a distorted housing market. Most crucially, ʿAbd al-Nasir-era rent controls allowed tenants to remain in their apartments at a marginal rent even when their family size was insufficient to fill the apartment. See Juan Eduardo Campo, "Domestications of Islam in Modern Egypt: A Cultural Analysis," in Chiara Briganti and Kathy Mezei (eds.), *The Domestic Space Reader* (Toronto: University of Toronto Press, 2012), 41.

63 "al-Ifta," *al-Daʿwa*, June 1979/Rajab 1399, 62.

64 Kepel, *The Roots of Radical Islam*, 86.

mufti, Muhammad ʿAbd Allah al-Khatib, fielded a question regarding young men who isolated themselves from society to preserve their faith. In response, he explained that "withdrawal and turning inwards" (*al-iʿtizāl wa-l-intiwā*) for the sake of ethical preservation is forbidden because a Muslim is obligated to "inform [people] and teach and guide them" (*al-balāgh wa-l-taʿlīm wa-l-irshād*) as part of the broader obligation to both spread the call of Islam (*daʿwa*) and to engage in jihad. Accordingly, self-isolation made the performance of these key individual obligations impossible.[65] Yet for those who rejected the path delineated by Shukri Mustafa – and the alienation from friends and family that it also entailed – hetero-sociability was the norm rather than the exception.

Calls for self-segregation were particularly unrealistic for young Egyptian men and women who were constantly on the move, whether traveling to school, work, or for leisure. Only a minority of these students and young workers, however, could afford either a driver or their own car; the majority used a combination of trains, subways, and buses to navigate Cairo, Alexandria, and the major cities of the Nile Delta. How could one avert one's gaze and separate one's body in this crowded context?

Middle-class Egyptians documented their frustrations and sought solutions. A March 1979 letter to *al-Daʿwa* by a youth from the Cairo suburb of Maʿadi complained about the crowding of the subway system, describing the experience of riding it as "[sexual] torment" (*al-ʿadhāb*).[66] Another letter from a male student at Cairo University's Faculty of Commerce elaborates: the bus and subway system lead to "[sexual] violation" (*intihāk*), as many women are forcibly pressed up against men; with this physical contact, "Satan begins to excite [sexual] desires."[67] The reader's target is not his fellow commuters but the government, which must set aside seats on public transportation for women and provide special buses for female workers at affordable prices. Though letters from *al-Iʿtisam*'s readers did not appear on this topic, its writers had grasped the difficulty. Muhammad Kamal al-Fiqhi, in an article entitled "Do Not Oppress Women," noted the social danger of men and women mixing on

[65] "al-Ifta," *al-Daʿwa*, February 1980/Rabiʿ al-Awwal 1400, 52.
[66] "Barid al-Daʿwa," *al-Daʿwa*, March 1979/Rabiʿ al-Thani 1399, 65.
[67] "Barid al-Daʿwa," *al-Daʿwa*, May 1980/Jumada al-Ukhra 1400, 64.

trains, subways, and buses.[68] The challenges for pious individuals, however, only multiplied when they disembarked.

On university campuses men and women had little space to breathe, let alone to maintain a distance from members of the other gender. The growth of the Egyptian university system between 1951 and 1976 from 1 to over 4 million students had not been accompanied by a proportional expansion of course selection, lecture halls, or leisure space. The readers of Islamic magazines lived this reality and the challenges it posed to the ideal of gender separation. A February 1980 letter to *Minbar al-Islam* asked whether friendship between young men and women was permitted, particularly at universities, due to the gender mixing therein. The State Mufti, Jadd al-Haqq, forbade friendship but permitted sitting together during lectures as a necessity of educational progress, on the condition that this did not involve "crowding or physical contact" (*tazaḥḥum aw iḥtikāk*).[69] Yet, in lecture halls that routinely seated several times the intended audience,[70] al-Haqq's fatwa did not speak to the lived experience of these students.

From Avoidance to Unexceptional Interaction

Letters and fatwa requests from young men and women not only testified to the limits of Islamist efforts to provide gender-segregated spaces, but also questioned whether an individual ethic of self-segregation was either sufficient or practical. Indeed, gender segregation was increasingly prevalent regionally, such as in the growing number of segregated beaches in Israel,[71] the expansion of exclusively male and female educational institutions in Saudi Arabia following the oil boom,[72] and the new professional and educational regulations

[68] Muhammad Kamal al-Fiqhi, "La Tazlumu al-Mar'a," *al-I'tisam*, April 1976/Rabi' al-Akhar 1396, 15.

[69] "Bab al-Ifta," *Minbar al-Islam*, February 1980/Rabi' al-Awwal 1400, 137.

[70] Mahmoud Abdel-Fadil reports that Egyptian universities enrolled approximately four times their capacity, with Arts, Law, and Commerce faculties particularly suffering in this regard. See Abdel-Fadil, *The Political Economy of Nasserism*, 354–55.

[71] In 1979 the Israeli parliament (the Knesset) passed a law stipulating that all waterfront municipalities must include a gender-segregated beach. See Weiss, "A Beach of Their Own," 39.

[72] Hertog, *Princes, Brokers and Bureaucrats*, 92.

instituted by the 1979 Islamic Revolution in Iran.[73] Yet, bereft of access to state power, Islamist elites and their Quietist Salafi counterparts would instead craft significant exceptions to their previous prescription of avoidance to grapple with both incomplete educational gender segregation and highly limited separation in professional workplaces and on public transportation.

In the face of these challenges, the late 1970s would see the Muslim Brotherhood explicitly permit "mixing with unrelated men" (*al-ikhtilāṭ bi-l-ajānib*) if a woman found it necessary (*idhā uḍṭarrat al-mar'a*).[74] Moreover, a woman's voice, once seen as an *ipso facto* source of *fitna*, was now only considered so if she deliberately accentuated its femininity (*al-khuḍū' bi-l-qawl*).[75] Along similar lines, the Jam'iyya Shar'iyya's leading scholars now permitted men to look at women "in cases of necessity or pressing need" (*fī ḥalāt al-ḍarūra aw al-ḥāja al-mulliḥa*)[76] and allowed female high-school students to look at and speak with their teachers in order to better comprehend their lessons.[77] Finally, Ibrahim Ibrahim Hilal of Ansar al-Sunna, previously a vocal advocate of domestic confinement, now argued that his earlier position had merely been a reaction to a broader moral environment in which women were pressed to dress in "unveiled and immodest dress" (*sāfira ghayr muḥtashima*); if women were free to dress modestly, their mere public presence would not threaten the social order.[78] It was the Supreme Council for Islamic Affairs, however, that pushed these concessions furthest, permitting male students to listen to and look at their female teachers, even when the latter engaged in "flaunting" (*al-tabarruj*).[79] Avoidance had turned, under the cover of necessity, to uneasy coexistence.

It is likely, however, that those who invoked necessity did not see it as a long-term solution. During the same period, leading scholars and thinkers of the Muslim Brotherhood and Jam'iyya Shar'iyya were

73 Sedghi, *Women and Politics in Iran*, 221–27.
74 "al-Ifta," *al-Da'wa*, September 1979/Shawwal 1399, 67.
75 "Nahwa Bayt Muslim," *al-Da'wa*, October 1979/Dhu al-Qa'da 1399, 32–36, at 34.
76 Ahmad 'Isa 'Ashur, "al-Fatawa," *al-I'tisam*, August 1978/Ramadan 1398, 41–42.
77 Zaynab 'Awad Allah Hasan, "Rukn al-Mar'a al-Muslima," *al-I'tisam*, February 1980/Rabi' al-Awwal 1400, 26–28.
78 Ibrahim Ibrahim Hilal, "al-Ta'lim wa-l-Tabarruj," *al-Tawhid*, December 1978/ Safar 1398, 4.
79 "al-Ifta," *Minbar al-Islam*, July 1980/Sha'ban 1400, 119.

engaged in continued negotiations with university administrators to provide gender-segregated learning spaces. Most prominently, *al-Da'wa* boasted of the provision of separate seating in lecture halls for male and female students at Asyut University.[80] In parallel, the Jama'a Islamiyya negotiated with the administration of Cairo University to provide separate spaces for men and women for university events hosted in the university's outdoor stadium.[81] Finally, *al-Da'wa* also touted an agreement with al-Azhar University to require that its female students and university employees wear "Islamic dress" on campus and in the university dorms as a landmark shift.[82] These proposals, however responsive to the needs of readers, were nonetheless limited: without the power to set university policy, the Brotherhood and the Jama'a Islamiyya negotiated piecemeal over policies at particular institutions.

Other Islamists turned to veiling as a technology of gender segregation. A fatwa in the February 1980 issue of *al-I'tisam* is illustrative in this regard, featuring the story of a female student who had turned to Islamic dress – whether she wore the hijab or niqab is left ambiguous – in order to escape sexual harassment. This young woman, in turn, "felt comfort and calm in the university and in the street and on public transportation ... people began to respect her and treat her according to [Islamic] norms of comportment (*yu'āmilūhā bi-l-adab*)."[83] These Islamist elites thus sought to activate these new models of *adab* to compensate for their inability to implement gender segregation.

It was thus of little surprise that the gendered vision of public space promoted by Islamist thinkers in 1970s Egypt remained on the cultural and institutional margins. Institutional change remained a challenge, even in ostensibly orthodox spaces: in February 1981 'Abd al-Hamid Kishk reported that the dean of the Women's College (Kuliyyat al-Banat) at al-Azhar had even rejected the notion that veiling with the hijab was a religious obligation.[84] Efforts to facilitate gender segregation were

80 "Akhbar al-Shabab wa-l-Jami'at," *al-Da'wa*, February 1980/Rabi' al-Awwal 1400, 62–63.

81 "Fasl al-Tullab 'an al-Talibat fi Tijarat al-Qahira," *al-Da'wa*, April 1981/ Jumada al-Ukhra 1401, 60.

82 "Akhbar al-Shabab wa-l-Jami'at," *al-Da'wa*, March 1981/Jumada al-Ula 1401, 58.

83 Muhammad Shu'ayr, "Mafhum Jadid li-Ayat al-Hijab," *al-I'tisam*, February 1980/Rabi' al-Awwal 1400, 28.

84 'Abd al-Hamid Kishk, *al-Hikma al-Ilahiya min Dhikr Qissas al-Anbiya fi al-Qur'an al-Karim*, rec. 6 February 1981, cassette, n.d.

equally likely to stall: A 1981 push to create a women's car on the Cairo subway system had failed due to a "lack of positive response." Yet, as *al-Da'wa* noted, the need was pressing, as female students and workers of "limited income" were forced to rely on a public transportation system that did not protect them from gender mixing.[85] It was in this context that the Muslim Brotherhood emphasized comportment over gender segregation: A September 1981 advice column by the leading female Islamist thinker Zaynab al-Ghazali noted that women could mix with men when necessary (*bi-l-ḍarūra*). Instead, al-Ghazali's central concern was that women should avert their gaze, not speak in an overly feminine fashion (*bi-lā khuḍū' fī al-qawl*), and avoid unnecessary "chatter" (*al-tharthara*).[86]

Efforts to craft a pious model of proper gender relations thus struggled in the face of limited access to state institutions, as well as the social and economic preferences and needs of Egyptian men and women. While the specific emphasis on individual comportment within public space as central to the preservation of public morality emerged in response to previous Islamist calls for gender segregation and a State Feminist project of female integration in public space, this project also reflected longstanding anxieties among Islamic scholars regarding modest comportment and gender relations. Crucially, male–female interaction – derisively termed "gender mixing" – was an assumed condition of these calls for conservative gender relations. At the intersection of male and female sexuality, religious mobilization and state institutions, an exceptional model of gender mixing became decidedly unexceptional.

Conclusion

The popularization of socially conservative practices of modesty and gender relations since the 1970s presents a paradox. On the one hand,

85 "Tajriba Yajib an Tu'ammam," *al-Da'wa*, May 1978/Jumada al-Thaniyya 1398, 44–46. It is unclear whether this particular program was put into broad practice, or whether it was another proposal that led to the creation of women-only sections on trains and subway cars in Egypt. Either way, this program of gender segregation was never applied to public buses.

86 Zaynab al-Ghazali, "Risala ila Kull Muhajjaba," *al-Da'wa*, September 1981/Dhu al-Qa'da 1401, 34.

the majority of women don either the hijab or the niqab,[87] and the Cairo subway and Egyptian rail system offer women-only cars at peak hours. If veiling and gender segregation have become normative, the decision to show one's hair in public or to ride the "mixed" car on the subway is seen as a challenge to the status quo. On the other hand, this same period saw increasing panic over an epidemic of sexual harassment in Egypt;[88] and harassment faced by Egyptian women as they traversed Egyptian cities alone at night reflects men's inability to avert their gaze.[89] As in the case of Samuli Schielke's study of Salafi youth in Upper Egypt, this paradox's core dynamic becomes clear when one appreciates that "a sexual morality based on the discipline of passions and the control of (primarily) women's bodies ... problematizes all contact between men and women to a degree that, for most young people, is impossible to enact."[90] The concurrent spread of highly gendered visions of piety and sexual harassment reflect the state of exception in which cross-gender interaction must exist.

The discourse of public morality on which this project pivoted also contributed to the creation of a gendered and classed vision of Egyptian public life that sought to balance between non-negotiable social and economic realities and an ideal of feminine domesticity. Among religious elites, not all participants spoke equally: though women such as Zaynab al-Ghazali and Zaynab ʿAwad Allah Hasan argued for female participation in public life both implicitly through the act of writing and explicitly through calls for female education and employment, they

87 There is no way to show statistically that the men and women who practice piety, whether through ritual or modest comportment, are a majority. What one can state is that secularist women who remain unveiled, such as the socialist intellectual and novelist Nawal al-Saʿadawi, are conspicuous in their decision to do so, and that any implication of impiety among politicians, even those running on secular platforms, is a source of concern. For an example of the latter dynamic, see "ElBaradei Claims 'Smear Campaign'," *Al Jazeera English*, Al Jazeera, 4 Sept. 2010, web, 18 July 2014.

88 For example, see Rasha Mohammad Hassan and Aliyaa Shoukry, *Sexual Harassment: From Verbal Harassment to Rape* (Cairo: Egyptian Center for Women's Rights, 2008), available at www.endvawnow.org/uploads/browser/files/ecrw_sexual_harassment_study_english.pdf.pdf, accessed 12 January 2018.

89 For a description of this dynamic, see Farha Ghannam, *Remaking the Modern: Space, Relocation, and the Politics of Identity in a Global Cairo* (Berkeley: University of California Press, 2002), 100.

90 Samuli Schielke, "Ambivalent Commitments: Troubles of Morality, Religiosity and Aspiration among Young Egyptians," *Journal of Religion in Africa*, 39: 2 (2009), 158–85, at 178.

did so within a broader debate defined by men, whether religious professionals or laymen, Islamists or state employees. Women's marginal status was reflected not merely in their position as a numerical minority, but also in how they spoke. While women could highlight challenges that daily life posed to this project of modesty, men had the opportunity not merely to articulate their own religious commitments, but also to voice their impious acts. These assumptions of gendered modesty emerged out of a male-centered textual elite and male-dominated readership; though women participated as both writers and readers, they faced obstacles to equal participation in both textual and public space.

The growing prominence of individual comportment that accepted the reality of gender mixing thus emerged at the intersection of sociological realities, a regime which balanced between religious claims and contradictory actions, and an Islamist opposition which seized on modesty to implicitly challenge the al-Sadat regime yet could not provide structures that would facilitate gender segregation. Such efforts to facilitate public morality, however, faltered not only because of a lack of state support, but also due to the challenges they engendered for mobile young men and women of limited means and even more limited marriage prospects. As participants questioned the strictures set forth by elites, they challenged them to provide programmatic solutions that could undergird this nascent community and aid their aspirations to piety. Yet, if women's presence in public was a concession in the early years of the Islamic Revival, it would soon become a necessary condition of public morality. How did this happen, and what can it reveal about the consolidation of this religious shift?

6 The Ambiguous Legacy of the Islamic Revival

How Women Emerged as a Barometer of Public Morality

Throughout the 1970s Muslim Brothers and Salafis inveighed against the social threat of gender mixing that had resulted from women's entrance into public educational institutions and the workplace. By 1990, however, the leading Brotherhood thinker Muhammad al-Ghazali appeared to sanction varied forms of male–female interaction when he warned against the specific threat of "chaotic mixing" (*al-ikhtilāṭ al-fawdawī*)[1] and, in 1996, a prominent Salafi preacher, Muhammad Hussayn Ya'qub (b. 1956), valorized women who wore the niqab in public as the "banner of Islam" (*liwā al-Islām*).[2] That a Muslim Brother would be concerned with particular forms of male–female interaction or that Salafis would trumpet the niqab was decidedly unremarkable. What was striking in these two visions of piety, however, was the unspoken assumption that women were in public to stay.[3]

The transformation of Brotherhood and Salafi ideals of women's public position did not occur in a vacuum. Between 1981 and 2011 they were joined by Statist scholars and Liberal Islamic intellectuals who debated how to regulate, rather than restrict, women's access to employment, education, and public space. In isolation, shifting

1 Muhammad al-Ghazali, *Qadaya al-Mar'a al-Muslima bayna al-Taqalid al-Rakida wa-l-Wafida* (Cairo: Dar al-Shuruq, 1990), 41.

2 Muhammad Hussayn Ya'qub, *Sifat al-Muslima al-Multazima* (Giza: Maktabat Suq al-Akhira, 1996), 57.

3 Elizabeth Thompson has rightly emphasized the necessity of establishing the ways in which the bounds of public and private space are locally constituted. While it remains for future research to trace these boundaries in twentieth-century Egypt, this chapter seeks to sidestep the specific question of where "private" ends and "public" begins by focusing on distinctly public sites (such as educational institutions and offices) or private domains (such as the home). See Elizabeth Thompson, "Public and Private in Middle Eastern Women's History," *Journal of Women's History*, 15:1 (2003), 52–69, at 52.

Brotherhood or Salafi visions of women's public presence could be read primarily as a concession to sociological and economic realities – specifically, the growth of female employment under Mubarak and the related challenges of making ends meet on one salary. While such a reading has merit, it obscures a larger story of how these two trends came to highlight women's presence as a barometer of public morality.[4]

The previous chapter traced the emergence of self-consciously Islamic norms of comportment in the shadow of a Secular Nationalist project of State Feminism that had begun under ʿAbd al-Nasir. This chapter, by complement, charts how Muslim Brothers and Salafis adopted the guiding logic of this Secular Nationalist project, which positioned women as necessarily public objects and agents of change, as they sought to consolidate the gains of the Revival under Mubarak. Specifically, their respective efforts to control women's bodies as they moved outside the home led to the elevation of women as an essential marker of their respective projects and, unexpectedly and perhaps unintentionally, to changing expectations of male domestic labor.

This chapter draws on a combination of Islamic legal texts, popular catechisms, and marriage manuals published since 1981 to trace the changing assumptions that undergird these arguments over women's position in Egyptian society. Such sources do not allow us to trace women's social practice, nor do they proportionately represent the religious visions of Egyptian women during this period.[5] They do, however, cast light on a central difference between the Islamic Revival's genesis and its consolidation: while the key practices spearheaded by the Islamist opposition at the dawn of the Revival used modernist logics of bodily practice and social change as a means to shape state and society, the Revival's consolidation entailed an adoption of this logic as an end unto itself. In the process, women's public

[4] By contrast, Ellen McLarney's study of women in Egypt's Islamic Revival foregrounds the centrality of domestic space and narrates women's entrance into the workforce in terms of its effect on the cultivation of an Islamic home. See McLarney, *Soft Force*, 180–218. Although McLarney notes the importance of veiling to women's participation in the workforce, she does not situate veiling within a broader project of comportment. For a limited reference to comportment, see McLarney, *Soft Force*, 200–01.

[5] While all these movements and ideological trends counted women within their ranks, men disproportionately shaped debates over public morality.

presence shifted from constituting a feared side-effect of an allegedly culturally alien project of Western feminism to representing an intrinsic aspect of Brotherhood and Salafi activism.[6]

The choice of gender relations, rather than either daily prayer or Islamic education, as the focus of this chapter stems from the fact that questions about women's place in public life continue to activate major political divides over public morality in contemporary Egypt. The significance of these battles lies not in their novelty – as Chapter 5 noted, women have long served as symbols of public morality both within and beyond Egypt[7] – but rather in what they reveal about the changing dynamics of Egypt's Islamic Revival as it became the norm, rather than the exception, under the rule of Hosni Mubarak. By contrast, the striking legacy of ritual practice and Islamic education in contemporary Egypt is that, irrespective of origin, they are no longer contested. Though participation in independent Islamic educational institutions and the performance of the *ẓuhr* prayer may both index particular religious commitments, neither represents a central point of contention for Egypt's diverse religious movements, nor a key concern for the ruling regime.

The centrality of Islamic norms of comportment to projects of public morality is not unique to Egypt. With the significant exception of the Gulf states, particularly Saudi Arabia and Iran,[8] gender segregation in educational institutions, offices, and sites of leisure (such as malls) has not been financially feasible, even in those cases in which it

[6] As Lila Abu-Lughod has noted previously, the Islamist project of gender relations represents a selective engagement with the Liberal bourgeois vision of the early twentieth-century Egyptian feminist movement. See Lila Abu-Lughod, "The Marriage of Feminism and Islamism in Egypt: Selective Repudiation as a Dynamic of Postcolonial Cultural Politics," in Lila Abu-Lughod (ed.), *Remaking Women: Feminism and Modernity in the Middle East* (Princeton: Princeton University Press, 1998), 243–69.

[7] This is not to suggest that efforts by men to control women's bodies are somehow unique to consciously Islamic projects of change, thus obscuring the highly gendered colonial and postcolonial projects of nation building. For example, see Elizabeth Thompson, *Colonial Citizens: Republican Rights, Paternal Privilege, and Gender in French Syria and Lebanon* (New York: Columbia University Press, 1999). Also see Beth Baron, *Egypt as a Woman: Nationalism, Gender and Politics* (Berkeley: University of California Press, 2005), esp. 40–56.

[8] For a Saudi example, see Le Renard, *A Society of Young Women*. For Iran, see Sedghi, *Women and Politics in Iran*.

was ideologically desirable. Whether in Egypt, Lebanon,[9] Palestine, or Algeria,[10] individual female modesty, of which wearing either the hijab or niqab is but one component, has emerged as an ethical practice that both challenges and helps to sustain a mixed public arena. The Egyptian case, in turn, helps to cast light more broadly on the relationship between the popularization of modesty and the expansion of opportunities for women regionally.

This chapter begins by tracing the relationship between the Revival's original project of individual comportment and three significant shifts of the early to mid-1980s: the linked assumptions that comportment was primarily a female concern, that women in public would veil in some form or fashion, and that female employment could be religiously legitimate in and of itself rather than a mere concession to necessity. Instead of seeing veiling and comportment as a necessary concession to women's public presence, I argue that, in 1980s Egypt, a call to modest comportment was a means by which religious elites could continually shape women's practice as they moved outside the home. The second section, which draws on texts published between 1987 and 2004, traces how the initial linkage between female labor and modest comportment would come to involve not only an expanded understanding of the permissible fields of female labor, but also the emergence of women as key objects and agents of public religious activism across the ideological spectrum.

Moving from this acceptance of women's public presence to debates over gender segregation between 2004 and 2011, the third section zones in on changing Salafi understandings of a practice that became central to this movement in the 1970s. Specifically, it shows how Egyptian Salafis trumpeted the centrality of the niqab as a technology of gender segregation in a manner that affirmed, rather than challenged, the claim made by their Liberal competitors that individual comportment was sufficient to ensure women's continued pious

[9] Deeb, *An Enchanted Modern*, 106–16.

[10] For Palestine, see Rema Hammani, "From Immodesty to Collaboration: Hamas, the Women's Movement, and National Identity in the Intifada," in Joel Beinin and Joe Stork (eds.), *Political Islam: Essays from Middle East Report* (Berkeley: University of California Press, 1997), 194–210. For Algeria, see Susan Slymovics, "'Hassiba Ben Bouali, If you Could See our Algeria': Women and Public Space in Algeria," in Beinin and Stork (eds.), Political Islam, 211–19. It is important to note that, like scholars of Egypt, these two authors both focus on the hijab.

presence in public space. The chapter concludes by drawing on Islamic marriage manuals published in Egypt throughout the period of Mubarak's rule to chart how a growing acceptance of female education and employment was accompanied by changing expectations of domestic labor. Far from being a story of Brotherhood and Salafi efforts to valorize a domestically rooted woman and Statist and Liberal advocacy of female employment, diverse religious elites would unite to highlight female public conduct as a means of furthering distinct ideological projects and of reaffirming their own authority to regulate female bodies and, by extension, public space.

The 1980s: When Pious Women in Public Become the Norm

In 1984 Muhammad Lutfi al-Sabagh (b. 1930), a professor at King Saud University in Riyadh, contributed a chapter to a commentary on Hasan al-Banna's *al-Mar'a al-Muslima* (The Muslim Woman), which was published by the Salafi Bookstore in Cairo. In this volume al-Sabagh sought to make the case that women's entrance into the Egyptian workforce had led not only to their employment in restaurants and bars, but also to unwanted pregnancies, abortion, and a spate of romantically fueled murders.[11] Al-Sabagh's primary target of criticism was the Egyptian government's failure to provide structural solutions such as separate classrooms to facilitate gender segregation and to restrict women from entering particular professions.

This critique would have been of little surprise to the Muslim Brothers and Salafis likely to purchase this volume. During the second half of al-Sadat's rule the Brotherhood had worked with the Islamic student movement to organize gender-segregated transportation by bus between Cairo University and the various areas of Egypt's sprawling capital city,[12] and had even secured a women's car on select train routes nationally.[13] These efforts to separate men and women in

[11] Muhammad b. Lutfi al-Sabagh, "al-Risala al-Rabi'a: Tahrim al-Khalwa b-il-Mar'a al-Ajnabiyya wa-l-Ikhtilat al-Mustahtar," in Hasan al-Banna, *al-Mar'a al-Muslima*, ed. Muhammad Nasr al-Din al-Albani (Cairo: Dar al-Kutub al-Salafiyya, 1987), 81–99, at 83–85. This volume was first published, by the same publishing house, in 1984.

[12] "Akhbar al-Shabab wa-l-Jami'at," *al-Da'wa*, March 1977/Rabi' al-Thani 1396, 45.

[13] "Tajriba Yajib an Tu'ammam," *al-Da'wa*, May 1978/Jumada al-Thaniyya 1398, 44–46.

public, however, were ultimately piecemeal and, in the aftermath of al-Sadat's October 1981 assassination, opportunities for cooperation with state institutions had ground to a halt.

An alternative answer to gender mixing was a return by women to the home. In the 1970s the Brotherhood, Jam'iyya Shar'iyya, and Ansar al-Sunna had all valorized a domestically rooted woman,[14] and, in the case of Ansar al-Sunna and Jam'iyya Shar'iyya, had explored proposals for domestic confinement.[15] At this time women's permanent incorporation into the labor force was not a foregone conclusion: in 1960 women represented 4.8 percent of the working population, a statistic that had risen only slightly, to 5.5 percent, by 1976. If anything, the broader slowdown in government employment – a key avenue of female employment – had made women's participation in the labor market even more challenging.[16]

The dawn of Hosni Mubarak's rule even saw a growing promotion of domestic labor by the state as central to national development. Al-Sadat had previously enacted a series of laws aimed at facilitating female employment in the private sector. By contrast, in 1985 Mubarak's government released *The Egyptian Woman*, a study that sought to "stake out women's important roles in the interrelated projects of economic development and family planning."[17] While both the State Feminist project under 'Abd al-Nasir and the neoliberal policies under al-Sadat had emphasized the role of women in national economic development, Mubarak now melded this emphasis with his Brotherhood and Salafi challengers' ideal of the woman as the religious center of the Egyptian home.[18] In this formulation, human development, which depended on sound domestic practice (however defined), was a precondition for national progress.

This growing consensus that women's domestic labor undergirded the future of the Egyptian nation, however, did not result in a decline in female employment. Instead, women's participation in the formal labor force grew, reaching 8.9 percent by 1986,[19] and 26 percent by

[14] The Brotherhood's emphasis on the woman as the "first teacher" of the next generation goes back to Hasan al-Banna. See Hasan al-Banna, "al-Risala al-Ula: al-Mar'a al-Muslima," in *al-Mar'a al-Muslima*, 5.

[15] Rock-Singer, "The Salafi Mystique," 295–301.

[16] Wickham, *Mobilizing Islam*, 41–42.

[17] McLarney, *Soft Force*, 204–05.

[18] McLarney, *Soft Force*, 206–07.

[19] Central Agency for Public Mobilization and Statistics (CAPMAS), *Preliminary Results of the Population, Housing and Establishment Census of 1986* (Cairo: Central Agency for Public Mobilization and Statistics, 1987), 7.

2006.[20] In this context, clerical work within government offices was a standout field, as women grew from 4.5 percent of this workforce in 1960 to 27.4 percent by 1976.[21] Work was not merely a choice, but increasingly a necessity, as the retrenchment of state-sponsored social welfare services inaugurated by al-Sadat had made the purchasing power enabled by two wages increasingly necessary for many families.

In the absence of viable structural solutions to gender mixing, and the continued growth and necessity of female employment, Muslim Brothers and Salafis doubled down on a call for embodied Islamic norms of comportment (*al-ādāb al-islāmiyya*), which enlisted individual discipline of men and women alike in the service of conservative gender relations. The regime of self-regulation through dress, speech, and gaze had first emerged during the second half of al-Sadat's rule as a responsibility of men and women alike. As in the 1970s, the call for particular models of comportment during the 1980s reflected the failure of efforts by Muslim Brothers, Salafi organizations, and the Islamic student movement to secure structural solutions to the challenge of gender mixing by providing gender-segregated educational institutions and public transportation, or, in the case of Salafis, barring women from employment.

Unlike in the 1970s, however, the call for proper comportment, even among Statist scholars, came to focus on women alone. Shortly after al-Sadat's October 1981 assassination Muhammad Ahmad al-Siba'i published *al-Mar'a bayna al-Tabarruj wa-l-Tahajjub* (The Woman between Flaunting and Veiling),[22] in which this Azhari scholar serving on the seminary's Islamic Research Academy emphasized the necessity of women veiling, averting their gaze, and avoiding all behavior that could draw unnecessary attention.[23] Along similar lines, a second member of the Islamic Research Academy and the Secretary General

20 World Bank, "Labor force participation rate, female," available at http://data.worldbank.org/indicator/SL.TLF.CACT.FE.ZS, accessed 13 March 2017.

21 Nadia Youssef, *A Woman-Specific Strategy Statement: The Case of Egypt* (Cairo: Aid Bureau of Program and Policy Coordination, 1980), cited in Macleod, Accommodating Protest, 49.

22 This book's year of publication is 1981 Gregorian and 1402 *hijrī*. If it was published on the very first day of 1402 (e.g. 1 Muharram 1402), then the book would have come out on 29 October 1981, several weeks after the assassination of Anwar al-Sadat and Hosni Mubarak's assumption of the presidency.

23 Muhammad Ahmad al-Siba'i, *al-Mar'a bayna al-Tabarruj wa-l-Tahajjub* (Cairo: Islamic Research Academy, 1981), 3–4, 163.

of Islamic Preaching (*al-da'wa al-islāmiyya*) at al-Azhar, 'Abd al-Waddud Shalabi (d. 2008), noted that the goal of donning the hijab and averting one's gaze was to facilitate women's public presence, rather than to restrict them to the home.[24] Statist scholars, who sought to uphold both the authority of state institutions to regulate society and their religious authority in the face of Brotherhood and Salafi challenges, had to negotiate a space for themselves between the State Feminist project's vision of women's active participation in public space and Brotherhood and Salafi calls for proper comportment.

By contrast, Liberal Islamic intellectuals challenged both the exclusive focus on women and the broader assumption that men and women could not coexist socially. Most notably, in 1984, Hussayn Ahmad Amin (b. 1932), the son of the Egyptian historian Ahmad Amin (d. 1954) and brother of the prominent economist and commentator Jalal Amin (d. 2018), argued that it was absurd to assume that men and women were incapable of sitting next to each other without being overtaken by sexual desires.[25] While Amin's opponents, presumably Salafi scholars, argue that such glances constitute an "arrow of Iblis" (*sahm min sihām iblīs*) and that women must thus cover their faces,[26] Amin argued that such a viewpoint is "abnormal" (*ghayr 'ādī*).[27] In this debate, however, Liberal Islamic intellectuals were a distinct minority, overshadowed by an implicit consensus among their Statist, Brotherhood, and Salafi competitors that female behavior was central to public morality.

The viability of an exclusive focus on female comportment was bolstered by the growing popularity of veiling during this period. Notwithstanding the limits of what normative visions of piety can tell us about social practice more broadly, one can nonetheless state that

24 'Abd al-Waddud Shalabi, *Fi Mas'alat al-Sufur wa-l-Hijab* (Cairo: Islamic Research Academy, 1985), 28. This book was first published as part of the June 1984/Ramadan 1404 issue of *al-Azhar*.

25 Hussayn Ahmad Amin, *Hawl al-Da'wa ila Tatbiq al-Shari'a al-Islamiyya wa Dirasat Islamiyya Ukhra* (Cairo: Dar Su'ad al-Sabbah, 1992), 68. This volume was first published in Beirut in 1985 by Dar al-Nahda al-'Arabiyya li-l-Tiba'a wa-l-Nashr.

26 This claim refers back to a Hadith report, originally reportedly narrated by Hudhayfa, a Companion of the Prophet. For a contemporary Salafi Friday sermon on this topic, recorded by the Egyptian Salafi website *Ana Salafi*, see Sa'id 'Abd al-'Azim, *al-Nazra Sahm min Sihham Iblis* (RAM, 46 minutes, available at www.anasalafy.com/play.php?catsmktba=10874, accessed 13 March 2017).

27 Amin, *Hawl al-Da'wa ila Tatbiq al-Shari'a al-Islamiyya*, 67.

religious scholars and thinkers across the ideological spectrum increasingly premised their calls for modesty on the assumption that veiling was a common, rather than a countercultural, practice. This optimism was new: during the 1970s Islamist and Salafi scholars and intellectuals had continually bemoaned the minority position of veiled women, arguing that the masses of scantily clad women (*nisā kāsiyyāt ʿariyyāt*) endangered public morality and must be returned to Islam.[28] Although this concern had certainly not disappeared by the early 1980s, Brotherhood and Salafi thinkers had increasingly come to direct their efforts to regulate how women looked at and spoke to unrelated men toward already-veiled women, specifically those who wore the hijab.[29]

An early observer and advocate of this trend was the former Leftist cultural-critic-turned-Islamic-activist Safinaz Kazim (b. 1937). In 1982 Kazim published *Fi Masʾalat al-Sufur wa-l-Hijab* (The Question of Unveiled Dress and the Hijab), in which she divided pious Egyptian women into three segments: hesitant women (*al-mutaraddida*), who veil simply in order to avoid conflict with society's dominant norms (*al-mujtamaʿ al-sāʾid*); those who wear the hijab yet do not see themselves as obligated to cover their hands or face; and those who go above and beyond by wearing a niqab.[30] While Kazim acknowledges that yet other Egyptian women do not veil at all, her reference to the pressures produced by society's dominant trends suggests a changing socio-religious landscape. Indeed, the call to reform the practices of already-veiled women reveals both the growing normativity of the hijab and the unspoken assumption that pious women would continue to frequent spaces in which it was necessary to don modest dress.

As the decade progressed, Egyptian Salafis, too, would adopt the assumption that the hijab had become the norm, and that women who

[28] For an example from the Jamʿiyya Sharʿiyya, see Hussayn Muhammad Yusuf, "al-Islam wa Qadiyat al-Hijab," *al-Iʿtisam*, December 1976/Dhu al-Hijja 1396, 24–26, at 26. For an example from Ansar al-Sunna, see Muhammad ʿAli ʿAbd al-Rahim, "Bab al-Sunna," *al-Tawhid*, June–August 1977/Rajab–Ramadan 1397, 10–13, at 11. For an example from the Muslim Brotherhood, see "Akhbar al-Shabab wa-l-Jamiʿat," *al-Daʿwa*, October 1979/Dhu al-Qaʿda 1399, 54–57, at 54.

[29] Such a focus is consistent with an ethnographic study from this period which noted a shift toward veiling as normative over the course of the 1980s. See Macleod, *Accommodating Protest*, 105.

[30] Safinaz Kazim, *Fi Masʾalat al-Sufur wa-l-Hijab* (Cairo: Maktabat Wahba, 1982), 5–6.

wore the hijab should be central targets of reform. In her 1987 *al-Mutabarrijat* (The Flaunters), a female Egyptian Salafi–Islamist thinker who had moved to Yemen, al-Zahra Fatima B. ʿAbd Allah, noted an epidemic of "flaunting" (*al-tabarruj*) among veiled and unveiled women alike.[31] Of particular concern were two classes of women: those who faithfully yet mistakenly veiled, and those "falsely veiling women" (*al-muḥajjabāt al-zāʾifāt*) who sought to exploit the veil to attraction male attention.[32] That same year the noted Salafi preacher Muhammad Hassan (b. 1962) published *Tabarruj al-Hijab* (The Flaunting of the Hijab), in which he warned of the growing popularization of the "modern hijab" (*al-ḥijāb al-ʿaṣrī*) over the "proper hijab" (*al-ḥijāb al-sharʿī*).[33] The battle among Statist scholars, Liberal intellectuals, and Brotherhood and Salafi thinkers was not a conflict between a vision of domestically centered modesty and a call for women's further integration into public space, but about how pious women would traverse public space in the absence of formal gender segregation. The terms of the debate had thus shifted: in contrast to the 1970s, competing claimants to authority within the Islamic Revival now assumed that women's ongoing presence in public was an irreversible fact.

This emphasis on veiling also led to a broader vision of religiously licit female employment. Brotherhood and Salafi thinkers had previously permitted female labor outside the home based on the religious principle of "necessity" (*ḍarūra*),[34] while Statist scholars had avoided dealing directly with this question even as they noted women's prominent medical and administrative roles in the early Muslim community's territorial conquests.[35] By contrast, in 1981 Statist scholar Muhammad

[31] al-Zahra Fatima b. ʿAbd Allah, *al-Mutabarrijat* (Cairo: Maktabat al-Sunna, 1987), 11.

[32] B. ʿAbd Allah, *al-Mutabarrijat*, 43.

[33] Muhammad Hassan, *Tabarruj al-Hijab* (Cairo: Dar al-Fajr al-Jadid, 1987), 13.

[34] The justification of necessity originated within the broader concept of the "common good" (*al-maṣlaḥa al-ʿāmma*), most notably in the work of the fourteenth-century Islamic scholar al-Shatibi (d. 790/1388). This concept was popularized – and transformed – in the modern period by Muhammad Rashid Rida (d. 1935). See Muhammad Qasim Zaman, "The ʿUlama of Contemporary Islam and their Conceptions of the Common Good," in Dale Eickelman and Armando Salvatore (eds.), *Public Islam and the Common Good* (London: Brill, 2004), 129–56, at 131–2. Also see Malcolm Kerr, "Rashid Rida and Islamic Reform: An Ideological Analysis," *The Muslim World*, 50:2 (April 1960), 99–109.

[35] For example, see Ibrahim al-Fahham, "al-Marʾa wa-l-ʿAmal fi al-Islam," *Minbar al-Islam*, January 1976/Muharram 1396, 162.

Ahmad al-Siba'i explained that female employment constituted a "right" (*li-l-mar'a al-ḥaqq fī al-'amal*)[36] undergirded by women's participation in public prayer, commerce, and war during the life of the Prophet Muhammad.[37] Moving beyond questions of employment, al-Siba'i argued that women had the right to leave the home to visit the hair salon, tailor, doctor, or friends.[38] This vision spread, albeit in attenuated fashion, to Salafis: in 1987 al-Zahra Fatima B. 'Abd Allah had allowed for the possibility of women serving as doctors and nurses under the premise that individuals in such professions often cover their faces.[39] Though B. 'Abd Allah's argument hardly glorified female employment, it tentatively accepted it without preconditions of necessity.

In the face of women's inescapable public presence, Salafi scholars reiterated the authority of men, particularly those with access to state power, to regulate women's behavior. As Darwish Mustafa Hasan noted in his 1987 *Fasl al-Khiṭab fi Mas'alat al-Hijab wa-l-Niqab* (Parsing the Discourse on the Question of the Veil): "The veil is an obligation of Muslim woman ... and the responsibility [for enforcing this obligation] is shared by the woman herself, the ruler (*al-ḥākim*), and her family." One can assess the ruler's success in fulfilling his designated role, in turn, based on the presence or absence of "protection from sexual instincts" (*al-amān al-gharīzī*).[40] This vision, though couched in a traditionalist idiom, departed significantly from premodern models of regulating public morality that emphasized the role of individual Muslims rather than the state,[41] and prior rulings regarding the specific question of gender relations that centered on preventing illicit sex (*zinā*).[42] However, such discussions would remain theoretical: in the absence of access to state power, Brothers and Salafis would

36 al-Siba'i, *al-Mar'a bayna al-Tabarruj wa-l-Tahajjub*, 8.
37 al-Siba'i, *al-Mar'a bayna al-Tabarruj wa-l-Tahajjub*, 31.
38 al-Siba'i, *al-Mar'a bayna al-Tabarruj wa-l-Tahajjub*, 166.
39 B. 'Abd Allah, *al-Mutabarrijat*, 127.
40 Darwish Mustafa Hasan, *Fasl al-Khiṭab fi Mas'alat al-Hijab wa-l-Niqab* (Cairo: Dar al-I'tisam, 1987), 3–4.
41 Michael Cook, *Commanding Right and Forbidding Wrong in Islamic Thought* (Cambridge and New York: Cambridge University Press, 2004), xii. Specifically, the obligation to command right and forbid wrong constituted a duty that rulers carried out through an official appointed censor (*muḥtasib*) and his role in regulating public conduct (*ḥisba*).
42 Tucker, *Women, Family and Gender in Islamic Law*, 175, 199.

focus on embodied practice, rather than on state enforcement, as the central means of preserving public morality and of affirming their own claims to regulate society.

Women as Public Agents of Revival

What did it mean for women to actively participate in public life in a time of Islamic revival? In the late 1980s Liberal intellectuals questioned the disproportionate burden placed by Muslim Brotherhood and Salafi intellectuals and scholars on women over the preceding decade-and-a-half. A Liberal intellectual who originally trained in medicine, Ahmad Shawqi Finjari (b. 1925), noted that while women should not frequent "bars or places that include nudity" (*makānan tudār fīhi khamr aw khalāʿa*), this prohibition applies equally to men.[43] More broadly, Finjari argued that a woman is qualified to hold all leadership positions, to acquire all forms of education, and to work in all jobs that don't impinge on her chastity (*ʿiffatihā*) or domestic responsibilities (*riʿāyat baytihā*).[44]

Yet, if al-Finjari's emphasis on men and women's joint responsibility to maintain propriety placed him in the minority, his call for female employment was far from exceptional. Only three years later a leading Muslim Brother, Muhammad al-Ghazali (d. 1966), argued that women are suited to work in teaching, medicine, nursing, social work, publishing, and writing.[45] The ground underneath this debate was unmistakably shifting and, in 1998, the noted Liberal Islamic thinker Jamal al-Banna (d. 2013) would push this vision of female employment further, arguing that, while historically female-dominated fields such as cosmetology, nursing, and women's medicine should be available, "women should not be deprived of the opportunity to study other topics" (*ḥirmānihā min al-dirāsāt al-ukhrā*).[46] Though one might have expected al-Finjari and al-Banna to agree, al-Ghazali's argument for female employment beyond the grounds of necessity underscored broadened Islamist participation in this debate over female employment.

43 Ahmad Shawqi al-Finjari, *al-Ikhtilat fi al-Din – fi al-Tarikh – fi ʿIlm al-Ijtimaʿa* (Cairo: al-Hayʾa al-Misriyya al-ʿAmma li-l-Kuttab, 1987), 24.

44 al-Finjari, *al-Ikhtilat fi al-Din*, 33.

45 al-Ghazali, *Qadaya al-Marʾa al-Muslima*, 38–39.

46 Jamal al-Banna, *al-Marʾa al-Muslima bayna Tahrir al-Qurʾan wa Taqayyud al-Fuqaha* (Cairo: Dar al-Fikr al-Islami, 1998), 186.

Indeed, the dominant shift of this period was the emergence of self-consciously affirmative visions of mixing across the ideological spectrum. Among Liberal Islamic thinkers, al-Banna sought to restore expectations of comportment to both men and women by arguing that the Quranic command to avert one's gaze (*ghaḍḍ al-naẓar* or *ghaḍḍ al-baṣar*, Q 24:30–31) had been misunderstood. The command to avert one's gaze was not a "comprehensive directive to members of both genders" (*tawjīh shāmil li-l-jinsayn*); instead, the Quran assumes that there will be instances in which specific individuals act in ways that "attract the gaze of those around them" (*mā yuthīr al-naẓar*), and that one must look away from such individuals.[47] Similarly, al-Finjari argued that men and women could coexist in mosques, schools, offices, on public transportation, during social celebrations, and even during jihad as long as they adhered to modest dress, physical behavior, and speech.[48]

The promotion of comparatively permissive visions of women's rights and responsibilities beyond Salafi circles coincided with increasingly stringent calls for modesty within them. Although Salafi scholars in 1970s had shown little consensus as to the obligatory nature of the niqab,[49] by 1989 Muhammad b. Isma'il al-Muqaddam (b. 1952), a leading Islamist–Salafi scholar within the Alexandria-based Salafi Call (al-Da'wa al-Salafiyya), argued that a woman's decision to show her face by wearing the hijab rather than the niqab now constituted "unveiled dress" (*al-sufūr*). Invoking a non-existent scholarly consensus, even within Salafi circles, al-Muqaddam assured his readers that "all scholars agree that women must cover their face and hands to protect against acts that could lead to corruption" (*saddan li-dharā'i' al-fasād*).[50] A prominent figure within this Salafi–Islamist organization, al-Muqaddam sought to distinguish the Salafi Call from fellow

47 al-Banna, *al-Mar'a al-Muslima bayna Tahrir al-Qur'an wa Taqayyud al-Fuqaha*, 189.

48 al-Finjari, *al-Ikhtilat fi al-Din*, 24.

49 For the view that the hijab is sufficient, see al-Albani, *Hijab al-Mar'a al-Muslima*, 6. For the view of the Jam'iyya Shar'iyya's leading female thinker, Zaynab 'Awad Allah Hasan, that the niqab is required if a woman has just applied makeup, see Zaynab 'Awad Allah Hasan, "Kayfa wa-Liman Tatazayyin al-Mar'a al-Muslima," *al-I'tisam*, October 1976/Dhu al-Qa'da 1396, 24. For a more stringent view on the necessity of the niqab when women venture out in public, see Sidqi, *al-Tabarruj*, 13.

50 al-Muqaddam, *Adillat al-Hijab*, 79.

Islamists who did not share a Salafi interpretative approach and offered a less stringent model of female modesty.

Seven years later a leading Salafi preacher, Muhammad Hussayn Yaʿqub, added a further explanation that hinted at the niqab's future centrality to Salafi understandings of gender mixing. As Yaʿqub explained: "The hijab is niqab and constitutes a form of worship (*ʿibāda*) ... it encompasses all behaviors, beliefs, and ritual practices that are related to a woman who covers her face (*jumlat tasarrufāt wa-iʿtiqādāt wa-ʿibādāt qurb mughaṭiyyat wajhihā*)."[51] The niqab, beyond representing a specific obligatory sartorial choice, now indexed a series of norms of Islamic comportment that assumed, rather than rejected, women's public presence.

While Salafis did not subscribe to the far more egalitarian visions of individual comportment offered by al-Banna and al-Finjari, Yaʿqub was no less focused on women's central role as public actors. Though he acknowledged the threat of the "unveiled women who had come to destroy Muslim youth,"[52] Yaʿqub simultaneously valorized the "committed sister" (*al-ukht al-multazima*) who raises the "banner of Islam" (*liwā al-islam*) by donning the niqab.[53] Instead of highlighting the danger of gender mixing – a common and well-accepted Salafi trope of the previous quarter-century[54] – Yaʿqub explained that "a committed sister upholds Islam's norms of comportment in all aspects of her life ... whether at home ... in the street ... in the mosque ... among her children ... with her parents ... [or] with her sister."[55]

Left unsaid was the obvious: mixing was now a sociological reality that leading figures across the religious spectrum accepted, whether implicitly or explicitly. The question was how to respond to this disjuncture between female modesty and the absence of gender

[51] Yaʿqub, *Sifat al-Muslima al-Multazima*, 45–46. By contrast, Muhammad Nasir al-Din al-Albani's prescription for proper behavior centered on dress, an approach cited (and reproduced) by Ansar al-Sunna in the 1970s. For the original citation for al-Albani, see al-Albani, *Hijab al-Mar'a al-Muslima*, esp. 4. For Ansar al-Sunna's reproduction of these conditions, see Sayyid Sabiq, "Min Qadaya al-Mujtamaʿ al-Muslim," *al-Tawhid*, October 1986/Dhu al-Qaʿda 1396, 24–26.

[52] Yaʿqub, *Sifat al-Muslima al-Multazima*, 8.

[53] Yaʿqub, *Sifat al-Muslima al-Multazima*, 16.

[54] Rock-Singer, "The Salafi Mystique."

[55] Yaʿqub, *Sifat al-Muslima al-Multazima*, 40–41.

segregation; in 1990 the Muslim Brotherhood's Muhammad al-Ghazali had taken a first step when he warned that women must avoid "chaotic mixing" (*al-ikhtilāṭ al-fawḍawī*).[56] Al-Ghazali, however, had left the crucial question of what lay beyond chaotic mixing unanswered.

"Forbidden Mixing": How Salafis Came to Accept Male–Female Interaction

If women were to be in public as objects and agents of religious change, which forms of mixing would be permitted, and how could this approach undergird particular projects of religiosity? The third section of this chapter will tackle these questions through a comparison of two ideologically opposed visions: a Liberal claim to the sufficiency of norms of comportment that rejects all forms of gender segregation; and a Salafi case for the plagues of gender mixing. As in previous debates over comportment, veiling, and female employment, Liberal and Salafi claims to women's bodies and public space evince a similar acceptance of women's public presence, an emphasis on embodied female modesty, and the assumption that male religious elites should regulate female practice.

In 2004 Mustafa Mu'awad 'Abd al-Ma'bud, a professor of Philosophy at 'Ayn Shams University's Women's Faculty in Cairo, authored *Fitnat al-Mar'a: Bayna al-Ikhtilat wa Sadd al-Dhari'a fi al-Fikr al-'Arabi al-Mu'asir* (The Temptation of Women: Between Mixing and Preemptive Prevention in Contemporary Arabic Thought). Taking aim at Salafi attempts to restrict women's public presence through invocation of the specter of temptation (*fitna*), 'Abd al-Ma'bud valorized gender mixing as the very basis of human civilization (*al-'umrān*), whether through professional employment, development, education, ritual worship, culture, arts, or sports. Indeed, free male–female interaction represented no less than the basis for "building, liberating and improving society and for cooperation in all domains of social and political life."[57] Whether the goal was women's development, successful marriage, the promotion of civil society, halting the spread of

[56] al-Ghazali, *Qadaya al-Mar'a al-Muslima*, 41.

[57] Mustafa Mu'wad 'Abd al-Ma'bud, *Fitnat al-Mar'a: Bayna al-Ikhtilat wa Sadd al-Dhari'a fi al-Fikr al-'Arabi al-Mu'asir* (Cairo: Dar al-Shams, 2004), 5.

homosexuality, or motivating men and women to greater professional productivity,[58] such interaction was an essential feature of a productive Islamic society.

This university professor was particularly concerned to intervene in a polarized debate that pitted Liberal intellectuals against Salafi scholars. While the former – most notably Jamal al-Banna and Hussayn Ahmad Amin – had previously denied that women represented *fitna* in any shape or form, the latter argued that that all mixing would lead to *fitna*, thus defining women primarily in terms of the danger posed by their femininity.[59] Seeking to square this circle, ʿAbd al-Maʿbud acknowledged that particular individuals were disproportionately prone to illicit relations stemming from gender mixing, yet the benefits derived by society more broadly from such interaction substantially outweighed this risk. Accordingly, the key to avoiding *fitna* is not gender segregation based on the principle of "damning the pretexts of sin" (*sadd al-dharīʿāt*),[60] but rather adherence to a detailed set of norms that include prohibitions against staring (*al-baḥlaqa*) at other men or women, immodest clothing, flirtatious speech (*al-luyūna wa-l-muyūʿa*), walking barefoot, and frequenting crowded areas in which men and women's bodies are pressed together (*iḥtikāk al-ajsād*).[61] Working within the Revival's emphasis on Islamic norms of comportment, ʿAbd al-Maʿbud argues that even if many people refuse to adhere to correct comportment, the benefits of mixing significantly outweigh its costs (*al-maṣāliḥ al-mutarattiba ʿalā al-ikhtilāṭ akbar bi-kathīr min al-mafāsid*). ʿAbd al-Maʿbud thus invoked the common good (*al-maṣlaḥa al-ʿāmma*) to expand, rather than restrict, the purview of individual behavior.[62]

By contrast, Shaykh Shahata Muhammad ʿAli Saqr (b. 1969) drew on previous Salafi models of public space and gender in his 2011 two-volume work *al-Ikhtilat bayna al-Rijal wa-l-Nisa: Ahkam wa Fatawa* (Mixing between Men and Women: Rulings and Fatwas). As a founder of the Salafi Call in Alexandria and a member of the organization's Consultative Council (*majlis al-shūrā*), this Islamist–Salafi could have straightforwardly condemned the moral ills produced by gender

58 ʿAbd al-Maʿbud, *Fitnat al-Marʾa*, 56–66.
59 ʿAbd al-Maʿbud, *Fitnat al-Marʾa*, 6–7.
60 ʿAbd al-Maʿbud, *Fitnat al-Marʾa*, 7.
61 ʿAbd al-Maʿbud, *Fitnat al-Marʾa*, 29–30.
62 ʿAbd al-Maʿbud, *Fitnat al-Marʾa*, 30.

mixing. Instead, he chose to expand on Muhammad al-Ghazali's 1990 warning against the dangers of "chaotic mixing" to introduce the category of "forbidden mixing" (*al-ikhtilāṭ al-muḥarram*).[63]

Saqr's elaboration of the varieties of mixing reveals both Salafi responses to women's increasing public prominence over the previous three decades and the continued efforts of male religious elites to assert their control over women's bodies:

> Forbidden mixing is any [mixed interaction] in a private place ... or at a site which promotes corruption ... or hosts acts forbidden by shari'a ... and involves men sitting alongside women as they would alongside their own wives or one of their female relatives ... in a manner that lifts the barrier between them ... and allows him to affect her if he so choose (*al-ta'thīr 'alayhā law arād*) ... it includes mixing within educational institutions and at private lessons ... as well as at work, at clubs, on public transportation, at markets, in hospitals, during neighborly visits, and at weddings and parties ... and when a male doctor examines a woman when a female doctor is available ... or during medical exams ... or at restaurants ... or in the case of male drivers transporting female passengers.[64]

The category of implicitly permitted mixing is comparatively small, centering on the case of niqab -wearing university students who arrive at campus in private transportation and then avert their gaze and speak softly in class.[65]

However, the primary significance of Saqr's statement lies not in his programmatic vision of "permitted" mixing – a term that is implied but not used – but rather in the reaction that this conceptual approach aroused. His study also contained multiple forewords, traditionally a genre that serves to praise the author's contribution. In the first

63 Though rare, the use of this category is not entirely unprecedented outside Salafi circles. For example, an article in the Syrian Islamic periodical *al-Tamaddun al-Islami* by a Hanafi scholar, Wahbi Suliman al-Albani (d. 2013), explained the dangers of "forbidden mixing," while arguing that women are permitted to attend holiday and mosque prayers. See Wahbi Suliman al-Albani, "al-Ikhtilat al-Muharram wa Adrarahu," *al-Tamaddun al-Islami*, Tishrin al-Thani (i.e. October) 1958/Rabi' al-Thani 1358, 298–303. While Muhammad Nasir al-Din al-Albani published regularly in this journal, its pages encompassed a range of views, many of which were distinct from Purist Salafism.

64 Shahata Muhammad 'Ali Saqr, *al-Ikhtilat bayna al-Rijal wa-l-Nisa: Ahkam wa Fatawa, Thimar Murra Qissas Mukhziyya, Kashf 136 Shubha li-Du'at al-Ikhtilat* (Cairo: Dar al-Yusr, 2011), vol. I: 65–71.

65 Saqr, *al-Ikhtilat bayna al-Rijal wa-l-Nisa*, vol. I, 220.

entry, transcribed by the publisher based on a handwritten document, a retired judge within the Saudi court system, Shaykh Muhammad b. Shami al-Shabih (b. 1955), blessed the book for its elucidation of the dangers of mixing and noted its place in the battle against those "preachers of mixing" (*du'āt al-ikhtilāṭ*).[66] Change, however, was afoot: instead of seeking to return women to the home, al-Shabih addressed himself to "every believing woman ... [calling on her] to veil around unrelated men (*an takūn muḥtajjaba 'an al-rijāl*) ... to distance herself from mixing with them ... and to avoid employment in mixed work spaces (*'amal mukhtalaṭ*)."[67] The assumptions of this Saudi Salafi scholar are unmistakable: Egyptian (though not Saudi) women are in public to stay and, as such, are responsible for successfully navigating the challenges of a mixed public arena.

While al-Shabih's foreword praised Saqr's indictment of gender mixing, the second introductory note, written by a senior preacher within the Salafi Call, Yasir al-Burhami (b. 1958), moved from praise to conceptual affirmation. Like Shabih, al-Burhami warned against the power of sexual desire (*al-shahwa al-jinsiyya*), stating that women's flaunting (*al-tabarruj*) posed a threat to the "chastity and purity" (*al-'iffa wa-l-ṭahāra*) of the Islamic *umma*.[68] The issue, however, was not merely flaunting: as al-Burhami noted, "forbidden mixing (*al-ikhtilāṭ al-muḥarram*) represents one of the most potent tools of civilizational war and of cultural and intellectual invasion by the West against Muslims."[69]

Most striking, however, is al-Burhami's novel interpretation of mixing, which casts light on the emergence of a distinction between forbidden and permitted forms of male–female coexistence:

> Our brother Shahata Saqr has pointed us in this study to the harms of forbidden mixing ... he has brought up well-known issues of our Egyptian society ... in our universities, schools, and professional workspaces ... which encompass numerous evil actions (*anwā' al-munkarāt*) including illicit looking (*al-naẓar al-muḥarram*), illicit speech (*al-kalām al-muḥarram*), illicit listening (*al-samā' al-muḥarram*), and the forbidden touch (*al-lams al-muḥarram*).[70]

66 Saqr, *al-Ikhtilat bayna al-Rijal wa-l-Nisa*, vol. I, 6.
67 Saqr, *al-Ikhtilat bayna al-Rijal wa-l-Nisa*, vol. I, 6.
68 Saqr, *al-Ikhtilat bayna al-Rijal wa-l-Nisa*, vol. I, 9.
69 Saqr, *al-Ikhtilat bayna al-Rijal wa-l-Nisa*, vol. I, 10.
70 Saqr, *al-Ikhtilat bayna al-Rijal wa-l-Nisa*, vol. I, 10–11.

Al-Burhami voices little concern about the implications of the term "forbidden mixing." Instead, he formalizes a space for women to move within in public by defining gender segregation as a set of embodied practices that center on Islamic comportment, rather than on physical separation between men and women. Yet, if this Salafi preacher had given up on the ideal of domestic seclusion or broadly enforced structures of gender segregation in state institutions or public space, his argument that a woman could quite literally segregate herself from the men in her midst through bodily practice continued to place the burden of public morality on her shoulders.

Salafi acceptance of this distinction between legitimate and illegitimate mixing, on the one hand, and the redefinition of gender segregation as comportment, on the other, would not pass without a challenge. In yet another foreword, Muhammad Yusri Ibrahim (b. 1966), an Egyptian Salafi based in Saudi Arabia at the Islamic University of Medina and the head of the volume's publisher, Dar al-Yusr, cautioned the author and his readers alike:

> Let us not say that there are permitted and forbidden forms of mixing (*inna al-ikhtilāṭ minhu mubāḥ wa minhu muḥarram*) ... instead, let us say: mixing is unequivocally forbidden by human nature, it is an educational failure that has been discarded by history. It brings down civilizations and is forbidden in the most absolute terms by Islamic law. [71]

From across the Red Sea, an Egyptian scholar working at the epicenter of a global Salafi movement scolded his counterpart in Egypt for the ideological and practical implications of this choice of words.

Just as striking, though, was the fact that it occasioned no similar response from Yasir al-Burhami. Instead, consciously or unconsciously, al-Burhami – and, prior to him, Muhammad Hussayn Ya'qub – had come to the conclusion that individual comportment was sufficient to preserve proper gender relations, and that women were central public actors in a Salafi project of religious mobilization. Gender segregation, in turn, now depended not on physical separation of men and women, but on the maintenance of distinct norms of comportment by women under the supervision of male Salafi scholars.

[71] Saqr, *al-Ikhtilat bayna al-Rijal wa-l-Nisa*, vol. I, 14.

Between Public and Private: The Emergence of an Islamic Case for Male Domestic Labor

The debate over women's public presence was not merely about shaping public space, but also about defining domestic roles. Despite a longstanding emphasis on the role of the mother as a homemaker dedicated to forming the next generation,[72] Brotherhood and Salafi thinkers increasingly articulated new expectations of domestic space which enlisted men and technology as key cogs in lessening the dual burdens of employment and domestic labor on Egyptian women.

The role of technology as a means of meeting this challenge was hardly new. In November 1963 the Conference on the Affairs of the Working Woman had recommended state support for the spread of gas stoves, semiautomatic washing machines, refrigerators, and electric irons,[73] and the state sponsored household-management classes that taught women how to use and maintain these appliances.[74] Prior to the 1980s, however, this question was secondary to Brotherhood and Salafi deliberations over domestic labor because both were committed to the ideal of a domestically rooted woman.

The first echo of changing expectations emerged in a 1987 manual devoted to building a "Muslim home" (*bayt muslim*). Authored by Sa'id Hawwa (d. 1989), an exiled Syrian Muslim Brother then living in Jordan and published in Cairo, *Qawanin al-Bayt al-Muslim* (The Rules of the Muslim Home) emphasized the importance of purity (*al-ṭahāra*) to an authentically Muslim domestic life:

> The Muslim man is keen to preserve purity and cleanliness (*al-ṭahāra wa-l-niẓāfa*) in his home ... and accordingly, pays attention to the purity and cleanliness of clothing and body. The Muslim man is keen to preserve the cleanliness of his furniture to the degree possible (*mā amkan*) ... and his prayer space (*makān al-ṣalāt*) ... and one should make sure that the waste basket (*salāl al-muhmalāt*) is sufficient[ly large] ... and pay particular

[72] For an example from this period, see Shabab Sayyidna Muhammad, *Dustur al-Mujtama' al-Muslim* (Cairo: Dar al-I'tisam, 1987), 28–31. This is not to suggest, however, that domestic space somehow lost its significance for the Islamic Revival; for a literary study of the centrality of the Muslim home to contemporary piety, see McLarney, *Soft Force*, esp. 219–54.

[73] United Arab Republic, *Mu'tamar Shu'un al-Mar'a al-'Amila* (Cairo: Permanent Council for Women's Affairs, 1963), 58–59, in Bier, *Revolutionary Womanhood*, 81.

[74] Bier, *Revolutionary Womanhood*, 82.

attention to the bathroom and the toilet . . . And just as cleanliness within the home is important, so too is cleanliness in the area surrounding the home (*mā yuḥīṭ al-bayt*).[75]

Even more striking than the extension of an emphasis on ritual purity to the home as a whole is the new division of labor to preserve this ritually pure and hygienic state: while women are to arrange specific times to wash clothing and dishes, the "members of the family" (*ahl al-bayt*) as a whole are responsible for the disposal of the trash and vacuuming,[76] and each individual member is responsible for his or her room remaining tidy (*murattaban*).[77]

This is not to argue that such domestic labor was unprecedented. As Arlene Macleod notes in her ethnography of 1980s Cairo:

Perhaps half of men admit, with some embarrassment, that they do in fact sometimes help their wives with housework. Usually they help with the food shopping or light cleaning and straightening up in the apartment. Very seldom [however] will a husband perform such tasks in front of guests, nor will his wife encourage him to do so.[78]

Instead, the shift is one of expectations as Hawwa sought to articulate a principle, rather than merely an exception, to justify male domestic labor.

Domestic labor was not simply a question of cleaning, but also one of cooking. Notwithstanding Hawwa's 1987 call for men to preserve the cleanliness of their homes, the easier solution to challenges of domestic labor was the purchase of home appliances. In the 1970s Egyptian women had begun to publish cookbooks geared toward working women who needed to make quick meals; a popular text from this period, produced in cooperation with the feminist *Hawwa* (no relation) magazine, was entitled *Atbaq Laziza wa-Asnaf Sari'a li-l-Mar'a al-'Amila* (Tasty Dishes and Quick Portions for the Working Woman).[79] The diffusion of gas stoves and refrigerators, in turn,

[75] Sa'id Hawwa, *Qawanin al-Bayt al-Muslim* (Cairo: Dar al-Salam, 1987), 49–50. This book was published together with a second work by Hawwa, *Ghada al-'Ubudiyya*.

[76] Hawwa, *Qawanin al-Bayt al-Muslim*, 50.

[77] Hawwa, *Qawanin al-Bayt al-Muslim*, 53.

[78] Macleod, *Accommodating Protest*, 87.

[79] See Nazira Naqula, *Atbaq Laziza wa-Asnaf Sari'a li-l-Mar'a al-'Amila* (Cairo: Hawwa Magazine, 1976). I wish to thank Anny Gaul for generously sharing this text with me.

enabled women to cook and then store large portions of food more easily.

Calls for female employment, in turn, increasingly reflected these technological advances. In his 1998 *al-Mar'a al-Muslima bayna Tahrir al-Qur'an wa Taqayyud al-Fuqaha* (The Muslim Woman between the Liberation of the Quran and the Limits of the Jurists), Jamal al-Banna argued that female employment was possible, pending the husband's agreement, because "the latest appliances (*al-ma'dāt al-ḥadītha*) for cooking, sweeping, and washing have made it possible for her to fulfill her domestic responsibilities and to work."[80] Although such appliances were certainly out of the reach of households belonging to the lower middle and working classes[81] – the precise segment of society that could least afford a single salary – they appeared to offer middle class Egyptian women a technological solution to the challenge of balancing employment and domestic labor.

Popular discourses of financial responsibility also opened up new spaces for the negotiation of domestic labor at the intersection of increased use of technology and male participation. Beginning in the 1990s and accelerating after 2000, self-help literature, though couched in terms of the Islamic tradition, offered a neoliberal model of subjectivity in which "individuals are in charge of their own lives, and responsible for their own economic, emotional, and mental well being."[82] Characteristic of this trend, a 2005 pamphlet by Akram Rida, a self-help author loosely affiliated with the Muslim Brotherhood,[83] advised couples on how to maintain a financially solvent household. Although Rida acknowledged the basic structure of the home – in which the man is responsible for earning money (known as the *nafaqa*) and the woman for administering it – he counsels men and women alike that this agreement does not preclude cooperation in fulfilling each other's respective responsibilities.[84] Other steps, meant to save money, also served to lessen

80 al-Banna, *al-Mar'a al-Muslima bayna Tahrir al-Qur'an wa Taqayyud al-Fuqaha*, 183.

81 See Macleod, *Accommodating Protest*, 66.

82 Jeffrey T. Kenney, "Selling Success, Nurturing the Self: Self-Help Literature, Capitalist Values, and the Sacralization of Subjective Life in Egypt," *International Journal of Middle East Studies*, 47 (2015), 663–80, at 665.

83 This book was published by the Muslim Brotherhood's official publishing house, Dar al-Tawzi' wa-l-Nashr al-Islamiyya.

84 Akram Rida, *Buyut Bi-La Duyun: Kayfa Tudabittuna Mizaniyat Buyutikum?* (Cairo: Dar al-Tawzi' wa-l-Nashr al-Islamiyya, 2005), 24.

the burden on women, from Rida's suggestion that weekly trips to the market would save women from buying more than they need,[85] to the recommendation that women should prepare meals that could last several days (and thus allow them to buy ingredients in bulk),[86] to the emphasis on using electric appliances such as washing machines.[87]

Akram Rida's 2005 call for cooperation, however, paled in its scope compared to the Salafi vision of domestic life offered by Mahmud al-Misri Abu ʿAmmar in his 2006 pamphlet *al-Zawaj al-Islami al-Saʿid* (The Happy Islamic Marriage).[88] A student of a leading Alexandrian Salafi shaykh, Muhammad b. Ismaʿil al-Muqaddam, this Islamist–Salafi's book on Islamic marriage stretches 912 pages and focuses on legal questions such as whom one is permitted to marry, the different varieties of licit marriage, the correct norms of an Islamic wedding celebration (*adāb al-zifāf*), and how to get divorced. Within this broader legal discussion, Abu ʿAmmar laid claim, albeit in fleeting fashion, to an authoritative model for male domestic labor: "The greatest man Muhammad Peace and Blessings upon Him ... who carried the burdens of the entire Islamic *umma* ... would help his wife with housework (*ʿamal al-bayt*)."[89] Based on this line of reasoning, male domestic labor was not merely a concession or an extra-Islamic practice, but a basic religious responsibility.

What did this authoritative model look like in practice? As Abu ʿAmmar explained, "the meaning of masculinity (*al-rujūla*) is not for the man to dominate his wife ... so that she feels his power and tyranny (*quwatihi wa jabrūtihi*) ... rather, masculinity is found in a man's ability to submerge his wife in tenderness, love, and mercy (*bi-ḥanānihi wa maḥabatihi wa raḥmatihi*)."[90] Speaking rhetorically, Abu ʿAmmar asks his male reader:

Dear brother, how would it hurt you to help your wife when she is sick or exhausted from the burdens of maintaining the home (*min aʿbā al-manzal*) ...

85 Rida, *Buyut Bi-La Duyun*, 54. 86 Rida, *Buyut Bi-La Duyun*, 84.
87 Rida, *Buyut Bi-La Duyun*, 173.
88 Al-Misri's lectures are featured on Ansar al-Sunna al-Muhamadiyya's website, and Maktabat al-Safa is a well-known publisher of Salafi authors. For Ansar al-Sunna's website, see "Mahmud al-Masri," *Ansar al-Sunna al-Muhamadiyya*, available at www.ansarsonna.com/category/الدروس-والخطب-المرئية/محمود-المصري/, accessed 13 March 2017.
89 Mahmud al-Misri Abu ʿAmmar, *al-Zawaj al-Islami al-Saʿid* (Cairo: Maktabat al-Safa, 2006), 619.
90 Abu ʿAmmar, *al-Zawaj al-Islami al-Saʿid*, 619.

> [how would it hurt you] to yourself prepare a meal or to help her in housework (*'amal min a'māl al-bayt*) . . . do not think that I am asking you to do this indefinitely . . . Such a task would be impossible for anyone (*hadha shay lā yastaṭī'ahu aḥadan*) due to [men's] limited time . . . and lest your the wife think that you are responsible for working both within and outside the home.[91]

Notwithstanding Abu 'Ammar's qualification that male domestic labor is a temporary endeavor, the basic structural conditions on which it depended are hardly temporary in contemporary Egypt.

The distinction between religious ideal and sociological reality is even clearer in Akram Rida's 2008 work *Rifqa bi-l-Qawarir* (Be Gentle to Women). Moving from his previous focus on economic efficiency to a more direct engagement with domestic gender roles, Rida argues that women's responsibility for "household affairs" (*shu'ūn al-bayt*) proceeds from the conscious decision of a woman to stay at home and for her husband to work outside the home rather than from her obligation to her husband to perform these duties (*ḥaqq al-zawj 'alā zawjatihi fī khidmat al-bayt wa-l-qiyām bi-shu'ūnihi*).[92] Accordingly, if a husband wishes for his home to function in a particular fashion while his wife chooses to work, he is obligated to not only purchase the relevant home appliances,[93] but also to either provide his wife with domestic help or to help her himself.[94] As men and women worked outside the home, Brotherhood and Salafi expectations of domestic labor were shifting in halting yet unmistakable ways.

Conclusion

While, at the dawn of the Islamic Revival, Muslim Brothers and Salafis sought to alert Egyptian society to the danger of women's public presence, by 2011 the question was how these same women could serve the Revival's cause by shaping society. Far from being a story of growing social conservatism restricting women to the home, modesty and expanded female prominence in both the workplace and Islamist and Salafi movements arose in tandem. The emergence of women as

91 Abu 'Ammar, *al-Zawaj al-Islami al-Sa'id*, 620.
92 Akram Rida, *Rifqa bi-l-Qawarir: al-'Ishra fi al-Bayt al-Muslim bayna al-Mawadda wa-l-Rahma* (Cairo: al-Andalus al-Jadida, 2008), 38.
93 Rida, *Rifqa bi-l-Qawarir*, 47. 94 Rida, *Rifqa bi-l-Qawarir*, 50–52.

key objects and agents of change, however, would not alter a basic dynamic by which male (religious) elites regulated female bodies.

What can this story tell us about the broader negotiation of religion and politics in contemporary Egypt? As in the 1970s, the story of religious change is not only about state power but also about daily life. As under al-Sadat, political adversaries continue to be intellectual bedfellows: While Brotherhood and Salafi efforts to form an Islamic society have successfully introduced alternative models of Islamic piety, their key concerns and themes were deeply shaped by a longer history of modernist order and discipline, the Secular Nationalist project of State Feminism, and dialogue with Statist and Liberal competitors. While normatively opposed, perhaps even irreconcilably so, these groups are intellectual cousins, joined at the hip by a shared belief that male religious elites can and should regulate individual comportment, and that women are objects and agents of religious change.

Far from being a story of an Islamist opposition driving a close tie between religion and politics closer, the ultimate story of Egypt's Islamic Revival is about the mutual interdependence and influence of the top-down religious ambitions of Statist institutions, the broad-based grassroots mobilization of Islamic movements, and their sometimes overlapping constituencies. While the 1970s saw Egypt's Islamist opposition successfully utilize modernist logic to entrench their projects within state institutions, the following three decades would see the logic of a Secular Nationalist project, State Feminism, come to define, rather than merely facilitate, the consolidation of the Revival. An Islamic revival that arose via calls for women to turn away from public space was consolidated through their entrenchment in precisely this space.

Conclusion

Religious Revival between the Local, National, and Regional

Egypt's Islamic Revival arose in the shadow of a détente between Anwar al-Sadat and the Muslim Brotherhood following the ideological polarization and political repression of ʿAbd al-Nasir's rule. Egypt's Islamist opposition found increasing room to operate under Hosni Mubarak between 1981 and 2011, and was joined by Statist institutions and Liberal Islamic intellectuals in defining the precise contours of the Revival. The ideological polarization of the post-2011 period, however, threatens to overshadow the shared history of the preceding four decades.

Over the past seven years Egypt's political landscape has veered between diametrically opposed leaders and ideological claims. From revolt against Mubarak to Mursi to al-Sisi, every choice seemed to present an alternative, whether it is the revolutionary chant of "Egypt for Egyptians" (*Miṣr l-il-Miṣriyyīn*), Mursi's "Islamic renaissance" (*nahḍa islāmiyya*), or a return to the pre-revolutionary status quo and promises of an "Islamic revolution" (*thawra islāmiyya*) under the Brigadier-General-turned-President, ʿAbd al-Fattah al-Sisi. Most tumultuous was the year between Mursi's election on 30 June 2012 and the 3 July 2013 coup. While in February 2013 Islamists had been excited to talk and optimistic about the future, by June 2014 al-Sisi had spearheaded a successful campaign to categorize all-Islamists as "terrorists."[1]

Al-Sisi's decision to place the Brotherhood beyond the pale politically and to outlaw it legally exacerbated tensions within an already polarized landscape. Indeed, when I contacted Badr Muhammad Badr, the former editor of the Youth and Student News (Akhbar al-Shabab wa-l-Jamiʿat)

[1] For the longer-term roots of this polarized discourse by which Islamists are uniformly constructed as "terrorists," see Walter Armbrust, "Media Review: *al-Daʿiyya* (The Preacher)," *Journal of the American Academy of Religion*, 82:3 (Sept. 2014), 841–56.

section of al-*Da'wa*, via Facebook to set up a follow-up phone conversation, he explained that his garage had suffered an arson attack several weeks earlier, and that he no longer used his phone. A burnt garage was only the tip of the iceberg: the August 2013 massacre of hundreds at Raba'a al-'Adawiyya mosque and the imprisonment of thousands of Muslim Brothers made it clear that there was little room for the Brotherhood to participate in Egyptian politics or society. In turn, a group identifying itself as the local branch of ISIS has taken to attacking government officials, naval ships, foreign embassies, and possibly even a Russian civilian plane. A minority voice within the Islamist movement has thus become its most active faction as Muslim Brothers (including Badr) sit in prison and Salafis struggle to balance political accommodation and religious principle. While the choice between al-Sisi and Islamism was not initially one of security over terror, the former's policies created a self-fulfilling prophecy.

These political tremors derailed the research of many of my colleagues. My project, by contrast, was less vulnerable to political vicissitudes, depending not on sustained access to Brotherhood or Salafi leaders, or to state institutions, but on print media that few saw as politically contentious. Once I had acquired the bulk of this material – whether at the Egyptian National Archives (Dar al-Kutub), the 'Azbakiyya Book Market in Cairo, the Moshe Dayan Center Media Arabic Press Archive at Tel Aviv University, Princeton's Firestone Library, or Columbia University's Butler Library – I could begin to tell a story of the religious contestation and pious practice that had emerged in the early years of the Islamic Revival. As the cooperation of this period grew more distant in the face of a violent polarization of Egyptian public discourse over Islam after 25 January 2011, the events of the 1970s became even more crucial to understanding negotiations of Islam in contemporary Egypt.

This book has told a story of the rise of the Islamic Revival that challenges depictions of this shift as either an exclusive story of the Islamist movement or as a "return" to piety in response to the 1967 war based on a diachronic tradition of Islamic ethics. Instead, novel models of religious thought and practice – distinguished by practices of and structures to facilitate religious education, the collective regular performance of the *ẓuhr* prayer, and self-consciously Islamic norms of public comportment – would emerge through intellectual cross-pollination, competition, and even cooperation among Statist and Islamist religious elites, and their local constituencies, between 1976 and 1981.

A focus on both Statist institutions and Islamist organizations reveals the analytical limitations of mapping the state–society division along the axis of religio-political regulation and change. Put differently, this story of the Revival's rise and consolidation suggests that religious change does not emerge from society to challenge limits enforced by the state. Instead, this turn to Islam emerged at key sites of intersection between state and society, including bureaucratic offices, schools, mass transportation, or the streets of Cairo, Alexandria, the Nile Delta, and Upper Egypt. Reorienting our gaze to the spaces in which projects of piety are born and lived reveals a complex story of religious change that challenges previous divisions between state and society, conflations of the regime and state institutions, and assumptions of uniformity within the Islamist opposition.

This methodological move helps to shape more nuanced understandings of an Islamic Revival that includes pious participants with varying political allegiances. While it shows significant overlap between those who turned to Statist institutions and those who embraced Islamist organizations when it comes to questions of religious obligation and practice, it also highlights divergent political approaches. Crucially, piety and either implicit or explicit support for the (non-Islamist) status quo can go hand in hand; the Quietist Salafis who performed the *zuhr* prayer for decades without politicizing it are no less committed to the project of mass religiosity than their Islamist competitors. Nevertheless, the ranks of the politically quietist pious extend beyond the Salafis to those who participated in Statist projects of religious respectability. Instead of considering the latter as somehow unprincipled or mere apologists, this study takes seriously the rise of a movement that dedicates itself to Statist visions of Islam and opposes Islamism. Religious principle can be lived not merely through resistance to an unjust regime, but also through attempts to morally shape society under the leadership of state-aligned scholars and intellectuals.

Conversely, Statist and Islamist projects emerge not only through cross-pollination among elites, but also through and between a dialogue between these elites and local constituencies. Complicating SMT studies that depict a "framing" process that is both conceptually and chronologically prior to mobilization, this study suggests that the frames themselves are formed at the intersection of elite programmatic visions and local practice. Neither can we separate these frames from broader intellectual trends: while the existing literature highlights the importance of neighborhood outreach and leading Islamist thinkers, participants in these projects are neither ideologically nor sociologically sealed. Instead, projects of piety were intimately linked to the particular conditions of the state institutions in which they arose, the longer history of modernist conceptions of time and order that structured these institutions, and the unexpected ways in which ideas and people move across supposedly clear-cut political and religious borders.

A practice-centered history of the Islamic Revival also reveals how the spread of competing projects of religious respectability produced a highly classed and gendered religious sphere in which ostensibly direct obedience to divine writ renders sustained critiques of class and gender impossible. The normativity of piety – whether education, ritual practice, or modesty – has continued to place the burdens of class on the shoulders of a middle class whose purchasing power has declined, and particularly on those women within it who bear disproportionate responsibilities. While religious elites offer short-term solutions – such as limited economic redistribution through *zakāt*, subsidized modest dress and books, gender-segregated subway cars, or regular prayer spaces – they lack the economic resources to fundamentally ease the burdens of piety or the politics of gender that structure them. Yet these participants are nonetheless privileged: the pious social respectability to which they lay claim is only available to those with sufficient literacy to purchase and read pamphlets and periodicals. These strictures affect even those who don't wish to participate: the choice is no longer to educate oneself religiously, pray, or veil, but rather to abstain from these practices.

This examination of religious change at the intersection of state institutions, Islamic movements, and local practice necessitates reconsidering Islamism as an analytic category. The solution is not simply to note the existence of competing religious claims by Statist institutions and Islamist movements. This approach, though it illustrates the diversity of contemporary contestations of Islam and politics, is primarily descriptive. Instead, we must understand Statist and Islamist claims in relational fashion: each is engaged in a religious project that draws on modernist state-sponsored conceptions of order and discipline, even as it makes selective use of the Islamic scholarly tradition. It is only by considering these projects as ideologically and spatially linked that we can appreciate the influence of each on the contemporary Middle East and the political game by which each seeks to obscure its ties to the other.

This approach also necessitates a reconsideration of Salafism and its relationship to the commonly used category "the Islamic opposition." While hybrid organizations such as the Jam'iyya Shar'iyya share the Muslim Brotherhood's approach to religious change with some within their ranks adhering to a distinctly Salafi approach to questions of theology and ritual practice, Quietist Salafi movements such as Ansar al-Sunna explicitly distance themselves from association with the kind of direct challenges to state authority and focus on state power characteristic of the Brotherhood. Put differently, Salafis only represent part of an Islamist opposition when they embrace the Brotherhood's approach to change; Quietist Salafis, by contrast, have as much in common with their quietist Statist counterparts (and the latter's commitment to advising the ruler) as they do with the Muslim Brotherhood.

It is a peculiar legacy of the Islamic Revival that social dominance, combined with a self-perception by both Statist and Islamist actors that they work in parallel universes, has begotten historical amnesia. Instead of being perceived as the collaborative labor of leading religious factions of the period, whether Statist or Islamist, the Revival is seen as the product of a fully formed and self-evident turn to Islam. It is in this context that Brothers, Salafis, and al-Sisi share religious references and commitments. Islamists no longer have an unmistakable upper hand; indeed, the question isn't whether al-Sisi prays, but where. Even more notable, however, is the transformation of Egypt's first lady: while both Jihan al-Sadat and Suzanne Mubarak consciously fashioned themselves as "Westernized" and left their heads uncovered, al-Sisi's wife Intisar 'Amer (like Mursi's wife, Najla Mahmud) dons the hijab.[2]

Indeed, the multiplication of claimants to Islam, part and parcel of the spread of the Islamic Revival, has challenged the Brotherhood's previous preeminent position. The speed with which Egyptians turned against the Muslim Brotherhood in June 2013 thus becomes easier to understand: at stake was not the election of an outwardly pious leader,

[2] Such a shift is the more notable given the historic marginalization of all pious markers from Egyptian media and culture. For more on this point with regard to films, see Walter Armbrust, "Islamists in Egyptian Cinema," *American Anthropologist*, 104:3 (2002), 922–30.

but rather which pious leader could govern Egypt's fractious political system. Political contestation in post-Mubarak Egypt – whether Mursi's rise and fall or al-Sisi's ascent – becomes legible when we foreground the changing goalposts of religiosity that have come to define Egyptian society.[3]

A shared history of Statist institutions and Islamist organizations and the ways in which they sought to mobilize and shape Egyptians who made their way through state institutions stands at the heart of the emergence of the Islamic Revival in Egypt. This story, however, is not limited to Egypt; rather, it speaks to the ways in which competition between Islamic movements and nation-states across the Middle East and South Asia to mobilize populations to piety has driven and will continue to drive an increasingly close tie between religion and politics across state and society.

[3] This is not to suggest, however, that all those Egyptians who live within post-Revival Egypt participate in a wholly coherent fashion. Instead, the demands of piety set forth by this shift in religious practice – and the social normativity of such piety – have produced their own contradictions. See Schielke, "Ambivalent Commitments." Indeed, the social dominance of the Revival broadly shapes not merely the processes of subject formation among its participants but also the articulations of "non-belief" among those who situate themselves outside its ranks. See Samuli Schielke, "Being a Nonbeliever in a Time of Islamic Revival: Trajectories of Doubt and Certainty in Contemporary Egypt," *International Journal of Middle East Studies*, 44:2 (2012), 301–20.

Bibliography

Arabic-Language Periodicals

Jaridat al-Ikhwan al-Muslimin (Cairo: Tantawi al-Jawhari, 1933–37, 1943–46, 1954).
Majallat al-Azhar (Cairo: Islamic Research Academy, 1933–81).
Majallat al-Da'wa (Cairo: Dar al-Da'wa, 1951–54, 1976–81).
Majallat al-Fath (Cairo: al-Maktaba al-Salafiyya, 1926–43).
Majallat al-Hadi a-Nabawi (Cairo: Ansar al-Sunna al-Muhammadiyya, 1936–69).
Majallat al-I'tisam (Cairo: Dar al-I'tisam, 1969–81, 1983–90).
Majallat al-Manar (Cairo: Dar al-Manar, 1898–1935).
Majallat Minbar al-Islam (Cairo: Supreme Council for Islamic Affairs, 1970–81).
Majallat al-Mujtama' (Kuwait City: Jam'iyyat al-Islah al-Ijtima'i, 1970–81).
Majallat al-Tamaddun al-Islami (Cairo: Jam'iyyat al-Tamaddun al-Islami, 1936–81).
Majallat al-Tawhid (Cairo: Ansar al-Sunnaa al-Muhammadiyya 1973–91).
Majallat al-Wa'i al-Islami (Kuwait City: Ministry of Justice, Endowments, and Islamic Affairs, 1970–81).

Television

al-Sha'rawi, Muhammad Mutwalli. *Khawatir al-Sha'rawi*. Prod. 'Abd Al-Mun'im Mahmud. Channel 1. Cairo, 18 July 1980–18 September 1981, television (98 episodes in total, 45 min each).

Audiocassette Sermons

Kishk, 'Abd al-Hamid.

Ahmad Ibn Hanbal. Rec. 25 March 1977. N.D. Cassette. (#9).
al-Badn al-Sabir wa-l-Zawja al-Muti'a. 24 May 1980. N.D. Cassette. (#36).

Fi Rihab Surat al-Qalam. 12 May 1978. N.D. Cassette. (#143).
Hafl Takhrij Adam. Rec. 27 March 1981. N.D. Cassette. (#157).
al-Hikma al-Ilahiyya fi Dhikr Qissas al-Anbiya fi al-Quran al-Karim. Rec. 6 February 1981. N.D. Cassette. (#281).
Hukm al-Islam fi al-'Ada al-Siriyya. 13 October 1978. N.D. Cassette. (#161).
al-'Ibra min Qissat Nuh 'Alayhi al-Salam. 6 March 1981. N.D. Cassette. (#270).
Janib al-'Ibra wa Janib al-Maw'iza fi Qissas al-Anbiya fi al-Quran. 27 February 1981. N.D. Cassette. (#148).
Kayfa Nafham al-Islam? 28 December 1979. N.D. Cassette. (#254).
Malikat Shabaa. Rec. 6 May 1977. N.D. Cassette. (#306).
Muhakamat al-Khalil Ibrahim. 2 November 1979. N.D. Cassette. (#2).
al-Qarar al-Ilahi al-Thalith. 3 April 1981. N.D. Cassette. (#359).
Qissat Ayyub 'Alayhi al-Salam. Rec. 10 June 1977. N.D. Cassette. (#261).
Sharh Hadith "Sab'a La Yuzzilluhum Allah fi Zillihi." 22 February 1980. N.D. Cassette. (#197).
al-Shart al-Khamis min Shurut Qubul al-Salat. 28 September 1979. N.D. Cassette. (#382).
al-Shart al-Rabi' min Shurut Qubul al-Salat. 21 September 1979. N.D. Cassette. (#381).
al-Shart al-Thalith min Shurut Qubul al-Salat. 14 September 1979. N.D. Cassette. (#380).
al-Shart al-Thani min Shurut Qubul al-Salat. 7 September 1979. N.D. Cassette. (#379).
Ta'at Allah wa Rasulahu. 28 March 1980. N.D. Cassette. (#235).

All sermons are available online on archive.org (numbers in parentheses correspond to website), https://archive.org/details/Abdel-Hamid_Kichk_Mawsoaa_Mp3_uP_bY_mUSLEm. Each sermon runs roughly ninety minutes. Dates are derived from an abridged written version of the sermons. See 'Abd al-Hamid Kishk, *al-Khutab al-Minbariyya li-Fadilat al-Shaykh 'Abd al-Hamid Kishk* (Cairo: Maktabat al-Sihafa, 2011), vols. I–XII, XVI.

Interviews

Badr, Badr Muhammad. Personal interview. Cairo: 24 February 2013.
Personal interview. Cairo: 26 February 2013.
Bashandi, 'Abd al-Salam. Personal interview. Cairo: 20 February 2013.
Hassan, Muhammad. Personal interview. Cairo: 20 February 2013.
Khafaji, 'Adil Rafi'i. Personal interview. Cairo: 26 February 2013.
Madbuli, Muhammad. Personal interview. Cairo: 24 February 2013.
Personal interview. Cairo: 28 February 2013.

Video Memoirs

al-Duktur Hisham al-Suli Mas'ul Ikhwan al-Isma'iliyya Ma'a Dhikrayat Jil al-Sab'inat. Perf. Hisham al-Suli, 2009. www.Ikhwantube.com.

Hadith Dhikrayat Ma'a al-Duktur Usama Nasr 'Adu Maktab al-Irshad ... Yuhadithuna 'an Mishwar Hayatihi Ma'a Da'wat al-Ikhwan al-Juz'a al-Awwal. Perf. Usama Nasr, 2010. www.Ikhwantube.com.

Hadith Dhikrayat Ma'a Khalid 'Abd al-Qadir 'Awda. Perf. Khalid 'Abd al-Qadir 'Awda. Ikhwantube, 2010. www.Ikhwantube.com.

Hadith Ma'a al-Duktur 'Ali Ahmad 'Umran ... wa Dhikrayatahu Ma'a Jama'at al-Ikhwan wa Ta'sis Da'wat al-Ikhwan bi-l-Minya. Perf. 'Ali Ahmad 'Umran, 2010. www.Ikhwantube.com.

Muhammad 'Abd al-Mun'im wa Tarikh Da'wat al-Ikhwan bi-l-Iskandariya al-Juz'a al-Awwal. Perf. Muhammad 'Abd al-Mun'im, 2010. www.Ikhwantube.com.

Sayyid al-Nuzayli wa Hadith 'an Dhikrayathu Ma'a Jama'at al-Ikhwan al-Juz'a al-Thalith. Perf. Sayyid al-Nuzayli, 2009. www.Ikhwantube.com.

Secondary Sources

Abaza, Mona. *Changing Consumer Cultures of Modern Egypt: Cairo's Urban Reshaping* (Boston: Brill, 2006).

'Abd al-'Azim, Sa'id. *al-Nazra Sahm min Sihham Iblis* (RAM, 46 minutes, available at www.anasalafy.com/play.php?catsmktba=10874, accessed 13 March 2017).

'Abd al-Ma'bud, Mustafa Mu'wad. *Fitnat al-Mar'a: Bayna al-Ikhtilat wa Sadd al-Dhari'a fi al-Fikr al-'Arabi al-Mu'asir* (Cairo: Dar al-Shams, 2004).

Abdel-Fadil, Mahmoud. *The Political Economy of Nasserism: A Study in Employment and Income Distribution Policies in Urban Egypt, 1952–72* (Cambridge: Cambridge University Press, 1980).

Abou el Fadl, Khaled. *Speaking in God's Name: Islamic Law, Authority and Women* (London: Oneworld Publications, 2014).

Abu 'Ammar, Mahmud al-Misri. *al-Zawaj al-Islami al-Sa'id* (Cairo: Maktabat al-Safa, 2006).

Abu-l-Futuh, 'Abd al-Mun'im. *'Abd al-Mun'im Abu-l-Futuh: Shahid 'ala Tarikh al-Haraka al-Islamiyya fi Misr, 1970–1984*, ed. Hussam Tammam (Cairo: Dar al-Shuruq, 2012).

Abu-Lughod, Lila. *Dramas of Nationhood: The Politics of Television in Egypt* (Chicago: University of Chicago Press, 2005).

"The Marriage of Feminism and Islamism in Egypt: Selective Repudiation as a Dynamic of Postcolonial Cultural Politics," in Lila Abu-Lughod (ed.), *Remaking Women: Feminism and Modernity in the Middle East* (Princeton: Princeton University Press, 1998), 243–69.

Veiled Sentiments: Honor and Poetry in a Bedouin Society (Oakland: University of California Press, 2016).

Afghani, Jamal al-Din and Muhammad ʿAbduh. *al-ʿUrwa al-Wuthqa: al-Athar al-Kamila*, ed. Hadi Khasru Shahi (Cairo: Maktabat al-Shuruq, 2002).

Agrama, Hussein Ali. *Questioning Secularism: Islam, Sovereignty and the Rule of Law in Modern Egypt* (Chicago: University of Chicago Press, 2012).

Ahmed, Jamal Mohammed. *The Intellectual Origins of Egyptian Nationalism* (Oxford: Oxford University Press, 1960).

Ahmed, Leila. *A Quiet Revolution: The Veil's Resurgence from the Middle East to America* (London: Yale University Press, 2011).

Ajami, Fouad. *The Arab Predicament: Arab Political Thought and Practice since 1967* (Cambridge: Cambridge University Press, 1992).

Alam, Anwar. *Religion and State: Egypt, Iran and Saudi Arabia* (Delhi: Gyan Sagar Publications, 1998).

al-Albani, Muhammad Nasr al-Din. *Hijab al-Mar'a al-Muslima fi al-Kitab wa-l-Sunna* (Cairo: al-Matbaʿa al-Salafiyya, 1374 H [1951]).

Al-Jazeera. "ElBaradei Claims 'Smear Campaign'," *Al Jazeera English*. Al Jazeera, 4 Sept. 2010, available at www.aljazeera.com/news/middleeast/2010/09/201094171456896412.html.

Amin, Hussayn Ahmad. *Hawl al-Daʿwa ila Tatbiq al-Shariʿa al-Islamiyya wa Dirasat Islamiyya Ukhra* (Cairo: Dar Suʿad al-Sabbah, 1992).

Anderson, Benedict. *Imagined Communities: Reflections on the Origin and Spread of Nationalism* (New York: Verso, 1991).

Anderson, Jon W. "Social Structure and the Veil: Comportment and the Composition of Interaction in Afghanistan," *Anthropos*, 77 (1982), 397–420.

Antoun, Richard. "On the Modesty of Women in Arab Muslim Villages: A Study in the Accommodation of Traditions," *American Anthropologist*, NS, 70:4 (Aug. 1968), 671–97.

Aran, Gideon. "Jewish Zionist Fundamentalism: The Bloc of the Faithful in Israel (Gush Emunim)," in Martin E. Marty and R. Scott Appleby (eds.), *Fundamentalisms Observed* (Chicago: University of Chicago Press, 1991), 265–344.

Kukizm: Shorshe Gush Emunim, Tarbut Hamitnahalim, Te'logya Tsiyonit, Meshihiyut bi-Zemanenu (Jerusalem: Karmel, 2013).

al-Arian, Abdullah. *Answering the Call: Popular Islamic Activism in Sadat's Egypt* (Oxford and New York: Oxford University Press, 2014).

Arjomand, Said Amir. *The Turban for the Crown: The Islamic Revolution in Iran* (New York: Oxford University Press, 1988).

Armbrust, Walter. "Islamists in Egyptian Cinema," *American Anthropologist*, 104:3 (2002), 922–30.

Mass Culture and Modernism in Egypt (Cambridge: Cambridge University Press, 1994).

"Media Review: *al-Da'iyya* (The Preacher)," *Journal of the American Academy of Religion*, 82:3 (Sept. 2014), 841–56.

Asad, Talal. *Genealogies of Religion: Discipline and Reasons of Power in Christianity and Islam* (Baltimore: Johns Hopkins University Press, 1993).

Formations of the Secular: Christianity, Islam, Modernity (Stanford: Stanford University Press, 2003).

Atiyeh, George. *The Book in the Islamic World: The Written Word and Communication in the Middle East* (Albany: State University of New York, Press, 1995).

al-'Awadi, Hisham. *In Pursuit of Legitimacy: The Muslim Brothers and Mubarak, 1982–2000* (New York: I. B. Tauris, 2004).

Ayalon, Ami. *The Press in the Arab Middle East* (New York: Oxford University Press, 1995).

Ayubi, Nazih M. *Bureaucracy and Politics in Contemporary Egypt* (London: Ithaca Press, 1980).

Badr, Badr Muhammad. *Sutur min Hayat al-Da'iyya al-Rabbani 'Umar al-Tilmisani* (Cairo: n.p.: n.d.).

al-Banna, Hasan, *al-Mar'a al-Muslima*, ed. Muhammad Nasr al-Din al-Albani (Cairo: Dar al-Kutub al-Salafiyya, 1987).

Nazarat fi Kitab Allah (Cairo: Dar al-Tawzi' wa-l-Nashr al-Islamiyya, 2002).

"al-Risala al-Ula: al-Mar'a al-Muslima," in *al-Mar'a al-Muslima*, ed. Muhammad Nasr al-Din al-Albani (Cairo: Dar al-Kutub al-Salafiyya, 1987), 1–22.

al-Banna, Jamal. *al-Mar'a al-Muslima bayna Tahrir al-Qur'an wa Taqayyud al-Fuqaha* (Cairo: Dar al-Fikr al-Islami, 1998).

Barak, On. *On Time: Technology and Temporality in Modern Egypt* (Berkeley: University of California Press, 2013).

Baron, Beth. *Egypt as a Woman: Nationalism, Gender and Politics* (Berkeley: University of California Press, 2005).

The Orphan Scandal: Christian Missionaries and the Rise of the Muslim Brotherhood (Stanford: Stanford University Press, 2014).

The Women's Awakening in Egypt (New Haven: Yale University Press, 1997).

Bayat, Asef. *Making Islam Democratic: Social Movements and the Post-Islamist Turn* (Stanford: Stanford University Press, 2007).

Bearman, P. T. Bianquis, C. E. Bosworth, E. van Donzel, and W. P. Heinrichs, eds. *Encyclopedia of Islam*, Brill Online, 2013.

Beattie, Kirk J. *Egypt during the Sadat Years* (New York: Palgrave Macmillan, 2000).

Beck, Colin J. "State Building as a Source of Islamic Political Organization," *Sociological Forum*, 24:2 (2009), 337–56.

Beetham, Margaret. "Towards a Theory of Periodical Publishing as a Genre," in Laurel Brake, Aled Jones, and Lionel Madden (eds.), *Investigating Victorian Journalism* (New York: St. Martin's, 1990), 19–32.

Beinin, Joel and Joe Stork (eds.). *Political Islam: Essays from Middle East Report* (Berkeley: University of California Press, 1997).

Bergerand, Maurits and Nadia Sonneveld. "Sharia and National Law in Egypt," in Michiel Otto (ed.), *Sharia Incorporated: A Comparative Overview of the Legal Systems of Twelve Muslim Countries in past and Present* (Leiden: Leiden University Press, 2010), 51–88.

Berkey, Jonathan. *Population Preaching and Religious Authority in the Medieval Islamic Near East* (Seattle: University of Washington Press, 2001).

Bier, Laura. *Revolutionary Womanhood* (Stanford: Stanford University Press, 2011).

Billig, Michael. *Banal Nationalism* (London: Sage Publications, 1995).

Bint ʿAbd Allah, al-Zahra Fatima. *al-Mutabarrijat* (Cairo: Maktabat al-Sunna, 1987).

Bourdieu, Pierre. "The Forms of Capital," in A. H. Halsey, Philip Brown, Hugh Lauder, and Amy S. Wells (eds.), *Education, Culture, Economy and Society* (New York: Oxford University Press, 1997), 46–58.

Bringa, Tone. *Being Muslim the Bosnian Way: Identity and Community in a Central Bosnian Village* (Princeton: Princeton University Press, 1995).

Brooke, Steven and Neil Ketchley. "Social and Institutional Origins of Political Islam," *American Political Science Review*, 112:2 (May 2018), 376–94.

Brown, Daniel W. *Rethinking Tradition in Modern Islamic Thought* (Cambridge: Cambridge University Press, 1999).

Brown, Nathan. "Shariʿa and State in the Modern Middle East," *International Journal of Middle East Studies*, 29:3 (1997), 359–76.

Campo, Juan Eduardo. "Domestications of Islam in Modern Egypt: A Cultural Analysis," in Chiara Briganti and Kathy Mezei (eds.), *The*

Domestic Space Reader (Toronto: University of Toronto Press, 2012), 40–44.

Central Agency for Public Mobilization and Statistics. *1976 Population and Housing Census* (Cairo: Central Agency for Public Mobilization and Statistics, 1980), vol. I.

al-Ihsa'at al-Thaqafiyya: al-Idha'a wa-l-Sihafa 1969 (Cairo: Central Agency for Public Mobilization and Statistics, 1970).

al-Ihsa'at al-Thaqafiyya: al-Idha'a wa-l-Sihafa 1979 (Cairo: Central Agency for Public Mobilization and Statistics, 1983).

Preliminary Results of the Population, Housing and Establishment Census of 1986 (Cairo: Central Agency for Public Mobilization and Statistics, 1987).

Statistical Yearbook: Arab Republic of Egypt 1952–1974 (Cairo: Central Agency for Public Mobilization and Statistics, 1975).

Statistical Yearbook: Arab Republic of Egypt 1952–1979 (Cairo: Central Agency for Public Mobilization and Statistics, 1983).

Cesari, Jocelyne. *The Awakening of Muslim Democracy: Religion, Modernity and the State* (Cambridge: Cambridge University Press, 2014).

Chartier, Roger. "The Biblioteque Blue and Popular Reading," in *The Cultural Uses of Print in Early Modern France*, trans. Lydia G. Cochrane (Princeton: Princeton University Press, 1988), 240–64.

"Texts, Printing, Readings," in Lynn Hunt (ed.), *The New Cultural History* (London: University of California Press, 1989), 154–75.

Clark, Janine A. *Islam, Charity and Activism: Middle-Class Networks and Social Welfare in Egypt, Jordan and Yemen* (Bloomington: Indiana University Press, 2004).

Cook, Michael. *Ancient Religions, Modern Politics: The Islamic Case in Comparative Perspective* (Princeton: Princeton University Press, 2014).

Commanding Right and Forbidding Wrong in Islamic Thought (Cambridge and New York: Cambridge University Press, 2004).

Cook, Steven. *The Struggle for Egypt: From Nasser to Tahrir Square* (New York: Oxford University Press, 2012).

Dallal, Ahmad. "The Origins and Objectives of Islamic Revivalist Thought, 1750–1850," *Journal of the American Oriental Society*, 113:3 (Jul.–Sept. 1993), 341–59.

Darnton, Robert. "First Steps Toward a History of Reading," in *The Kiss of Lamourette: Reflections in Cultural History* (New York: W. W. Norton, 1990), 154–90.

Dasuqi, 'Abduh Mustafa and al-Sa'id Ramadan 'Abbadi. *Tarikh al-Haraka al-Tullabiyya bi-Jama'at al-Ikhwan al-Muslimin 1933–2011* (Cairo: Mu'assasat Iqra li-l-Nashr wa-l-Tawzi' wa-l-Tarjama, 2013).

Dawud, Muhammad ʿAbd al-ʿAziz. *al-Jamʿiyyat al-Islamiyya fi Misr wa Dawraha fi Nashr al-Daʿwa al-Islamiyya* (Cairo: al-Zahra l-il-Iʿlam al-ʿArabi, 1992).

Deeb, Lara. *An Enchanted Modern: Gender and Public Piety in Shiʿi Lebanon* (Princeton: Princeton University Press, 2006).

Doumato, Eleanor Abdella and Gregory Starrett (eds.). *Teaching Islam: Textbooks and Religion in the Middle East* (London: Lynne Rienner Publishers, 2007).

Eickelman, Dale and Armando Salvatore (eds.). *Public Islam and the Common Good* (London: Brill, 2004).

Eickelman, Dale and Jon Anderson. *New Media in the Muslim World: The Emerging Public Sphere* (Bloomington: Indiana University Press, 2003).

Eickelman, Dale F. and James Piscatori. *Muslim Politics* (Princeton: Princeton University Press, 1996).

Eisenstein, Elizabeth. *Print Culture and Enlightenment Thought* (Chapel Hill: Hanes Foundation, 1986).

Erlich, Haggai. *Students and University in Twentieth Century Egyptian Politics* (New York: Taylor & Francis, 2005).

Esposito, John. *Islam and Politics* (Syracuse: Syracuse University Press, 1998).

"Tradition and Modernization in Islam," in Charles Wei-hsun Fu and Gerhard E. Spiegler (eds.), *Movements and Issues in World Religions* (New York: Greenwood Press, 1987), 89–106.

Euben, Roxanne and Muhammad Qasim Zaman. *Princeton Readings in Islamist Thought* (Princeton: Princeton University Press, 2009).

Fahmy, Khaled. *All the Pasha's Men: Mehmed Ali, His Army and the Making of Modern Egypt* (Cairo: American University in Cairo Press, 2002).

Fahmy, Ninette S. *The Politics of Egypt: State–Society Relationship* (New York: RoutledgeCurzon, 2002).

Fahmy, Ziad. *Ordinary Egyptians: Creating the Modern Nation through Popular Culture* (Stanford: Stanford University Press, 2011).

Farag, Iman. "Private Lives, Public Affairs: The Uses of Adab," in Armando Salvatore (ed.), *Muslim Traditions and Modern Techniques of Power* (Münster: Lit Verlag, 2001), 93–120.

Farquhar, Michael. *Circuits of Faith: Migration, Education, and the Wahhabi Mission* (Stanford: Stanford University Press, 2016).

al-Finjari, Ahmad Shawqi. *al-Ikhtilat fi al-Din – fi al-Tarikh – fi ʿIlm al-Ijtimaʿa* (Cairo: al-Hayʾa al-Misriyya al-ʿAmma li-l-Kuttab, 1987).

Flippen, J. Brooks. *Jimmy Carter, the Politics of Family, and the Rise of the Religious Right* (London: University of Georgia Press, 2011).

Fourt, Maynard H. "A Survey of Printing Facilities in Egypt." Technical Assistance Division, Education Division, US Information Service (USIS), February 1978.

Friedan, Betty. *The Feminine Mystique* (New York: W. W. Norton & Company, 2013).
Fritzche, Peter. *Reading Berlin 1900* (Cambridge, MA: Harvard University Press, 1996).
Fyfe, Aileen. *Science and Salvation: Evangelical Popular Science Publishing in Victorian Britain* (Chicago: University of Chicago, 2004).
Gaffney, Patrick. "The Changing Voices of Islam: The Emergence of Professional Preachers in Contemporary Egypt," *Muslim World*, 81:1 (1991), 27–47.
The Prophet's Pulpit: Islamic Preaching in Contemporary Egypt (Berkeley: University of California Press, 1994).
Gauvain, Richard. *Salafi Ritual Purity: In the Presence of God* (London: Routledge, 2013).
Geertz, Clifford. *Islam Observed: Religious Development in Morocco and Indonesia*. (Chicago: University of Chicago Press, 1968).
Gellner, Ernest. *Muslim Society* (Cambridge: Cambridge University Press, 1981).
Gershoni, Israel and James P. Jankowski. *Redefining the Egyptian Nation, 1930–1945* (Cambridge: Cambridge University Press, 1995).
al-Ghazali, Muhammad. *Qadaya al-Mar'a al-Muslima bayna al-Taqalid al-Rakida wa-l-Wafida* (Cairo: Dar al-Shuruq, 1990).
al-Ghubashi, Shu'ayb. *Sihafat al-Ikhwan al-Muslimin: Dirasa fi-l-Usul wa-l-Funun* (Cairo: Dar al-Tawzi' wa-l-Nashr al-Islamiyya, 2004).
Gonzalez-Quijano, Yves. *Les gens du livre: édition et champ intellectuel dans l'Égypte républicaine* (Paris: Centre national de recherche scientifique, 1998).
Graham, William. "Traditionalism in Islam: An Essay in Interpretation," *Journal of Interdisciplinary History*, 23:3 (1993), 495–522.
Gribetz, Sarit Kattan. "Conceptions of Time and Rhythms of Daily Life in Rabbinic Literature, 200–600 CE" (unpublished dissertation, Princeton University, 2013).
el-Guindi, Fadwa. "Veiling Infitah with Muslim Ethic: Egypt's Contemporary Islamic Movement," *Social Problems*, 28:4 (1981), 465–85.
Haddad, Mahmoud. "Arab Religious Nationalism in the Colonial Era: Rereading Rashid Rida's Ideas on the Caliphate," *Journal of the American Oriental Society*, 117:2 (1997), 253–77.
Haddad, Yvonne. "Islamists and the 'Problem of Israel': The 1967 Awakening," *Middle East Journal*, 46:2 (Spring 1992), 266–85.
Haj, Samira. *Reconfiguring the Islamic Tradition: Reform, Rationality, and Modernity* (Stanford: Stanford University Press, 2009).
Hallaq, Wael B. *Authority, Continuity and Change in Islamic Law* (Cambridge: Cambridge University Press, 2004).

Halperin-Kaddari, Ruth. *Women in Israel: A State of their Own* (Philadelphia: University of Pennsylvania Press, 2004).

Hammani, Rema. "From Immodesty to Collaboration: Hamas, the Women's Movement, and National Identity in the Intifada," in Joel Beinin and Joe Stork (eds.), *Political Islam: Essays from Middle East Report* (Berkeley: University of California Press, 1997), 194–210.

Hamzah, Dyala. "Muhammad Rashid Rida or: The Importance of Being (a) Journalist," in Heike Bock, Jörg Feuchter, and Michi Knecht (eds.), *Religion and its Other: Secular and Sacral Concepts and Practices in Interaction* (New York: Campus, 2008), 40–63.

"From *'Ilm* to *Sihafa* or the Politics of the Public Interest (*Maslaha*): Muhammad Rashîd Rida and his Journal *al-Manar* (1898–1935)," in Dyala Hamzah (ed.), *The Making of the Arab Intellectual (1880–1960): Empire, Public Sphere and the Colonial Coordinates of Selfhood* (London: Routledge, 2012), 90–127.

Hasan, Darwish Mustafa. *Fasl al-Khitab fi Mas'alat al-Hijab wa-l-Niqab* (Cairo: Dar al-I'tisam, 1987).

Hasan, Salah al-Din. *al-Salafiyyun fi Misr* (Giza: Awraq li-l-Nashr wa-l-Tawzi', 2012).

Hassan, Mona. "Women Preaching for the Secular State: Official Female Preachers (Bayan Vaizler) in Contemporary Turkey," *International Journal of Middle East Studies*, 43:3 (August 2011), 451–73.

Hassan, Muhammad. *Tabarruj al-Hijab* (Cairo: Dar al-Fajr al-Jadid, 1987).

Hassan, Rasha Mohammad and Aliyaa Shoukry, *Sexual Harassment: From Verbal Harassment to Rape* (Cairo: Egyptian Center for Women's Rights, 2008), available at www.endvawnow.org/uploads/browser/files/ecrw_sexual_harassment_study_english.pdf.pdf.

Hatina, Meir. *'Ulama', Politics, and the Public Sphere* (Salt Lake City: University of Utah Press, 2010).

Hawwa, Sa'id. *Qawanin al-Bayt al-Muslim* (Cairo: Dar al-Salam, 1987).

Hayba, Muhammad Mansur Mahmud. *al-Sihafa al-Islamiyya fi Misr: Bayna 'Abd al-Nasir wa-l-Sadat* (Mansura: Dar al-Wafa l-il-Tiba'a wa-l-Nashr wa-l-Tawzi', 1990).

Haykel, Bernard. "On the Nature of Salafi Thought and Action," in Roel Meijer (ed.), *Global Salafism: Islam's New Religious Movement* (New York: Columbia University Press, 2009), 33–57.

Helfont, Samuel. *Compulsion in Religion: Saddam Hussein, Islam, and the Roots of Insurgencies in Iraq* (Oxford: Oxford University Press, 2018).

Hertog, Steffen. *Princes, Brokers, and Bureaucrats: Oil and the State in Saudi Arabia* (London: Cornell University Press, 2010).

Hijazi, Muhammad Mahmud. *al-Tafsir al-Wadih* (Cairo: Dar al-Fikr al-'Arabi, 1969).

Hilmi, Ahmad Shalabi and ʿAbd al-ʿAzim Muhammad Ibrahim Ramadan. *Fusul min Tarikh Harakat al-Islah al-Ijtimaʿi fi Misr: Dirasa ʿan Dawr al-Jamʿiyya al-Khayriyya al-Islamiyya* (Cairo: al-Hayʾa al-Misriyya al-ʿAmma li-l-Kuttab, 1988).

Hinnebusch, Raymond. *Egyptian Politics under Sadat: The Post-Populist Development of an Authoritarian-Modernizing State* (Cambridge: Cambridge University Press, 1985).

Hirschhorn, Sara Yael. *City on a Hilltop: American Jews and the Israeli Settler Movement* (Cambridge, MA: Harvard University Press, 2017).

Hirschkind, Charles. *The Ethical Soundscape: Cassette Sermons and Islamic Counterpublic* (New York: Columbia University Press, 2004).

Hoffman-Ladd, Valerie. "Polemics on the Modesty and Segregation of Women in Contemporary Egypt," *International Journal of Middle East Studies*, 19:1 (1987), 23–50.

Hoodfar, Homa. "Return to the Veil: Personal Strategy and Public Participation in Egypt," in Nanneke Redclift and M. Thea Sinclair (eds.), *Working Women: International Perspectives on Labour and Gender Relations* (New York: Routledge, 1991), 105–26.

Hourani, Albert. *Arabic Thought in the Liberal Age, 1798–1939* (New York: Cambridge University Press, 1983).

Hull, Matthew S. *Government of Paper: The Materiality of Bureaucracy in Urban Pakistan* (Berkeley: University of California Press, 2012).

Huwayda, ʿAdil. "Harakat al-Islam al-Siyasi," in ʿAbd al-Ghaffar Shukr (ed.), *al-Jamʿiyyat al-Ahliyya al-Islamiyya fi Misr* (Cairo: Dar al-Amin li-l-Nashr wa-l-Tawziʿ, 2002), 39–72.

Ibn ʿArabi al-Hatimi al-Taʾi, Abu ʿAbd Allah Muhammad Ibn ʿAli Ibn Muhammad. *Tahdhib al-Akhlaq li-Ibn ʿArabi*, ed. ʿAbd al-Rahman Hasan Mahmud (Cairo: ʿAlam al-Fikr, 1986).

Ibn Kathir, Abu-l-Fada Ismail b. ʿUmar. *Tafsir al-Qurʾan al-ʿAzim* ed. Muhammad ʿAli Basyuni (Beirut: Dar al-Kutub al-ʿIlmiyya, 1999).

Tafsir al-Qurʾan al-ʿAzim, ed. Sami b. Muhammad al-Salama (Riyadh: Dar Tayba li-l-Nashr wa-l-Tawziʿ, 1999).

Ibrahim, Saad Eddin. *Egypt, Islam and Democracy: Twelve Critical Essays* (Cairo: American University in Cairo, 1996).

Ikram, Khald. *The Egyptian Economy, 1952–2000: Performance, Policies and Issues* (New York: Routledge, 2006).

Ismail, Salwa. *Rethinking Islamist Politics: Culture, the State and Islamism* (London: I. B. Tauris, 2006).

Ivanyi, Katharina Anna. "Virtue, Piety and Law: A Study of Birgivī Meḥmed Effendī's *al-Ṭarīqa al-Muḥamadiyya*" (unpublished dissertation, Princeton University, 2013).

al-Jahiz, Abu ʿUthman b. Bahar. *Tahdhib al-Akhlaq*, ed. Ibrahim b. Muhammad (Cairo: Maktabat al-Sahaba, 1989).

al-Jindi, Anwar. *Tarikh al-Sihafa al-Islamiyya* (Cairo: Dar al-Ansar, 1983).

Jouili, Jeanette S. *Pious Practice and Secular Constraints* (Stanford: Stanford University Press, 2015).

Kafafi, Husayn. *Ruʾya ʿAsriyya li-l-Mudun al-Sanaʿiyya fi Misr* (Cairo: Egyptian Public Institute for Books, 1985).

Kalmbach, Hilary. *Islamic Knowledge and the Making of Modern Egypt* (Cambridge: Cambridge University Press, forthcoming [2019]).

Kandil, Hazem. *Inside the Brotherhood* (Walden, MA: Polity, 2015).

Katz, Marion Holmes. *Women in the Mosque: A History of Legal Thought and Social Practice* (New York: Columbia University Press, 2014).

Kazim, Safinaz. *Fi Masʾalat al-Sufur wa-l-Hijab* (Cairo: Maktabat Wahba, 1982).

Keddie, Nikki. *Sayyid Jamal ad-Din al-Afghani: A Political Biography* (Berkeley: University of California Press, 1972).

Kenney, Jeffrey T. "Selling Success, Nurturing the Self: Self-Help Literature, Capitalist Values, and the Sacralization of Subjective Life in Egypt," *International Journal of Middle East Studies*, 47 (2015), 663–80.

Kepel, Gilles. *The Roots of Radical Islam*, trans. Jon Rothschild (London: Saqi, 2005).

Kerr, Malcolm. "Rashid Rida and Islamic Reform: An Ideological Analysis," *The Muslim World*, 50:2 (April 1960), 99–109.

Khaled, Adeeb. *The Politics of Muslim Cultural Reform: Jadidism in Central Asia* (Berkeley: University of California Press, 1998).

Khatib, Line. *Islamic Revivalism in Syria: The Rise and Fall of Baʿthist Secularism* (New York: Routledge, 2011).

Koselleck, Reinhart. *Futures Past: On the Semantics of Historical Time*, trans. Keith Tribe (New York: Columbia University Press, 2004).

The Practices of Conceptual History: Timing History, Spacing Concepts, trans. Todd Samuel Presner et al. (Stanford: Stanford University Press, 2002).

Kraemer, Gudrun. *Hasan al-Banna* (Oxford: Oneworld, 2010).

Lacroix, Stéphane. *Awakening Islam: The Politics of Religious Dissent in Contemporary Saudi Arabia*, trans. George Holoch (London: Harvard University Press, 2011).

Lane, Edward William. *An Arabic–English Lexicon* (Beirut: Libraire du Liban, 1968), vol. V.

Lauzière, Henri. *The Making of Salafism: Islamic Reform in the Twentieth Century* (New York: Columbia University Press, 2016).

Lav, Daniel. “Radical Muslim Theonomy: A Study in the Evolution of Salafī Thought” (unpublished dissertation, Hebrew University of Jerusalem, 2016).

Le Renard, Amélie. *A Society of Young Women: Opportunities of Place, Power and Reform in Saudi Arabia* (Stanford: Stanford University Press, 2014).

Lerner, Daniel. *The Passing of Traditional Society: Modernizing the Middle East* (London: The Free Press of Glencoe, 1958 [1969]).

Lockman, Zachary. *Contending Visions of the Middle East: The History and Politics of Orientalism* (New York: Cambridge University Press, 2004).

“Exploring the Field: Lost Voices and Emerging Practices in Egypt, 1882–1914,” in Israel Gershoni, Hakan Erdem, and Ursula Woköck (eds.), *Histories of the Modern Middle East* (London: Lynne Rienner Publishers, 2002), 137–54.

Lutfi, Huda. “Manners and Customs of Fourteenth-Century Cairene Women: Female Anarchy versus Male Sharʿi Order in Muslim Prescriptive Treatises,” in Nikki Keddie and Beth Baron (eds.), *Women in Middle Eastern History: Shifting Boundaries in Sex and Gender* (New Haven: Yale University Press, 1991), 99–121.

Macleod, Arlene. *Accommodating Protest: Working Women, the New Veiling, and Change in Cairo* (New York: Columbia University Press, 1991).

Mahmood, Saba. *The Politics of Piety: The Islamic Revival and the Feminist Subject* (Princeton: Princeton University Press, 2005).

Religious Difference in a Secular Age: A Minority Report (Princeton: Princeton University Press, 2016).

Mahmud, Mustafa. *ʿAsr al-Qurud* (Cairo: Dar al-Nahda al-ʿArabiyya, 1978).

Hiwar Maʿa Sadiqi al-Mulhid (Cairo: Dar al-ʿAwda, 1974).

Nar Tahta al-Ramad (Cairo: Dar al-Maʿarif, 1995).

“Mahmud al-Masri,” *Ansar al-Sunna al-Muhammadiyya*, available at www.ansarsonna.com/category/الدروس-والخطب-المرئية/محمود-المصري/, accessed 13 March 2017.

Malkiel, Nancy Weiss. *“Keep the Damned Women Out”: The Struggle for Coeducation* (Princeton: Princeton University Press, 2016).

Maʾmun, Hasan. “Kalimat Fadilat al-Imam al-Akbar Shaykh al-Azhar al-Shaykh Hasan Maʾmun fi Iftitah al-Muʾtamar,” in *Kitab al-Muʾtamar al-Rabiʿ li-Majmaʿ al-Buhuth al-Islamiyya: al-Muslimun wa-l-ʿUdwan al-Israʾili* (Cairo: Islamic Research Academy at al-Azhar, 1968), 9–15.

Marty, Martin E. and R. Scott Appleby (eds.). *Fundamentalisms Observed* (Chicago: University of Chicago Press, 1991).

Fundamentalisms and the State: Remaking Politics, Economies, and Militancy (London: University of Chicago Press, 1993).

Masquelier, Adeline. *Women and Islamic Revival in a West African Town* (Bloomington: Indiana University Press, 2009).

Mas'ud, Muhammad 'Ali. *al-Jam'iyya al-Shar'iyya li-Ta'awun al-'Amilin bi-l-Kitab wa-l-Sunna al-Muhammadiyya 'Aqidatan wa Minhajan wa Sulukan* (Cairo: al-Jam'iyya al-Shar'iyya, 1982).

Masud, Muhammad Khalid, Brinkley Messick, and David Powers, "Muftis, Fatwas, and Islamic Legal Interpretation," in Muhammad Khalid Masud, Brinkley Messick, and David Powers (eds.), *Islamic Legal Interpretation: Muftis and their Fatwas* (Cambridge, MA: Harvard University Press, 1996), 3–32.

McFadden, Tom Johnston. *Daily Journalism in the Arab States* (Columbus: Ohio State University Press, 1954).

McLarney, Ellen Anne. *Soft Force: Women in Egypt's Islamic Awakening* (Princeton: Princeton University Press, 2015).

Meijer, Roel. *Cosmopolitanism, Identity and Authenticity in the Middle East* (London: Curzon Press, 1999).

Messick, Brinkley. *The Calligraphic State: Textual Domination and History in a Muslim Society* (Berkeley: University of California Press, 1992).

Miliji, al-Sayyid 'Abd al-Sattar. *Tarikh al-Haraka al-Islamiyya fi Sahat al-Ta'lim* (Cairo: Maktabat Wahba, 1994).

Ministry of Education and Central Organization. *Manahij al-Dirasa al-Muwahhada: Li-l-Marhala al-Ibtida'iyya* (Cairo: Dar al-Kutub al-'Arabi, 1961).

Ministry of Endowments and Azhar Affairs, *al-Azhar: Tarikhuhu wa-Tatawwuruhu* (Cairo: Ministry of Endowments and Azhar Affairs, 1964).

Ministry of Endowments, *Wizarat al-Awqaf bayna al-Madi wa-l-Hadir … wa-l-Mustaqbal* (Cairo: Ministry of Endowments, n.d.).

Mitchell, Richard P. *The Society of the Muslim Brothers* (New York: Oxford University Press, 1993).

Mitchell, Timothy. *Colonising Egypt* (Berkeley: University of California Press, 1991).

Mittermaier, Amira. *Dreams That Matter: Egyptian Landscapes of the Imagination* (Berkeley: University of California Press, 2011).

Moaddel, Mansoor. *Jordanian Exceptionalism: A Comparative Analysis of State–Religion Relationships in Egypt, Iran, Jordan, and Syria* (New York: Palgrave Macmillan, 2002).

Mouline, Nabil. *The Clerics of Islam: Religious Authority and Political Power in Saudi Arabia*, trans. Ethan S. Rundell (New Haven: Yale University Press, 2014).

Muhammad, Muhammad ʿAbd al-Jawwad. *Hayat Mustafa Mashhur kama ʿAshatha Usratahu* (Cairo: Dar al-Tawziʿ wa-l-Nashr al-Islamiyya, 2005).

al-Muqaddam, Muhammad b. Ismaʿil. *Adillat al-Hijab: Bahth Jamiʿ li-Fadaʾil al-Hijab wa Adillat Wujubihi wa-l-Radd ʿala Man Abaha bi-l-Sufur* (Alexandria: Dar al-Iman, 2002).

Naor, Moshe. *Social Mobilization in the Arab–Israeli War of 1948: On the Israeli Home Front*, trans. Shaul Vardi (New York: Routledge, 2013).

Naqula, Nazira. *Atbaq Laziza wa-Asnaf Sariʿa li-l-Marʾa al-ʿAmila* (Cairo: Hawwa Magazine, 1976).

Nasr, Seyyed Vali Reza. *Islamic Leviathan: Islam and the Making of State Power* (Oxford: Oxford University Press, 2001).

Mawdudi and the Making of Islamic Revivalism (New York: Oxford University Press, 1996).

Nelson, Cynthia. *Selected Writings from Cynthia Nelson* (Cairo: American University in Cairo Press, 2007).

Ohmann, Richard M. *Selling Culture: Magazines, Markets and Class at the Turn of the Century* (New York: Verso, 1996).

Ong, Aihwa. *Spirits of Resistance and Capitalist Discipline: Factory Women in Malaysia* (Albany: State University of New York Press, 1987).

Oren, Michael. *Six Days of War: June 1967 and the Making of the Modern Middle East* (New York: Oxford University Press, 2002).

Ozgur, Iren. *Islamic Schools in Modern Turkey: Faith, Politics, and Education* (New York: Cambridge University Press, 2012).

Parker, John B. and James R. Coyle. *Urbanization and Agricultural Policy in Egypt*. Rep. no. PB92-109034, vol. 169 (Washington DC: Economic Research Service, 1981).

Podeh, Elie. *The Politics of National Celebration in the Arab Middle East* (Cambridge: Cambridge University Press, 2011).

Pohl, Florian. *Islamic Education and the Public Sphere: Today's Pesantren in Indonesia* (Münster: Waxmann Verlag GmbH, 2009).

Porter, Donald. *Managing Politics and Islam in Indonesia* (London: Routledge Curzon, 2002).

Powaski, Ronald E. *The Cold War: The United States and the Soviet Union, 1917–1991* (New York: Oxford University Press, 1998).

Pykett, Lyn. "Reading and the Periodical Press: Text and Context," in Laurel Brake, Aled Jones, and Lionel Madden (eds.), *Investigating Victorian Journalism* (New York: Macmillan, 1990), 3–18.

al-Qaradawi, Yusuf. *Min Fiqh al-Dawla* (Cairo: Dar al-Shuruq, 1997).

Risalat al-Azhar (Cairo: Maktabat Wahba, 1984).

al-Sahwa al-Islamiyya bayna al-Ikhtilaf al-Mashruʿ wa-l-Tafarruq al-Madhmum (Cairo: Dar al-Shuruq, 2001).

al-Tarbiya al-Islamiyya wa Madrassat Hasan al-Banna (Cairo: Maktabat Wahba 1979).
Thaqafat al-Da'iya (Cairo: Maktabat Wahba, 1978).
Qutb, Sayyid. *Ma'alim fi-l-Tariq* (Cairo: Dar al-Shuruq, 1979).
Fi Zilal al-Qur'an (Riyadh: Minbar al-Tawhid wa-l-Nur, n.d.), vol. IV.
Rafeq, Abdel-Karim. "Public Morality in 18th Century Damascus," *Revue du Monde Musulman et de la Méditerranée*, 55–56 (1990), 180–96.
Rahnema, Ali (ed.), *Pioneers of Islamic Revival* (London: Zed Books, 1994).
Ramadan, Abdel Azim. "The Strategies of the Muslim Brotherhood and the Takfir Groups," in Martin E. Marty and R. Scott Appleby (eds.), *Fundamentalisms and the State: Remaking Politics, Economies, and Militancy* (London: University of Chicago Press, 1993), 152–83.
al-Razi, Fakhr al-Din Muhammad ibn 'Umar. *Tafsir al-Fakhr al-Razi: al-Mushahhar bi-l-Tafsir al-Kabir wa-Mafatih al-Ghayb* (Beirut: Dar al-Fikr, 2005), vol. XXIII.
Reid, Megan. *Law and Piety in Medieval Islam* (Cambridge: Cambridge University Press, 2013).
"Richard P. Mitchell," *Faculty History Project: University of Michigan*, available at http://um2017.org/faculty-history/faculty/richard-p-mitchell/memorial, Accessed 27 September 2016.
Richards, Alan. "Higher Education in Egypt," Policy Research Working Papers. Washington: Education and Employment Division, 1992.
Rida, Akram. *Buyut Bi-La Duyun: Kayfa Tudabittuna Mizaniyat Buyutikum?* (Cairo: Dar al-Tawzi' wa-l-Nashr al-Islamiyya, 2005).
Rifqa bi-l-Qawarir: al-'Ishra fi al-Bayt al-Muslim bayna al-Mawadda wa-l-Rahma (Cairo: al-Andalus al-Jadida, 2008).
Rida, Rashid. *Tafsir al-Manar* (Cairo: Dar al-Manar, 1948), 12 vols.
Rinaldo, Rachel. *Mobilizing Piety: Islam and Feminism in Indonesia* (New York: Oxford University Press, 2013).
Rock, Aaron. "Amr Khaled: From Da'wa to Political and Religious Authority," British Journal of Middle East Studies, 37:1 (2010), 15–37.
Rock-Singer, Aaron. "Censoring the Kishkophone: Religion and State Power in Mubarak's Egypt," *International Journal of Middle East Studies*, 49:3 (July 2017), 437–56.
"A Pious Public: Islamic Magazines and Revival in Egypt, 1976–1981," *British Journal of Middle Eastern Studies*, 42:4 (2015), 427–46.
"Prayer and the Islamic Revival: A Timely Challenge," *International Journal of Middle East Studies*, 48:2 (April 2016), 293–312.
"The Salafi Mystique: The Rise of Gender Segregation in 1970s Egypt," *Islamic Law and Society* 23:3 (June 2016), 279–305.
"Scholarly Authority and Lay Mobilization: Yusuf al-Qaradawi's Vision of Da'wa, 1976–1984," *The Muslim World*, 106:3 (July 2016), 588–604.

Rozehnal, Robert. *Islamic Sufism Unbound: Politics and Piety in Twenty-First Century Pakistan* (New York: Palgrave Macmillan, 2007).
Russel, Mona. *Middle East in Focus (Egypt)* (Oxford: ABC-CLIO, 2013).
Rutherford, Bruce. *Egypt after Mubarak: Liberalism, Islam and Democracy in the Arab World* (Princeton: Princeton University Press, 2013).
al-Sabagh, Muhammad b. Lutfi. "al-Risala al-Rabiʿa: Tahrim al-Khalwa b-il-Marʾa al-Ajnabiyya wa-l-Ikhtilat al-Mustahtar," in Hasan al-Banna, *al-Marʾa al-Muslima*, ed. Muhammad Nasr al-Din al-Albani (Cairo: Dar al-Kutub al-Salafiyya, 1987), 81–99.
Sallam, Azza Mohamed Ahmed. "The Return to the Veil among Undergraduate Females at Minya University, Egypt" (unpublished dissertation, Purdue University, 1980).
Salvatore, Armando. "Mustafa Mahmud: A Paradigm of Public Islamic Entrepreneurship?" in Armando Salvatore (ed.), *Muslim Traditions and Modern Techniques of Power* (Münster: Lit Verlag, 2001), 211–24.
"The Reform Project in the Emerging Public Spheres," in Muhammad Masud, Armando Salvatore, and Martin van Brunessen (eds.), *Islam and Modernity* (Edinburgh: Edinburgh University Press, 2009), 186–205.
"Social Differentiation, Moral Authority and Public Islam in Egypt: The Path of Mustafa Mahmud," *Anthropology Today*, 16:2 (April 2000), 12–15.
"Staging Virtue: The Disembodiment of Self-Correctness and the Making of Islam as a Public Norm," in *Bielefeld Yearbook of the Sociology of Islam* (Hamburg: Lit Verlag, 1998), vol. I, 87–119.
Saqr, Shahata Muhammad ʿAli. *al-Ikhtilat bayna al-Rijal wa-l-Nisa: Ahkam wa Fatawa, Thimar Murra Qissas Mukhziyya, Kashf 136 Shubha li-Duʿat al-Ikhtilat* (Cairo: Dar al-Yusr, 2011), 2 vols.
Schäfer, Axel R. *Countercultural Conservatives: American Evangelicalism from the Postwar Revival to the New Christian Right* (Madison: University of Wisconsin Press, 2001).
Schielke, Samuli. "Ambivalent Commitments: Troubles of Morality, Religiosity and Aspiration among Young Egyptians," *Journal of Religion in Africa*, 39:2 (2009), 158–85.
"Being a Nonbeliever in a Time of Islamic Revival: Trajectories of Doubt and Certainty in Contemporary Egypt," *International Journal of Middle East Studies*, 44:2 (2012), 301–20.
Egypt in the Future Tense: Hope, Frustration and Ambivalence before and after 2011 (Bloomington: Indiana University Press, 2015).
Scott, David. *Conscripts of Modernity: The Tragedy of Cultural Enlightenment* (Durham, NC: Duke University Press, 2004).
Scott, James. *Seeing Like a State: How Certain Schemes to Improve the Human Condition Have Failed* (New Haven: Yale University Press, 1998).

Scott, Rachel. *The Challenge of Political Islam: Non-Muslims and the Egyptian State* (Stanford: Stanford University Press, 2010).

Sedghi, Hamideh. *Women and Politics in Iran: Veiling, Unveiling, Reveiling* (New York: Cambridge University Press, 2007).

Semerdjian, Elyse. *Off the Straight Path: Illicit Sex, Law, and Community in Ottoman Aleppo* (Syracuse: Syracuse University Press, 2008).

Shabab Sayyiduna Muhammad. *Dustur al-Mujtama' al-Muslim* (Cairo: Dar al-I'tisam, 1987).

Shahidian, Hammad. *Women in Iran: Gender Politics in the Islamic Republic* (London: Greenwood Press, 2002).

al-Shakry, Omnia. *The Great Social Laboratory: Subjects of Knowledge in Colonial and Postcolonial Egypt* (Stanford: Stanford University Press, 2007).

Shalabi, 'Abd al-Waddud. *Fi Mas'alat al-Sufur wa-l-Hijab* (Cairo: Islamic Research Academy, 1985).

Shalata, Ahmad Zaghlul. *al-Hala al-Salafiyya al-Mu'asira fi Misr* (Cairo: Maktabat Madbuli, 2011).

Shamikh, Amr. *al-Waqa'i' al-Ikhwaniyya* (Cairo: Dar al-Tawzi' wa-l-Nashr, 2012).

Sharkey, Heather J. *American Evangelicals in Egypt: Missionary Encounters in an Age of Empire* (Princeton: Princeton University Press, 2008).

Shechter, Relli. "From Effendi to Infitahi? Consumerism and its Malcontents in the Emergence of Egyptian Market Society," *British Journal of Middle Eastern Studies*, 36:1 (April 2009), 21–35.

Shehata, Samer S. *Shop Floor Culture and Politics in Egypt* (Albany: State University of New York Press, 2009).

Shephard, William E. "Sayyid Qutb's Doctrine of Jāhiliyya," *International Journal of Middle East Studies*, 35:4 (Nov. 2003), 521–45.

al-Siba'i, Muhammad Ahmad. *al-Mar'a bayna al-Tabarruj wa-l-Tahajjub* (Cairo: Islamic Research Academy, 1981).

Sidqi, Ni'mat. *al-Tabarruj* (Cairo: Dar al-I'tisam, 1975).

"al-Sisi: Nahtaj ila Thawra Diniyya Tukhlis al-Islam min al-Tatarruf." al-'Arabiyya, 2 Jan. 2015, available at www.alarabiya.net/ar/arab-and-world/egypt/2015/01/02/السيسي-نحتاج-إلى-ثورة-دينية-تخلص-الإسلام-مما-علق-به.html.

Sivan, Emanuel. *Radical Islam: Medieval Theology and Modern Politics* (New Haven: Yale University Press, 1990).

Siyam, 'Imad. "al-Haraka al-Islamiyya wa-l-Jam'iyyat al-Ahliyya fi Misr," in 'Abd al-Ghafar Shukr (ed.), *al-Jam'iyyat al-Ahliyya al-Islamiyya fi Misr* (Cairo: Markaz al-Buhuth al-'Arabiyya, 2006), 73–150.

Skeggs, Beverly. *Formations of Class and Gender: Becoming Respectable* (London: Sage, 1997).

Skovgaard-Petersen, Jakob. *Defining Islam for the Egyptian State: Muftis and Fatwas and Dār al-Iftā'* (New York: Brill, 1997).

Slymovics, Susan. "'Hassiba Ben Bouali, If you Could See our Algeria': Women and Public Space in Algeria," in Joel Beinin and Joe Stork (eds.), *Political Islam: Essays from Middle East Report* (Berkeley: University of California Press, 1997), 211–19.

Spadola, Emilio. *The Calls of Islam: Sufis, Islamists, and Mass Mediation in Urban Morocco* (Bloomington: Indiana University Press, 2014).

Starkey, Paul. "Modern Egyptian Culture in the Arab World," in *The Cambridge History of Egypt*, vol. II: *Modern Egypt from 1517 to the End of the Twentieth Century*, ed. M. W. Daly (Cambridge: Cambridge University Press, 1998), 394–426.

Starrett, Gregory. "The Political Economy of Religious Commodities in Cairo," *American Anthropologist*, 97:1 (March 1995), 51–68.

Putting Islam to Work: Education, Politics and Religious Transformation in Egypt (Berkeley: University of California Press, 1998).

Stein, Ewan. *Representing Israel in Modern Egypt: Ideas, Intellectuals and Foreign Policy from Nasser to Mubarak* (London: I. B. Tauris, 2012).

Stein, Salley. "The Graphic Ordering of Desire: Modernization of a Middle-Class Women's Magazine, 1914–1939," in Richard Bolton (ed.), *The Contest of Meaning: Critical Histories of Photography* (Cambridge, MA: MIT Press, 1992), 145–62.

Stolz, Daniel A. *The Lighthouse and the Observatory: Islam, Science and Empire in Late Ottoman Egypt* (Cambridge: Cambridge University Press, 2018).

al-Subki, Mahmud Muhammad Khattab and Amin Muhammad Khattab, *al-Din al-Khalis: Irshad al-Khalq ila Din al-Haqq* (Beirut: Dar al-Kutub al-'Ilmiyya, 2007), vol. VIII.

al-Sufi, Abu al-'Abbas Ahmad b. Muhammad b. al-Mahdi b. 'Ajiba al-Anjari al-Fasi. *al-Bahar al-Madid fi Tafsir al-Qur'an al-Majid*, ed. Ahmad 'Abd Allah al-Qarshi Raslan (Cairo: Hassan 'Abbas Zaki, 1999), vol. IV.

Sulaiman, Imam Hafiz Abu Dawud. "Bab al-Jum'a li-l-Mamluk wa-l-Mar'a," in *Kitab al-Sunnan: Sunnan Abi Dawud* (Mecca: Dar al-Qibla li-l-Thaqafa al-Islamiyya, 1998), vol. II, 92–93.

Kitab al-Sunnan: Sunnan Abi Dawud (Mecca: Dar al-Qibla li-l-Thaqafa al-Islamiyya, 1998).

Sunan Abu Dawud, trans. Nasiruddin al-Khattab (Jeddah: Maktabat Dar-us-Salam, 2008).

Sullivan, Earl L. *Women in Egyptian Public Life* (Syracuse: Syracuse University Press, 1986).

Sutton, Matthew Avery. *American Apocalypse: A History of Modern Evangelicalism* (Cambridge, MA: Harvard University Press, 2014).

al-Tabari, Muhammad b. Jarir b. Yazid b. Kathir b. Ghalib al-ʿAmali Abu Jaʿfar. *Jamiʿ al-Bayyan fi-Tafsir al-Qurʾan*, ed. Ahmad Muhammad Shakir (Cairo: Muʾasassat al-Risala, 2000), vol. XIX.

Tahir, Ahmad Muhammad. *Jamaʿat Ansar al-Sunna al-Muhammadiyya: Nashaʾtuha–Ahdafuha–Manhajuha–Juhuduha* (Mansura: Dar al-Fadila li-l-Nashr wa-l-Tawziʿ/Dar al-Hadi al-Nabawi, 2004).

Thompson, Elizabeth. *Colonial Citizens: Republican Rights, Paternal Privilege, and Gender in French Syria and Lebanon* (New York: Columbia University Press, 1999).

"Public and Private in Middle Eastern Women's History," *Journal of Women's History*, 15:1 (2003), 52–69.

Tucker, Judith. *Women, Family and Gender in Islamic Law* (New York: Cambridge University Press, 2008).

United Arab Republic. *Muʾtamar Shuʾun al-Marʾa al-ʿAmila* (Cairo: Permanent Council for Women's Affairs, 1963).

Voll, John O. "Muḥammad Ḥayyā' al-Sindī and Muḥammad ibn ʿAbd al-Wahhāb: An Analysis of an Intellectual Group in Eighteenth-Century Madīna," *Bulletin of the School of Oriental and African Studies*, 38:1 (1975), 32–39.

al-Wakil, ʿAbd al-Rahman. *Daʿwat al-Haqq* (Cairo: n.p., 1952).

Ware, Rudolph T. *The Walking Quran: Islamic Education, Embodied Knowledge, and History in West Africa* (Chapel Hill: University of North Carolina Press, 2014).

Weiss, Shayna. "A Beach of their Own: The Creation of the Gender-Segregated Beach in Tel Aviv," *Journal of Israeli History*, 35 (2016), 39–56.

Wensinck, A. J. "Mīḳāt," in *Encyclopedia of Islam, First Edition (1913–1936)*, ed. M. T. Houtsma, T. W. Arnold, R. Basset, and R. Hartmann. Brill Online, 2015.

White, Jenny. *Islamist Mobilization in Turkey: A Study in Vernacular Politics* (Seattle: University of Washington Press, 2002).

Wickham, Carrie Rosefsky. *Mobilizing Islam: Religion, Activism, and Political Change in Egypt* (New York: Columbia University Press, 2002).

The Muslim Brotherhood: Evolution of an Islamist Movement (Princeton: Princeton University Press, 2013).

Wiktorowicz, Quintan. "Anatomy of the Salafi Movement," *Studies in Conflict and Terrorism*, 29 (2006), 207–39.

Islamic Activism: A Social Movement Theory Approach (Bloomington: Indiana University Press, 2004).

The Management of Islamic Activism: Salafis, the Muslim Brotherhood, and State Power in Jordan (Albany: State University of New York Press, 2001).

Williams, John Alden. "A Return to the Veil in Egypt," *Middle East Review*, 11:3 (1979), 49–54.

Wood, Graeme. "What ISIS Really Wants," *The Atlantic*, March 2015, available at www.theatlantic.com/features/archive/2015/02/what-isis-really-wants/384980/.

World Bank, "Labor force participation rate, female," available at http://data.worldbank.org/indicator/SL.TLF.CACT.FE.ZS.

Ya'qub, Muhammad Hussayn. *Sifat al-Muslima al-Multazima* (Giza: Maktabat Suq al-Akhira, 1996).

Youssef, Nadia. *A Woman-Specific Strategy Statement: The Case of Egypt* (Cairo: Aid Bureau of Program and Policy Coordination, 1980).

Zahid, Mohammed. *The Muslim Brotherhood and Egypt's Succession Crisis: The Politics of Liberalisation and Reform in the Middle East* (New York: I. B. Tauris, 2010).

el-Zain, Abdul Hamid. "Beyond Ideology and Theology: The Search for the Anthropology of Islam," *Annual Review of Anthropology*, 6 (1977), 227–54.

al-Zamakshari, Mahmud b. 'Umar, *al-Kashshaf 'an Haqa'iq Ghawamid al-Tanzil wa-'Uyun al-Aqawil fi Wujuh al-Ta'wil*, ed. 'Adil Ahmad 'Abd al-Mawjud and 'Ali Muhammad Mu'awwad (Riyadh: Maktabat al-Obeikan, 1998), vol. IV.

Zaman, Muhammad Qasim. *Modern Islamic Thought in a Radical Age: Religious Authority and Internal Criticism* (Princeton: Princeton University Press, 2012).

"The 'Ulama of Contemporary Islam and their Conceptions of the Common Good," in Dale Eickelman and Armando Salvatore (eds.), *Public Islam and the Common Good* (London: Brill, 2004), 129–56.

The Ulama in Contemporary Islam: Custodians of Change (Princeton: Princeton University Press, 2002).

al-Zanira, Najah. *al-Majlis al-A'la li-l-Shu'un al-Islamiyya* (Cairo: Ministry of Endowments, 1995).

Zeghal, Malika. *Gardiens de l'Islam: les oulémas d'al-Azhar dans l'Egypte contemporaine* (Paris: Presses de Sciences Po, 1996).

"Religion and Politics in Egypt: The Ulema of al-Azhar, Radical Islam and the State (1952–94)," *International Journal of Middle East Studies*, 31:3 (1999), 371–99.

Zerubavel, Eviatar. *Hidden Rhythms: Schedules and Calendars in Social Life* (Berkeley: University of California Press, 1985).

Zuhur, Sherifa. *Revealing Reveiling: Islamist Gender Ideology in Contemporary Egypt* (Albany: State University of New York Press, 1992).

Index